KT-199-874

PENGUIN BOOKS

DON'T STOP ME NOW

Jeremy Clarkson began his writing career on the *Rotherham Advertiser*. Since then he has written for the *Sun*, the *Sunday Times*, the *Rochdale Observer*, the *Wolverhampton Express and Star*, all of the Associated Kent Newspapers, and *Lincolnshire Life*. Today, he is the tallest person working in British television.

Jeremy Clarkson's other books are *Clarkson's Hot 100*, *Clarkson on Cars*, *Motorworld*, *Planet Dagenham*, *The World According to Clarkson*, *I Know You Got Soul* and *And Another Thing: The World According to Clarkson Volume 2*.

Don't Stop Me Now

JEREMY CLARKSON

PENGUIN BOOKS

PENGUIN BOOKS

Published by the Penguin Group
Penguin Books Ltd, 80 Strand, London WC2R 0RL, England
Penguin Group (USA) Inc., 375 Hudson Street, New York, New York 10014, USA
Penguin Group (Canada), 90 Eglinton Avenue East, Suite 700, Toronto, Ontario, Canada M4P 2Y3
(a division of Pearson Penguin Canada Inc.)
Penguin Ireland, 25 St Stephen's Green, Dublin 2, Ireland
(a division of Penguin Books Ltd)
Penguin Group (Australia), 250 Camberwell Road, Camberwell, Victoria 3124, Australia
(a division of Pearson Australia Group Pty Ltd)
Penguin Books India Pvt Ltd, 11 Community Centre, Panchsheel Park, New Delhi – 110 017, India
Penguin Group (NZ), 67 Apollo Drive, Rosedale, North Shore 0632, New Zealand
(a division of Pearson New Zealand Ltd)
Penguin Books (South Africa) (Pty) Ltd, 24 Sturdee Avenue, Rosebank, Johannesburg 2196, South Africa

Penguin Books Ltd, Registered Offices: 80 Strand, London WC2R 0RL, England

www.penguin.com

First published by Michael Joseph 2007
Published in Penguin Books 2008
1

Copyright © Jeremy Clarkson, 2007
All rights reserved

The moral right of the author has been asserted

Typeset by Rowland Phototypesetting Ltd, Bury St Edmunds, Suffolk
Printed in England by Clays Ltd, St Ives plc

Except in the United States of America, this book is sold subject
to the condition that it shall not, by way of trade or otherwise, be lent,
re-sold, hired out, or otherwise circulated without the publisher's
prior consent in any form of binding or cover other than that in
which it is published and without a similar condition including this
condition being imposed on the subsequent purchaser

ISBN: 978–0–141–02611–4

www.greenpenguin.co.uk

Penguin Books is committed to a sustainable future
for our business, our readers and our planet.
The book in your hands is made from paper
certified by the Forest Stewardship Council.

To everyone except John Prescott

The contents of this book first appeared in Jeremy Clarkson's *Sunday Times* motoring column. Read more about the world according to Clarkson every week in the *Sunday Times*.

Contents

Peugeot 206 GTi

Look, can we get one thing clear this morning? Your butcher is no better than my butcher. Your local branch of Morrison's is no better than my local Tesco and your favourite village in France is no better than my favourite village in France. It's very rare these days that you find one product that is demonstrably better than its competition: Pepsi and Coke, O_2 and Vodaphone, Miyake and Armani, Eton and Harrow, Tory and Labour.

And if you do find something that has a clear advantage over its rivals, I'll wager that there's something wrong with it. Skiing in America is a classic case in point.

Sure, the runs are less busy and more varied than the runs you get in Europe. There are shorter queues too. But don't think this means you spend less time standing in them.

It's not that Americans won't fit through the turnstiles – their skiers are actually like twigs: it's the politeness.

'Hey, buddy, after you.' 'No way, friend, you were here first.' 'I sure was not.' 'I'm in no rush.' 'Me neither. Say, you on vacation?' 'Sure am. Soaking up some rays.' 'You know it.' 'Hey.' 'Say.' And so it goes on.

In the time it takes two Americans to decide who should get into the chairlift first you could have got half of Germany up the Matterhorn.

Living in the south-east is another example: it's better in every way.

But then you do get more for your money up north. And all the best countryside's up there.

So, you see, things are never so clear-cut.

Except when it comes to the new Mini. First, everyone likes it. This is Michael Palin and David Attenborough rolled into one cutesy bite-size package. Even non-car people are drawn to it like vegetarians to a bacon sandwich.

The looks and the cheeky chappiness would have been enough to win it many, many friends, but it's also fabulous fun to drive. The basic One is a hoot, the Cooper is hysterical and the Cooper S is a riot.

They're even doing a 200-bhp Works version these days. And that is the motoring equivalent of fish and chips at the Ivy: it appeals on every single conceivable level.

Maybe, if I'm hypercritical, the back of the Mini's a bit cramped and maybe the image has been tarnished a bit in London by an estate agency that has bought thousands. But if you don't live in the capital and you don't have children who are 15 feet tall, I can't think of a single reason why you would consider, even for a moment, buying anything else. Think of it as the Yorkshire Dales with Liverpool house prices in Chelsea. Or Vail run by the Swiss.

That's exactly what I was thinking on Monday morning as I peered out of my bedroom window at the 180-bhp Peugeot 206 GTi that was being delivered. It seemed so pointless. No, really. Why would anyone be interested in such a thing when for a little bit less money they could have a slightly more accelerative Mini Cooper S? By the time I'd finished my coffee and was ready to leave for the week in London I'd pretty much decided to leave it where it was and use the Mercedes instead. Well, it was a lovely day and I saw no point in spending time in a hot box.

I don't know why I changed my mind. Guilt perhaps? A sense that I have to drive everything, no matter how stupid or pointless it might seem? Or maybe it's because I spotted the air-conditioning button on the Pug's dash and thought: 'Oh, it won't be that bad.'

Whatever, I loaded my suitcases in the back and with the temperature nudging 75°F headed for London.

After half a mile I was suspicious. After a mile I was angry. It may have an air-conditioning button but it sure as hell doesn't have air-conditioning. The Rolls-Royce system works with the power of 30 domestic refrigerators. Peugeot's works with the power of an asthmatic in Bangladesh blowing at you through a straw.

There are some other issues, too. For instance, the hand-stitched instrument binnacle. Imagine one of those 14-year-old boys who hang around provincial bus stops at two in the morning. That's what the interior of the Pug looks like. Now imagine him in a pair of hand-made Church's shoes. And that's what a hand-stitched instrument binnacle looks like in there. Like it's been nicked.

Plus, I'm blessed with stupidly tiny feet. For someone so tall, it's absurd that I have to totter around on a pair of size nines. However, they were too big to fit on the clutch properly. And goddam, it's hot in here. It's noisy, too,

because now I'm having to drive down the damn motorway with the damn window down. Why the hell didn't
I take the Mercedes? In some ways this was all a bit
depressing. I used to love hot hatchbacks because they
did two jobs for the price of one. They were cheap to
buy, cheap to run and as practical as the shopping trolleys
on which they were based. But, then, on the right road,
at the right time, they could set fire to passing woodland.

I'm getting old, though. I don't want a practical shopping trolley and I don't much want to set fire to the
woods either. Furthermore, those who are young enough
to want both things could not possibly afford to insure
this car. Anyway, who'd want to when they could
have a better-made, better-equipped, faster, cheaper and
cheekier Mini? With air-con-bloody-ditioning.

The next day the Pug drove me even madder. Have
you tried to drive through London in a car with a manual
gearbox while talking on the phone? It's like rubbing your
head and patting your tummy while defusing a bomb.

On Wednesday I used the 206 to go to the *Top Gear*
base and, I have to admit, on a quiet country road it was
quite good fun. Nothing like the hot hatches of yesteryear
that sang soprano; it was more a torquey tenor. But that's
okay when you're 43; it means you don't have to stir the
gearbox so much.

It wasn't the speed that impressed most, though, it was
the handling. It would sail round corners at velocities I
would deem silly or even suicidal in other cars, some of
which cost an awful lot more than £14,995.

I must confess, I found myself driving this little pocket

rocket much faster than was entirely sensible. And I loved it. By the time I arrived I felt 18 years old again.

All day, as we made the show, I kept walking past the 206 and thinking: 'Actually, that's a very pretty little car.' And it is. Less cute than a Mini but prettier, certainly, and, with those huge alloys and fat tyres, more businesslike.

On Thursday I drove it round the *Top Gear* track and it was simply staggering. I'm loath to use the word perfect, but the combined effect of variable-assistance power steering, dual-rate springs, sharp dampers and truly magnificent front seats that nail you in place is that you can absolutely fly.

The Mini's good but the Peugeot's in a different class. It's like comparing Iron Maiden to Led Zep.

And part of the difference is down to weight. The Mini really is an Iron Maiden and the Peugeot really is a hot-air balloon.

Sadly, on Thursday night I went to a party where I quaffed champagne until I didn't know my name any more. This meant that when I woke up in Chipping Norton today I couldn't for the life of me remember where the Peugeot was. I miss it.

Sunday 15 June 2003

Volvo S60 R

Have you ever wondered what happened to all the engineers? Two hundred years ago, the world must have been full of men in frock coats inventing new ways of doing everything.

Conversation at the pub now is terribly dull. 'What did you do at work today?'

'Oh, nothing much. Tried to look up the secretary's skirt for a bit, then did some filing.'

Imagine, however, what it must have been like in 1750.

'What did you do at work today?'

'Well, I invented a steam engine and then this afternoon I developed a new way of keeping time. You?'

'Oh, same old same old. I came up with a new way of tunnelling and then I designed the pressure cooker.'

All over the world there were people saying, 'See how that sparrow makes its nest, using its beak to intertwine the twigs? It has given me an idea for something I shall call a washing machine.'

I've been watching Adam Hart-Davis's new series on BBC2. It's called *What the Tudors and Stuarts Did for Us* and it's been going on, unnecessarily, for weeks. It seems the answer could have been given in two seconds: 'Everything.'

In the space of a gnat's blink, we went from a species that ate mud to full-on civilisation, with blast furnaces, steam engines and new ways of making sure the roof on your house didn't fall down.

It must have been easy when the Victorians came along to look at what had already been achieved and think: 'Well, there's nothing left for us to invent.' But, unbelievably, they kept on going with their railway engines and their iron ships and their electricity.

Even as the twentieth century trundled into life, you couldn't go for a walk on any cliff top without bumping into someone who was muttering and making notes. John Logie Baird, for instance. He started out by inventing self-warming socks, then he developed jam before, on a stroll through Hastings, deciding to come up with radiovision – or television, as we now call it.

To us that seems incomprehensible. I mean, I went for a stroll this morning and decided to design a time machine, but I have no clue how I might go about it. Baird, on the other hand, went into a shop, bought a hat box and two knitting needles and, hey presto, the next thing you know we have Robert Kilroy-Silk.

Those were exciting times. The Victorians had the Great Exhibition of 1851 to showcase their wares and their brilliance. They saw mechanical engineering as the future of the world, the one thing that separated us from the beasts and the flies.

Now we have electronic engineering, which is not only stratospherically dull but also fills us with fear and dread. Ever since 1968, when Hal went bonkers and ate the crew of Discovery One, we've been brought up to be frightened of it.

Computers, we were told by James Cameron in *The Terminator*, would one day finish mankind, and Prince Charles agrees. He sees a time when nano-robots will learn to push buttons and end the world in a nuclear holocaust.

I'm not so sure. In fact, I have no fears at all about a robot the size of a human hair climbing on to a table – how, exactly? – and pushing the erase key, because we can be guaranteed that either the robot or the computer will have broken long before the bomb ever goes boom.

Think about it. Paddington station is still as beautiful and as functional as it was when Brunel built it, almost 150 years ago. Now compare that with the mobile phone you bought last September. Ugly, isn't it? And where's the camera and the electronic diary and the video facility? Not that it matters, because it started out by not working in Fulham and now it doesn't work at all.

Have you still got the video recorder you bought back in 1985, or the camera? Of course not. They went wrong years ago. And it's the same story with DVDs. I bought one of the first portable players for a monstrous £850, and already it's fit only for the bin.

And this brings me to the new Volvo S60 R. Apparently it's a four-wheel-drive, four-door answer to BMW's M3. Hmm. A slightly optimistic boast when you look under the bonnet and find the 2.5-litre turbo engine develops 300 bhp. That's a lot, for sure, but if the M3 is your Gare du Nord, 300 is only halfway through the Channel tunnel.

And I'm sorry, but turbocharging is positively James Watt.

Volvo ploughs on, however, saying the S60 R has, and I quote, 'the most advanced chassis of any road car'. It's called the Skyhook system because in comfort and sport modes it feels as though the car is suspended from above rather than propped up on such crudities as the wheels and suspension.

There's more, too, in the shape of active yaw control, two traction controls and a setting called advanced that, we're told, turns the S60 into a pure racing car.

It all sounded too good to be true. And it was. I borrowed one, drove it to the *Top Gear* test track and selected the advanced setting that unhooks the car from the sky. But way before I had a chance to decide whether I liked it or not, in fact way before I'd got round the first corner, the whole thing broke. A message on the dash said simply: 'Chassis settings. Service.'

Another car was duly delivered and I spent a day pushing buttons so that now I have a definitive verdict for you. Comfort makes the car comfortable. Sport makes the car less comfortable. And advanced makes it uncomfortable.

So far as handling's concerned, it didn't seem to make any difference what setting I selected so, after much careful deliberation (three seconds), I put the whole thing in comfort and went home.

That said, I rather liked the Volvo. In the past I've never really seen the point of the S60. Buying one was like deliberately sleeping with the plain, boring girl rather than her bubbly, pretty German friend, but the R version with its new nose and big alloy wheels is pretty too.

Strangely, it doesn't feel that fast. Oh, I've read the

figures and I'm sure they're right, but this is not a rip-snorting terrier, constantly surging up to corners faster than you'd like.

All cars have a motorway cruising speed at which they settle when you're not really concentrating. Mostly, it's 80 or so, though when you get up to something like the Mercedes S 600 it's more like 110. In the Volvo, however, I kept finding myself doing 60.

On country roads I'd remind myself that I was at the wheel of a turbocharged four-wheel-drive sports saloon and overtake the car in front, with consummate ease, it must be said. But then, a mile or so later, it'd be up behind me, its driver wondering why I was suddenly going so slowly.

As a result, it's a relaxing car to drive. Certainly you have no need to worry about being ambushed by a speed camera. Either you're concentrating, in which case you'll see it, or you're not, in which case you'll be doing 3 mph.

I loved the interior too. The seats are fabulously comfortable, the stereo is as good as you'll find in any car, and I would never tire of watching the sat nav screen slide out of the dash, as if installed by Q. It'll break, obviously, but while it's working it's wonderful.

What we have then is a comfortable, safe, well-equipped, well-priced car that, if you can really be bothered, is quite fast as well.

As a thriller it misses the BMW by a mile, but as an ownership experience I'd take the Volvo over the M3 every time. It's so much less – how can I put this politely? – plonkerish.

More importantly, however, it also misses the Audi S4. Like the Volvo, this has a turbo motor, four doors and four-wheel drive. Like the Volvo, it's quiet, comfortable and unassuming when you just want to get home. Unlike the Volvo, when conditions are right, the Audi picks up its lederhosen and absolutely flies.

Even though it's a couple of grand more expensive, I'd buy the Audi; it's more mechanical somehow. But if you want the Bill Gates Volvo, don't worry, you are not getting a bad car.

Sunday 29 June 2003

Koenigsegg CC

Jeremy Paxman. Very much the embodiment of twenty-first-century man. Civilised, urbane, well read and quick-witted. Yet underneath the polished veneer of sophistication pulsates the brain of a tree shrew. Yup. Underneath that £50 haircut Paxman is no different from the bass guitarist with AC/DC or your dog or even the brontosaurus.

Last week he rolled up at the *Top Gear* Karting Challenge wearing the sort of disdainful sneer that makes him such a terrifying adversary on *Newsnight*. 'I've never even seen a go-kart before,' he drawled before the race.

By rights he should have hated every moment of it. Here, after all, was one of the most respectable and respected men on television, all dolled up in a stupid racing suit and squeezed into a noisy, pointless bee of a thing.

But no, he loved it. Karting is cold, uncomfortable and a little bit dangerous. Uncultured, uncouth and yobbish, it is the diametric opposite of *University Challenge*. But it is guaranteed to send a shiver up the spine of even the most donnish romantic because, sitting down there, close to the ground, it feels fast.

Speed, we're forever being told, kills. Slow down, say the advertisements on television and the digital boards on motorways. Flash flash go the speed cameras. The message is clear and constant, but I'm afraid you might as well try to teach a lamp post how to tie shoelaces.

We need speed like we need air and food and water.

And I'm not talking about the usefulness of going quickly either. Obviously, the faster you travel, the sooner you get to where you're going. So you can see more and do more and learn more. Speed, as I've said many times before, makes you cleverer.

Nor am I being flippant. Though, yes, speed does mean you can now go to see your mother-in-law – but you don't have to stay the night.

What I'm being is scientific. Thousands of years ago, what caused man to come out of his cave and think: 'I wonder what's in the next valley'? The risks of going to find out were immense, but obviously he went ahead or we'd all still be living in Ethiopia.

More recently, what caused Christopher Columbus to sail across the Atlantic, or Neil Armstrong to fly to the moon? Why do people bungee jump? Well, it's simple: we like risk.

Deep at the root of any brain in the animal kingdom is the limbic system, a sort of slug-like sticky thing that controls our instincts.

When we do something dangerous, it dumps a load of dopamine into our heads that makes us euphoric. You see the effects of this on the face of a footballer after he's scored a goal. He's taken a chance, got away with it, and for a moment or two he is completely out of control, lost in a sea of pure ecstasy.

When you take cocaine, the drug causes dopamine to be released. It's why people become so addicted, why it's so moreish. But you don't need to clog up your nose and become a crashing bore to get exactly the same effect. All you need to do is get out there and put your foot down.

Next weekend is the Festival of Speed, an event where some of the best cars in the world drive past huge crowds of spectators in the grounds of Goodwood House.

If you're able to pop along, I urge you to go to the start line, where you will see all sorts of respectable middle-aged men from the world of rock music and big business. They always say, before they set off, that it's not a race and that they won't be trying hard.

But the instant the visor snaps shut on their helmets, the brain screams: 'Give me some dopamine,' the red mist comes down and they shoot off in a whirl of smoke and noise.

So what do the spectators get out of it? Well, the same deal, really. When the car comes roaring towards you, bellowing the V8 bellow, your body is thinking: 'Hello.'

And when the unseeing limbic system senses danger it goes berserk. When you hear a noise in the house in the middle of the night you remain stock still, just like a springbok when it thinks it senses a predator. Blood is fed to the muscles, which is why your face goes white.

Next time you see Paxman, then, having a ding-dong on *Newsnight*, consider this: his outer human brain is thinking of an intelligent response, but his inner tree-shrew brain is thinking, 'Where's the nearest tree?' His blood is a mass of endorphins and adrenalin that make him strong and awake; and so is yours as the Ferrari GTO barrels towards you at 120.

And so was mine the other day when I decided to see how fast I could make the new Koenigsegg go on our test track in Surrey.

Mr Koenigsegg is a completely bald inventor from Sweden who decided one day to make a supercar. Ferrari and Lamborghini should be afraid. Very afraid.

Sweden's odd like that. Only 172 people live there, but when they turn their attention to something the world tends to notice. Sweden produced one of the greatest Wimbledon champions of all time and one of the biggest-selling pop acts. Sweden is where you go for your self-assembly furniture.

Anything anyone can do, the Swedes can do better. Only a few years after someone failed to assassinate Ronald Reagan, someone shot the Swedish prime minister, Olaf Palme. And, unbelievably, they still haven't caught him.

So, what's the new car like? Well, it's almost the same weight as a McLaren F1, it is a little bit more aero-dynamically efficient, and with 655 bhp in the boot it's a little bit more powerful. The result is, quite simply, the fastest road car in the world.

They're talking about a top speed of 240 mph, and that's about 30 mph faster than Michael Schumacher drives when he's at work.

My limbic system was impressed. And it was even more impressed when I came back from my first speed run to say the front was feeling a little light. 'No problem,' said Mr Koenigsegg. 'We will jack up the back of the car a bit. And do you mind if we put some gaffer tape round the windscreen?' Wow. It's risky enough to drive any car at more than 170 mph, but to do it in a car that's been jacked up a bit and has a windscreen held in place with duct tape . . . There were so many chemicals coursing around my arterial route-map that if you'd cut me I'd have bled pure acid.

Eventually, I got it up to 174 mph, 4 mph faster than I'd managed in any other car on the test track. And then the dopamine came. Speed kills? Maybe, but it doesn't half thrill as well.

So does the Koenigsegg. It's an absolute beast, as hot as the centre of the Earth and as noisy as a foundry. It's like working out on the footplate of a steam train, but the rewards are huge.

Pile up to a corner, change down on the ridiculously narrow-gated gearbox, brake hard. Already your clutch leg is aching from the effort. Now turn the wheel. There's power assistance, but not much. Your arms are straining to hold the front in line, so you apply some power to unstick the back end. Grrrrr, goes the 4.7-litre V8. Weeeeeeeeee goes the supercharger. And eeeeeeeee go the tyres as they lose traction.

Whack on some opposite lock to catch the slide. Whoa, it's still going. More lock needed. More effort. Your arms are really hurting now and you're desperately trying to balance the throttle, to find the sweet spot that will hold the back end in check.

There. There it is. Smoke is pouring off the tyres now, but the car is powering sideways and under perfect control through the bend. Inside, you have sweat in your eyes, you feel like you've been arm-wrestling a mountain all morning, but with the dopamine coming you don't notice a thing.

Welcome, then, to the world of the super-fast supercar. They are utterly stupid, of course. Just like the people who drive them. Us.

Sunday 6 July 2003

Caterham Seven Roadsport SV

The week before last, during that mini heatwave, I left work at about eight o'clock and cruised, top down, up to the traffic lights under the A40 flyover in west London.

A right turn would take me back to my flat, a super-heated box with neither garden nor air. Then I'd be forced to lie awake all night long, stuck fast to the sheets, listening to policemen tearing up and down Westbourne Grove while testing their sirens.

A left turn, however, would take me to the tranquillity of the Cotswolds and my family. Here I would be able to sleep with nothing to wake me save the shush-hush of the barley and the pitter-patter of tiny foxes nibbling at the chicken run. And that's why I went left.

It was a good decision, too. Because after some 40 minutes I turned off the motorway and, with the sun a six-inch coin of brilliant scarlet light in an utterly clear, deep-blue sky, I mashed my foot into the SL's thick, velvety carpet . . .

. . . and went absolutely barking mad. I braked hard into each corner, nudging the gear lever once, twice and sometimes three times to keep the revs right up, until I hit the apex of the corner, and buried the throttle once more.

The tarmac was hot and sticky, and it crackled slightly

as the new Michelins cut through it like waterskis on a windless lake. And rising above it all, as wave after wave of power and torque surged down the prop shaft, came the hard-edged, machine-gun, staccato roar of that super-charged Mercedes V8 engine.

It was enough to make a man quite chubby with excitement. And with the sun beginning to kiss the western horizon I remember thinking, 'Well, if I hit a tree now, I'll at least be going out on a high.'

It was a wonderful drive home. Me and the machine, not just singing in perfect harmony but fused in a bout of gaily abandoned man-love. This was the raw, undiluted pleasure of driving almost for driving's sake.

Except, of course, that's rubbish, because it wasn't raw or undiluted at all. The Mercedes puts up a firewall comprising about a million gigabytes of silicon between the driver and the business end of things. It's got a braking assistance system and computer-controlled air suspension, along with traction control, power steering and a fly-by-wire throttle. I was driving a fascimile of a car, rather than the real thing: it moaned and groaned and twitched and flinched just like the true item, but in my heart of hearts I knew that I was making love to little more than a hologram.

All modern cars isolate you from the road, they cocoon you in a safe, quiet world of velour and Radio 2 and air-conditioning. The wind that ruffles your hair in a modern convertible isn't wind at all, rather a gentle breeze that has been massaged by an aerodynamics engineer somewhere in Frankfurt. And the nice rorty little rasp from your exhaust at 5,000 rpm was in fact put there by someone in an anechoic chamber in Stuttgart. So when you're in a car, you're really in the Matrix.

In the past I've never been able to get out, to smell real air and hear real engine noises. I was never able to do the Keanu Reeves thing because at 6ft 5in. I've always been much too tall to fit into a Caterham Seven.

Now, though, there's a longer, wider version available for the chap with the fuller, longer figure. And last weekend I gave it a whirl.

Bloody Hell Fire and Holy Mother of Christ: apart from being bigger, it was a whole lot more powerful to boot. In fact, it offers up 442 bhp per ton, and nothing else on the road gets even close to doing that. A Ferrari 575, for instance, produces a figure of only 298 bhp per ton, while the Lamborghini Murciélago manages 319 bhp per ton.

At first you'll wonder where the power has gone. But that's because you'll be changing up when the noise and the vibrations become intolerable. But don't. In fact, you change up when blood is spurting out of your ears and your right foot has been shaken clean off your ankle. Then you discover where the power is – hiding its massive bulk in the uppermost reaches of the rev band.

Go there and, no matter what you happen to be driving right now, you'll be surprised at the punch it delivers. I know I was.

What's more, you can actually see the suspension working, and the brakes too, and when you turn the wheel the road wheels move, right in front of your eyes. You can place this car bang on target every time. Not just near the white line, as you would in a painfully slow Lambo or a pedestrian Ferrari, but bang on that line.

I've always assumed that a car like this would feel like an extension of your hands and feet, but it's the other way round.

I felt like a part of it: an organic component, but a component nevertheless.

You use a normal car to take you somewhere, and it tries to make that journey as pleasant as possible. But you would never use a Caterham as a means of transport, because this is driving for the buzz of it, and as a result you're not a passenger. You are there to do a job, which means you are no more and no less important than one of the pistons or the windscreen wipers.

This is the real deal. Everything that happens happens because it happens. Not because some German in a white coat thinks it should happen. The marketing department has not created the noises, the jolts and the acceleration. They're there because this is a light, powerful sports car and these are the characteristics you must expect of such a thing.

I didn't like it. Partly because I still don't fit properly – the steering wheel sits on my thighs, which means I simply could not apply any opposite lock in an emergency. Also, while Caterham will build a car for you, it's designed to be a kit that you build yourself. That's why it bypasses regulations on noise, safety and emissions. Great, but I'd never fully trust anything I'd built myself: I'd always assume that a wheel was about to fall off.

Most of all, though, I didn't like the Caterham because

it was like camping. The roof looks so terrible that you can't possibly drive around with it up. But then again, it's so fiddly that you can't possibly drive with it down either. Plainly, it was designed by a man who likes to sleep out at night, possibly with some Boy Scouts, far from anywhere, with just a thin layer of canvas between him, the boys and the rain.

And then there's the business of what you should wear when driving the Caterham.

This is the only car that demands a trip down to Millets before embarking on even the shortest journey.

You need a woolly bobble hat, an anorak and some Rohan trousers. There's an almost wilful lack of style to this kind of motoring, you see. A. A. Gill described his run from the station in my wife's Caterham last year as 'the worst five minutes of my life'.

The problem here is that we are in the very furthest corner of motoring enthusiasm. And, as is the way with all hobbies, things go off the rails when people start to take them too seriously.

Everyone likes to dangle a worm in the water from time to time. But the Caterham is the equivalent of getting up at three in the morning and sitting in the rain, on a canal bank, until it goes dark again.

Everyone looks up when Concorde flies over, but the Caterham is the equivalent of flying to Greece to snap some Olympic 737s. Would you risk getting locked up for your love of this car? Man at Millets would.

I'm interested in motor racing but I don't want to be a marshal. I find stamps pretty but I don't want an album.

I like music but I'm not going to build my own instruments. And I like driving but I'm far too old, rich, soft and poncey – and still slightly too big – for what, without any doubt, is the ultimate driving machine.

Sunday 27 July 2003

Lamborghini Gallardo

Suppose you had a priceless Ming vase, you wouldn't use it as a dice shaker or a vessel for serving punch at Boxing Day parties.

In a similar vein you wouldn't use a racehorse to hack out, and you wouldn't use a pearl-handled butter knife to pick a lock. So it's faintly ridiculous to suppose a supercar can co-exist in the real world alongside young men from Kazakhstan in Nissan Laurels and even younger men from Albania on pizza-delivery mopeds.

So what is it for then, exactly? Getting down and growly on the world's racetracks? Well, yes, obviously, but even here things can go awry.

Just recently I attempted to see how fast the new Koenigsegg supercar could accelerate from 0 to 60 mph. But as I let the clutch in, one of the many belts that drives something important in the engine bay shredded and I was left in a world of noise and smoke, going nowhere.

Last week I attempted a similar test with a £320,000 Pagani Zonda, and again it all ended in tears. As I floored the throttle and the 7.3-litre Mercedes V12 engine girded its considerable loins for an assault on the horizon, the clutch shouted, 'For God's sake,' and exploded. There was a lot of smoke. Hence the tears.

Lamborghinis are especially good at this. Once, to

amuse the crowds at Goodwood, I decided to do a massive wheel-spinning start off the line. But this was a Diablo, with four-wheel drive and tyres bigger than the rings of Saturn, so the only thing that could possibly spin was the clutch. It did. And I had to drive up the hill with the V12 tearing its heart out, but only doing four or five miles per hour.

It has always been thus. I once drove the world's first supercar, a Lamborghini Miura, but I cannot tell you how fast it went since it oiled its plugs at every set of lights, and stalled. And there wasn't enough juice in the battery to get it going again.

A friend recently described his old Bentley as being like a middle-aged man, oohing and aahing its way through life because bits of it which worked perfectly well yesterday had suddenly decided to give up the ghost today.

Supercars, on the other hand, are like athletes, forever suffering from hamstring injuries and groin strains.

No, really. My wife goes to the gym every morning and as a result is permanently broken in some way. The bathroom cabinet looks like Harry Potter's potion store. Whereas I, whose only exercise is blinking, am never ill at all.

So, if you can't go quickly in a supercar, and you can't use it for everyday chores like shopping and taking the children to school, what can you do with it?

Go out for dinner? Oh puh-lease. Where are you going to leave it? In the street? In a multi-storey car park? And what shape do you suppose it will be in after you've finished your Irish coffee and mints?

I once parked my old Ferrari outside a restaurant, with the roof off. It didn't seem like a problem, since I was in the Cotswold village of Deddington where the crime statistics talk of some scrumping in 1947 – and that's it. But when I came back, the interior had been used for what I can only assume was the world championship gozzing competition. I have never seen so much phlegm.

Sure, you can take such a car to a friend's house for a party. But then, how are you going to get home? Driving a bright yellow Lamborghini at two in the morning is as obvious as weaving down the street with a traffic cone on your head.

Of course, one day you'll be in your supercar on a wonderful, sweeping mountain road, and suddenly all will become clear.

But not for long, because pretty soon you'll round a corner to find a party of ramblers or cyclists, or maybe both. Do you think they're going to (a) point appreciatively at your car or (b) shout obscenities?

And later, when you have broken down, or smashed the low-riding front end clean off on a dip in the road, do you think they'll (a) stop to help or (b) laugh at you until they need hospital treatment?

Buy a supercar, and your neighbours won't like the noise. Your wife won't be able to climb aboard in a short skirt, your friends will be jealous, and other road users will make signals. It's hard to think of any group or body that likes a man in a supercar; small boys, perhaps. But is that what you want? Probably not, I suspect.

None of this, of course, stops us wanting supercars, so

I was therefore intrigued by the new Lamborghini Gallardo. Unlike all the previous Lambos, there is no rear wing big enough to land helicopters on, and no air vents that slide out of the side when the going gets hot.

Yes, it looks sporty, but it's not like rocking up for work in a gold lamé jacket and tartan trousers. In a dark colour you might even call it discreet.

Inside, there's been another break from Lamborghini tradition. I fit. And the air-conditioning works, and you can see out of the back window, and there's a stereo that you can hear.

Oh, the engine makes a noise all right, but it doesn't prompt the sort of purple prose I normally use for cars of this type. There's no spine-tingling howl. It doesn't sound like Brian Blessed on the verge of an orgasm or Tom Jones making man-love for the first time.

There's a very good reason for all this. Italian politicians may think their German counterparts are humourless, strutting Nazis, and the Germans may have responded by taking their towels off the beaches of Tuscany this year. But all is well between the two nations in the world of car-making, because Lamborghini has been bought by Audi (itself part of the Volkswagen group), who have brought a dollop of common sense to the most lovably idiotic carmaker on earth.

As a result, the engine is an Audi V8 unit with two extra cylinders welded on to the end to create a 5-litre V10. It drives all four wheels via a six-speed gearbox, but you don't need to be a man-mountain to control everything. The clutch is light. The steering wheel moves easily. And you can change gear with one hand! Normally I have to get my super-fit wife to drive the Lamborghinis that we have on test. But even I, with arms like pipe cleaners, could manage the Gallardo.

I liked it, too, hugely. I liked it even more than the Ferrari 360 because it's better balanced and easier to control at the limit. It changes direction like a fly, grips like a barnacle and goes like a jet fighter on combat power. At one point I saw 175 mph on the clock, and there was plenty more where that came from.

It is a technological *tour de force*, a genuinely very good car, even if it is a trifle pricey at £115,000. But it left me feeling under-whelmed: there was no sense of occasion, like I felt when I first stepped into a Ferrari 355, or a Diablo, or a Zonda even.

This is important, because supercars appeal to the small boy in us all. We may hate the bastards who have them and we may know they make no sense at all, but that doesn't stop us wanting one. And there's the thing: I don't particularly want a Gallardo.

As I stepped out of it after a two-day stint, there was no pulsating desire to get back in again, and keep going. Although this may have had something to do with the fact that, after three hard minutes on the test track, the clutch was a thin veneer of dust on the main straight.

There we are, then. The message remains the same. If you want to go really, really fast, buy a plane ticket.

Sunday 21 September 2003

Mazda RX-8

When women crest the brow of middle age and start on the high-speed, unstoppable plunge to an osteoporotic, alopecia-ravaged death, there are many ways to pretend that it isn't happening. Breasts, ravaged by gravity and babies, can be re-upholstered. Tummies distorted by pregnancy can be vacuumed away. And shops such as SpaceNK and Boots sell exotic creams that soothe wrinkles and cellulite.

I have watched Joan Collins walk into a restaurant and noted how all the women stare in open-mouthed wonderment. Here she is, aged 70, and she doesn't look a day over 58. You certainly wouldn't give up your seat on a bus, were she to step on board with some heavy bags.

Now, compare and contrast the fortunes of Ms Collins with the plight of Barry Manilow. We hear he's had plastic surgery and what do we think? Poof. Mickey Rourke is said to have had Botox put in his face. Poof. Jay Kay wins a prize for most stylish man. Poof. A. A. Gill. Poof. Paul Smith. Poof.

Men who wear 'product' in their hair, whatever the hell that is. Poofs. Men who put on suncream in England. Poofs. Men who have combs or hairdryers. Poofs. Men who wash their cars. Poofs. Men in sandals. Poofs. Men who go to the dentist when they don't have toothache. Poofs.

Men who take vitamin tablets. Raving poofs. And backs to the wall, everyone: there's a jogger in the room.

Any attempt, whatsoever, to delay the visible signs of old age is met with a torrent of barracking and cruel jibes. And rightly so.

I wear clothes so that people cannot see my genitals. I have a stomach like a Space Hopper because I like eating food. My teeth are yellow because I drink 100 cups of coffee a day. My hair is cut with scissors. My bathroom scales are broken. I haven't combed my hair since I was 12, and I last washed a car in 1979.

I'd like, therefore, to say that I'm all man, but in my heart of hearts I know this to be untrue. Because a huge hole has appeared in the back of my hair and it's driving me insane with worry.

Baldness is bad enough when it appears from the front, but when it starts at the back, creating a big pink crater, it looks stupid. And what makes it worse is that the mirror lies. It tells you that you still have a full rug. It tells you that all is well. Your hole is as invisible as the hole in the ozone layer, but you know it's there all right, like a huge crop-circle, amusing people who sit behind you in cinemas.

Last weekend, a girl at a party tried to reassure me, saying that bald men smell nicer than those with a full crop. To demonstrate the point, she sniffed the shiny pate of Shaun Woodward, who happened to be near by, and declared the aroma to be 'lovely'. Whereas what's left of my curly top, she said, was 'horrid'. So much for the morning-pine goodness of my jojoba-tree shampoo.

I wasn't fooled, though. I know that baldness has to be masked. But how? I could go down the Dylan Jones route and give myself a number one. But then Dylan is editor of *GQ* magazine, and as such must be a poof.

Nothing works. Have a hair transplant, and you end up with something that looks like a Scottish forest on your head. Go for a scrape-over and you're marooned in your house every time there's a light breeze. And as for the wig? Forget it. Elton John has all the money in the world, and he still looks like he has a Huguenot carpet tile on his bonce.

If men were women, someone from Alberto Balsam would have thought of a cure for this terrible affliction. But we're not. So they haven't. I have, though. Simply hide your barnet under a car.

Plainly, if you're the sort of person who worries about hair loss, there is a trace of vanity, a hint of poofery in your make-up, so it needs to be something with a bit of panache and pizzazz. Though, obviously, it can't be a convertible.

A coupé, a car that puts style way above substance, is perfect. Not that long ago there were many from which to choose. Volkswagen did the Corrado, Nissan the 200SX, and Honda the Prelude. And there was the wonderful Fiat Coupé, a raft of cheap Porsches and the 6-series BMW. But one by one they all died away. Killed off, as people began to realise they were paying more for what was basically a saloon car in a funny hat.

Now, though, they're coming back. Joining the ancient Alfa GTV, the Toyota Celica – which is very good, incidentally – and the Hyundai Coupé – which is even better – will be the Chrysler Crossfire (a Mercedes SLK in a fairly pretty shell) and the Nissan 350Z, which is better looking but a bit of a pig to drive. It's just so wearing. Best of all, though, is the new Mazda RX-8, partly because of its rear doors, which open backwards to create a hole in the side of the car as big as the hole in the back of my head, and partly because it is so much fun talking about its Wankel rotary engine.

You've no need to explain how this works, because after you've said the name people are usually too busy laughing to be listening.

In essence, though, you get a sort of triangular-shaped 'piston' which spins round in a vaguely circular cylinder. The upside is uncanny smoothness – a buzzer sounds when you're up past 9,000 rpm to warn you that a gear-change might be in order – but the downsides have always been thirst and unreliability.

The problem is that the tips of the triangular 'piston' spinning round in the cylinder 9,000 times a minute have to be as tough as diamonds, but obviously not as expensive. I have no idea what Mazda has used – the residue of a Weetabix that's been left in a cereal bowl for a week, probably. That's the toughest substance I've ever encountered.

Whatever, Mazda says it has addressed all the problems in its new car, and that's good, because the upsides are better than ever. It may be only a 1.3-litre engine (in normal engine terms) but the power it delivers is astonishing: 231 bhp. And it just gets better and better as the revs begin the climb. Get past 7,000 rpm and it's like you've pressed a hyperspace button.

It handles, too. Unlike most coupés this one sends its power to the proper end of the car – the back. So the front does the steering, the rear does the driving, and you sit in the middle wondering why all cars don't feel this way; so balanced, so right and omigod I've just gone past 7,000 rpm again and it's all gone blurry.

As a practical proposition: well, it's not a people carrier, but you do get a decent boot and two smallish seats in the back. And with those doors, even the fattest children in the world can get in.

The best thing about this car, though, is the price: £22,000 is remarkable value for money, especially as my car had an interior that was not only nicely trimmed but also equipped like the innards of Cheyenne Mountain.

This is a very good car with an exceptional engine. But the whole point of a coupé is to bring a bit of style to your humdrum hairdo with its big hole at the back. It has to be a toupee with tyres, a weave with windscreen wipers, a syrup that can go sideways.

And on that front the RX-8 is a bit questionable. It's as though they had a styling suggestion box at the factory, and every single idea was incorporated. It's not ugly, and it's certainly not plain. But it is messy.

There is, however, an upside to this. People will be too busy examining the curved front, the striking back and the endless detailing, to notice the driver's a poof.

Sunday 14 September 2003

Noble M12 GTO-3R

The Audi TT has had a pretty undistinguished life so far. I thought, when it was launched, that it was as cute as a newborn lamb but that its steering was as woolly and as vague as a sheep. It turned out to be worse than that. After just a few months it began to emerge that on motorway slip roads the Pretty Titty, as I like to call it, would spin round and slam into the nearest solid object.

That was fixed, but worse was to come, because the redesigned cars, identifiable by their tail spoilers, were bought by young men who care just a little too much about their hair. So while it might not be quite so hell-bent on actually killing you, it would murder you socially by making you look like an estate agent.

To try to inject some new life into what's quite an old car now, Audi recently fitted the 3.2-litre V6, which is a good thing, and two gearboxes, which makes it rather jerky around town.

The idea is that when you select, say, third, the second gearbox prepares fourth, making the change almost seamless. Apparently each shift is done in something like 0.001 of a second, saving you 0.03 of a second every time you change gear.

Now you might think that it's an awful lot of bother,

fitting an extra gearbox just to save a thirtieth of a second. But after this week I'm not so sure.

Last Sunday I caught an afternoon flight to America and spent until 1 a.m. filming in Detroit. Then I drove west for 100 miles to be ready for a dawn photo-shoot.

After that was over, I filmed the new Ford GT40 for *Top Gear* – it's very, very good – and caught the overnight flight back again.

On Tuesday morning I raced home from Gatwick, wrote 3,000 words, quickly, because there was a school meeting that night, and on Wednesday I needed to write two television scripts, before flying to the Isle of Man for three filming days. I could have done with more time, but on Saturday night I needed to be in Berlin ready for a Sunday appointment with the new Porsche Carrera GT.

Next week things get really busy, with two overnight shoots, three columns, two features, two commentary records and trips to Surrey, London and St Tropez.

Never have I needed a fast car more. So, of course, the Mercedes broke down. The gearbox has decided it wants to be a ball gown or a potato, anything but a bucket of cogs, and naturally the spare parts have to come from Germany. I mean, it'd be far too much to expect Mercedes in Britain to clutter the place up with replace-ment bits and pieces. It might look ugly in the profit-and-loss accounts.

That's why I've been in the Audi, and on balance I must say I like the new gearbox(es). To hell with the horrid steering and the cherrywood chassis and the estate agent Bauhaus styling; every second counts, and if I can save one after just 30 gear-changes, good.

It is for this reason that there are currently men in the house fitting some kind of wireless transmitter device that allows me to access our new broadband connection.

Just this morning I needed to know when high water was in the Solomon Islands. Now, in the past, that would have necessitated a trip to the library, in a car with only one gearbox, but then along came the internet and suddenly you could get the answer in 10 seconds. But now, 10 seconds is an aeon. With broadband I can get the Solomons' tidal charts in one, leaving me time to download Gerry Rafferty's new album and have a spot of virtual sex with a young lady in Kiev.

At work I'll take the stairs rather than use a lift that has no 'door close' button. Standing there for three seconds waiting for them to shut automatically will make me late for the next appointment and the one after that until, eventually, I'll miss the heart attack I have scheduled for 2005.

On the roads I don't curse speed cameras because of the civil liberty issues. I curse them because they slow me down. Every time a traffic light goes red I want to get out and smash it up. On Monday I glowered at a poor woman whose horsebox had turned over on the M25. 'I don't care about your horse. I've had to swerve round you and that's cost me 3.27 seconds.'

But I reserve my special level of hatred, my mental Defcon 4, for people who drive up the A44 at 40 mph. I don't think we should be allowed to kill people who drive too slowly; it is never right to take a life. But I do think we should be allowed to torture them a bit. Saw their legs off, maybe, or shove a powerful air hose up their jacksies. Forty may have been all right in 1870, but it's simply unacceptable now. If all the world did 40, it wouldn't work any more.

This week, however, I found a woman coming up the A44 at 30 and I went beyond incandescence into a semi-catatonic state of pure rage. My blood turned to acid and fizzed. My heart was filled with hate. I very nearly followed her home, just so that I could burn it down. But there wasn't time. And, to make matters worse, the Pretty Titty didn't quite have the oomph to get past. Oh, it had the right gear in a jiffy, but the 3.2 wasn't enough of a heavyweight to exploit the gaps. God, I wanted my Mercedes. Or, better still, the new Noble M12 GTO-3R.

This doesn't accelerate when you press the pedal. It explodes. In the time it takes an Audi to select a gear, or the SL to gird its considerable loins, the lightweight Noble has added 10 mph to its speed, your eyeballs are fastened to the back of your skull and your left kidney has come off.

It may only have a 3-litre Mondro engine, but the addition of two turbochargers means it will accelerate from 0 to 60 in, oh, I don't know, four seconds. Maybe a bit less. And you'll reach the end of the road long before it reaches its top speed of 170 mph.

Speed, however, is only part of the fruit cocktail. The best thing about the old car, with the old 2.5-litre V6, was its handling. It simply didn't understand the concept of understeer, gripping like an American in Hurricane Isabel, and then oh so gently allowing the rear to slide in a glorious bout of power oversteer.

The new one is ever so slightly less good. Because there's so much more grunt from the extra half a litre, it's hard to get the throttle position just right. And it only takes your big toenail to grow a little and oomph, the rear wheels light up and you wind up going backwards in what feels like the smoking room at Detroit airport.

There's another problem, too. The new engine, and the addition of a six-speed gearbox, has pushed the price up to more than £50,000, and it's hard to justify that. Yes, it does appear to be well made and you do get leather trim, but there are no luxuries at all, apart from air-conditioning. You even have to wind your own windows down.

Sure, it's faster than a Carrera 2, and more fun as well, but it's not a Porsche, and you can never quite get it out of your head that it was built from plastic in South Africa and assembled on an industrial estate in Leicestershire.

I sort of don't mind, though, because it is just so very, very fast. And very, very pretty. And who cares if it doesn't handle quite as well as the old car. Coming second to that would be like coming second to Tom Jones in a singing competition.

The boss of TVR has referred to the Noble as 'the South African three-wheeler' ever since its suspension broke in a recent *Autocar* test. But that shows he's worried about it.

And rightly so. TVR has been doing its thing for

10 years and nobody has thought to help themselves to a slice of the cake. Now Noble has come along and taken the icing and the cherry, leaving only the sponge.

In a world obsessed with image, you can't beat a Porsche. But in a world obsessed with time, a Porsche is a library. A TVR is the internet. And the Noble is broadband.

Sunday 28 September 2003

TVR T350C

Whenever an actor is asked to slip into a toga he sees it as an excuse to go all swivel-eyed and bonkers. When it comes to the Romans, no speech defect is too preposterous, no gait too far-fetched.

We've had Derek Jacobi with his club foot and his stutter, and Malcolm McDowell helping himself to every bride, groom and farmyard animal in Rome. Oh, and let's not forget the one with the funny mouth who stabbed Russell Crowe in *Gladiator*.

If you believed everything you've seen about Rome on the silver screen, you'd wonder how on earth they managed to find the lavatory in the morning. Let alone work out how such a thing might be flushed and how the effluent might be carried away in a sewerage system, the like of which wasn't to be seen in the world again for another 1,800 years.

But it is an unwritten law that all empires, whether the Borg, the British, big business, or even the BBC, are bad. Fuelled by greed and policed with violence, they wreak havoc on the pipsqueaks, raping, pillaging and forcing them to eat genetically modified suppers while watching programmes like *Britain's Worst Toilet*.

So I wasn't expecting the Romans to be portrayed in a particularly rosy light in *Boudica* on ITV last Sunday.

And sure enough, in boinged Nero wearing lipstick. We didn't actually see him gnawing on a panda's ear and then using a slave's severed head to wipe away the goo, but the hint was there all right.

Meanwhile, back in plucky old England, Boudica was busy delivering speeches about freedom and democracy. She was the Afghan farmer whose poppies have been devastated by Monsanto. She was Nelson Mandela, William Wallace, Che Guevara and Gandhi all rolled into a one-cal, bite-sized Sunday evening, Charlie Dimmock-style glamourpuss.

Unfortunately, in real life she was none of these things. She was, in a word, British, which is just a whisker away from Brutish. The Romans may have brought peace, along with their baths and their roads, but behind the cloak of civilisation and poetry we were still a nation who loved to get our swords dirty.

When the Romans left, we reverted to type. As Simon Schama says in *A History of Britain*: 'War was not a sport; it was a system. Its plunder was the glue of loyalty binding noble warriors and their men to the king. It was the land, held in return for military service that fed their bellies, it was the honour that fed their pride and it was the jewels that pandered to their vanity. It was everything.'

In other words, the Brits love a good scrap. And it's still going on today. While the rest of the world hangs its head in despair over Iraq, Tony Blair comes out from behind the health-food counter and shouts: 'I'm proud of what we have done.'

Most countries, except perhaps France, will fight to

protect their borders or their way of life. But Britain will fight to protect someone else's borders and someone else's way of life. Poland. Kuwait. Korea. Don't worry, we'll be there, fists flying.

What's more, we're the only nation that likes to fight in its spare time. You'll see more brawls on a British high street in one night than you will in the whole of Italy in an entire year.

I went out the other night with a bloke who freely admitted that he likes nothing more than to finish off the night with a fight. While chaps elsewhere in the world hone their chat-up lines, hoping to go home with a girl, he has developed a range of provocations so that he can go home with a chair leg sticking out of his arm.

Think about it. If someone in Italy says, 'Are you looking at me?', you're on for some rumpy-pumpy. If someone says it in England, you're on for a ride in an ambulance. And have you ever heard a Frenchman say, 'Est-ce que vous upsettez mon vin?'

We are supposed to be a pot-pourri of Saxon, Goth, Roman, Norman, Celt and Viking. But actually we're just thugs and vandals. When the Romans went home, we pulled down their buildings, ripped up their roads and settled down for 400 years of bloodshed and mayhem known as the Dark Ages. Those were the days, eh?

And they're still going on. In Birmingham recently I encountered a group of lads pushing one of our television cameras along the street.

'Where are you going with that?' I asked.

'We're going to push it into the canal,' they replied, as

though it were the most natural thing in the world to do.

Beauty and love have no place in Britain. Which is why we are responsible for the most brutal and savage car of all: the TVR. An Alfa Romeo will try to woo you with poetry. A TVR will bend you over the Aga, rip off its kilt and give you one, right there and then.

A Volkswagen will make you a lovely shepherd's pie and light a fire to make your evening warm and cosy. Whereas a TVR will come home and bend you over the Aga again. A TVR would nick the lifeboat charity box on the bar, empty it, then shove it up your jacksie. A TVR would fight for its life, its honour, its family and, most of all, its pint.

Put a TVR on *Desert Island Discs* and it would take a flamethrower and a selection of hits from Wayne County and the Electric Chairs. Then it would bend Sue Lawley over the mixing desk and make animal love until it broke wind.

You don't get paint on a TVR; it's woad. And instead of being made from steel or aluminium, it's wattle and daub. It's an Iron Age fort with a Bronze Age engine. It's Boudica, only with less femininity and more rage in its heart.

And look at the names TVRs have had over the years: Griffith, Chimaera, Cerbera – all terrifying mythological creatures with goat heads and seven sets of teeth.

That's why I'm unnerved by the latest version, the T350C. What kind of a name is that? It makes it sound like an electric toothbrush. And while a toothbrush has a revolving head and bristles, it's not as scary as, say, a hammerhead shark. Could this mean, then, that the new car has lost some of its bite?

Two things back this up. First of all, it's a coupé with a boot and a hatchback, and I'm sorry but I just don't equate the concept of TVR motoring with all this stuff. It's like trying to imagine a Saxon despot in a cardigan.

Then there's the handling. Push any of the other TVRs into a corner too fast, and in an instant, with no warning, you're in a world of smoke and hate. Getting your entry speed wrong in a TVR is as dangerous as spilling a Glaswegian's pint. But the toothbrush just understeers, like a Golf or a Focus.

There's other stuff, too. For all the racing heritage and volume of a straight-six engine, it simply doesn't sound as terrifying as a V8. And this is the first TVR I've driven in ages with a substandard interior. In recent years we've become used to all sorts of swoops and oddities, but in this one it just doesn't work. It feels daft for no reason.

And yet, by some considerable margin, this is the best TVR I've ever driven. With its integral roll cage it feels stiffer and more together, like all four corners are working in harmony, rather than in discord. And the brakes are just astonishing.

So's the power. You may only get 3.6 litres and no forced induction, but you end up with a better power-to-weight ratio than you get from a Lamborghini Murciélago. That means it is seriously, properly, eye-poppingly fast.

And because it doesn't try to bite your head off every time you make a mistake, you can use more of the power for more of the time.

Finally, there's the question of money. To get this kind of performance, you have to be looking at a Porsche GT3 for £72,000, or a Murciélago for £163,000. Even the Noble I wrote about last week is over £52,000. But the TVR is just £38,500. Plus another two if you want lift-out roof panels.

So what we have here is a TVR with all the savagery of the olde worlde coupled with the practicality of a usable boot and a soft ride. It's an ancient Briton with Roman overtones, and as a result Alan Rickman wouldn't be able to play it properly in a film. He'd be too mad. Think more in terms of Alan Titchmarsh – a little bit raunchy, but actually a little bit not.

Sunday 5 October 2003

Porsche Carrera GT

There have been a handful of scientific breakthroughs in the past few weeks that I suspect may have slipped under your radar.

A couple of Dutch boffins, for instance, have developed a new kind of fabric that could be used as a television screen. So pretty soon you'll be able to watch *Matrix Reloaded* on your tie.

Then we have the British satellite that can spot rainfall and vegetation growth in Algeria. As a result, farmers there will be able to bring some shock and awe to the locust breeding grounds before the insect sex even takes place.

Or what about the vibrating shoes that have been developed in America? Apparently these compensate for a loss of balance in the elderly and will cut the number of falls and broken hips.

Best of all, we have the 2580 service on your mobile. Dial the number, hold the phone against a speaker and within 30 seconds, for just 9p, you'll be sent a text saying what the song is and who it's by.

So now you can wave goodbye to the misery of trying to find out what it was you heard on the radio by attempting to sing it to your friends. 'You must have heard it. It's brilliant. It goes ner-ner-ner de-dum-dum on the beach.'

Even China is riding the techno wave. We were told this week that the sheer weight of skyscrapers being built in Shanghai is squashing the rock on which the city is founded.

And we mustn't forget that extraordinary dam that will provide limitless power for everyone until the end of time, or their rocket, which next week will keep the red flag flying in space.

Nearer to home, scientists have developed a heat-resistant plastic which they're using to make a light that goes on in a handbag every time it's opened. Wonderful. No more standing around on the doorstep for 15 minutes while our wives rummage for the keys.

And then there's the world of computers. Seismologists have been able to work out just how big the tidal wave will be when Tenerife splits in half and falls into the sea. Very, seems to be the answer.

They've even been able to determine why tortoises on the Galapagos Islands are all mental. It seems there was a genetic bottleneck 100,000 years ago when a volcano went off, and only the biggest, daftest tortoises survived.

It's astonishing. We can trace a tortoise's family tree without trawling through parish records and looking at gravestones. We can watch moving pictures on our clothes of locusts 'dogging', safe in the knowledge that our mothers have not fallen over while we weren't looking.

And there's so much more. We can genetically modify crops, we can measure the smell of cheese, we can track stolen cars from space and teach our television sets to skip the adverts. We can do anything. We are invincible. And yet we are still being propelled from place to place by a series of small explosions.

It doesn't matter whether you drive a McLaren or a McDonald's delivery van, you are still relying on exactly the same technology that was dreamed up more than 100 years ago. In some ways this is a good thing, because when change is slow there's a chance for engineers to plane away at the rough edges, leaving you with something close to perfection.

If there had been a completely new type of technology invented every 20 years or so, none would have been refined to the same extent as the internal combustion engine we have now.

And the most refined, most planed-away, most astonishing engine I have ever encountered is currently to be found sitting in the middle of Porsche's new Carrera GT. This is 100 years of human achievement crammed into three cubic feet of titanium, magnesium, aluminium and raw, unadulterated, visceral, screaming power.

You're told, before you set off, that in no circumstances should you apply any throttle at all while engaging the clutch. The mountain of torque, apparently, would catapult you and your £320,000 hypercar into the nearest piece of foliage.

The Porsche engineers talk about the clutch pedal as though it's the trigger for a nuclear bomb. It may as well be.

The engine started out as a 5.5-litre V10 that was all set to be used in the back of a racing car at Le Mans. But a last-minute rule-change favoured smaller turbo units, so the programme was scrapped.

Nearly. In fact, Porsche's racing division handed over its stillborn engine to the road-car people, who had to worry about emission regulations. That meant adding a third piston ring, which meant fitting longer pistons, which took the engine up from 5.5 to 5.7 litres.

But the ceramic clutch remained. The Skunkwork stealth materials remained. The racing power remained too, all 612 brake horses of it. And you should hear the noise this thing makes. It's like driving around with the bastard love child of Jaws and Beelzebub in the boot.

Strangely, though, it's not the engine that impresses most of all about the Carrera GT. It's the weight. Unlike any other road car ever made, all of it − the body, the tub, even the support struts for that monster V10 − are made from stuff that sure as hell wasn't in the periodic table last time I looked.

The result is an extraordinary lightness. The targa-style roof, for instance, lifts out in two panels, each of which is light enough to be carried away by a strong ant. The seats weigh less than a bag of sugar. This car is so light I would be loath to leave it parked in a high wind. Certainly you'd feel guilty driving it after a big lunch.

The result is simple. Mix an anorexic body with a heart made of pure fire and you are going to go with a savagery that's hard to explain.

I've been in some pretty fast machinery over the years, but nothing prepared me for the neck-snapping, spleen-bursting, hammer-blow explosion of power that came the first time I floored the Carrera's throttle.

I was on an arrow-straight forest road in eastern

Germany and it was like I was caught up in a *Doctor Who* special effect. Nought to 60 was dealt with in 3.9 seconds. Nought to 100 took 8, and then it really started to fly. Even at 175 there was no let-up, no sense that the engine was having to fight the headwind. There was just more power, more acceleration, more speed and more of that amazing noise.

What made the experience even more bizarre was the way the engine lost its revs between gear-changes. Because the ceramic clutch is so light, there's nothing for it to fight. You just get that wawawawa, like you do from a Formula One engine.

Now, we have seen this kind of blood-and-guts stuff before, from Ferrari and McLaren and even some of the new boys like Pagani and Koenigsegg. But the Porsche feels different from any of them.

It feels finished. The quality of the body is as good as you'd expect from a Toyota Corolla and inside there's exactly the right blend of luxury, style and weight saving. Ferrari just tends to nail a speedo to the dash and leave it at that. Pagani uses too much chintz. The Carrera is perfect.

And there is no doubt that from any angle it is utterly beautiful. I had a long discussion recently with a friend about the difference between art and design. And without wishing to sound like Alan Yentob, the Carrera seems to sit at a point where the two disciplines meet.

It looks like the result of a liaison between Henry Moore and Isambard Brunel. It is engineering at its artsy-fartsy best.

The next time a car comes along that is better than this, it will be using a completely different technology. Because when you're limited to what we have now, this, quite simply, is as good as it gets.

Sunday 12 October 2003

Honda Accord Tourer Type S

With the audience figures for Radio 1's *Breakfast Show* in free fall, bosses have decided to replace the DJ Sara Cox with someone else whose name escapes me. The Queen, probably.

It won't make the slightest bit of difference. No one tunes in to a music radio station because of the announcer. We tune in because of the music, and the music on Radio 1 is from a never-ending stream of increasingly angry black men who, so far as I can tell, wouldn't know a piano if one were to land on their heads.

No, I do not sound like my father. He couldn't tell the difference between Ted Nugent and Karen Carpenter; it was all rubbish to his ears. Whereas today there is simply no difference between 50 Cent, Wyclef Jean and Black Eyed Peas. Except for the number of times each of them has been shot.

I have been paying rather more attention than usual to music recently because Sue Lawley invited me on *Desert Island Discs*.

The luxury good was easy. I decided I'd take a jet ski, though I was tempted, when I met Sue, to ask her along instead. She's hugely attractive.

The book was harder. You're given the *Complete Works* of Shakespeare – to get your fire going, presumably – and the Bible. But you're allowed to take one other. That's impossible. Not being five, I find all books dull after I've read them once.

But the most impossible thing of all was the music. Like everyone else, my list of Top 10 greatest all-time songs features around 250 tracks. Fourteen of which are the best ever.

And to make matters worse, some of the 14 best-ever songs are not the sort of things I would care to share with the nation. Telling the audience that one of your favourite tunes is 'Clair', by Gilbert O'Sullivan, is not that far removed from walking into the pub and telling everyone you have genital sores.

For instance, I've always had a soft spot for Sad Café. In the wee small hours I can admit that to myself, along with a fondness for Camel and Yes and Supertramp. But not in a studio, at 11 a.m. on a Tuesday morning. Not to Sue Lawley.

It was for this reason I also decided to steer clear of anything classical. Unlike some of the guests on the show, who prove themselves to be interesting and mysterious by choosing pieces in B flat by someone unpronounceable from Transylvania, the only classics I know are from adverts. And I fear I may have looked a bit of a fool if I'd asked for that piece from the Pirelli tyre commercial. Or worse, that one they all clap along to at the Horse of the Year Show.

So what I ended up with was my best-ever eight songs (that I'll admit to liking). And you know what? The most recent was Bowie's 'Heroes' from 1977. This makes me a very, very old man, and that means I'm feeling well qualified this week to write about Honda's new Accord Tourer Type S.

Over the years Honda has tried and tried to give itself a youthful appeal. It has injected its cars with Botox, collagen and testosterone. It has even slotted 190 bhp engines under the bonnet of a Civic, but this was like fitting a spoiler to a plastic hip. All it did was increase the speed the old lady was going when she hit the tree.

It came up with a funky small car which it called the Jazz. It even offered it in the same shade of metallic pink as a nine-year-old's nail varnish. And what happened? My mother bought one.

There were sports cars in the 1960s, and Honda does a wonderful sports car now: the S2000. There have been three prolonged lunges for glory in Grand Prix racing and even a foray into the world of supercars.

But it's to no avail. I was busy admiring an electric-blue NSX on the A40 last week when, with no warning whatsoever, it veered across my bows and shot up a slip road. And who was driving it? Well, it was Mr Bean himself, Rowan Atkinson.

At first I thought the new Accord Type S might be yet another attempt to woo thrusting young executives out of their BMWs and Audis. It has the requisite black interior and the de rigueur fake carbon-fibre cubbyhole covers, so that inside it looks like a gentleman's electric razor. In addition it has a huge orange speedometer that goes up to 160 mph, twin exhausts, lights like Butler &

Wilson jewellery and a titanium gear lever that offers a selection of six forward gears.

'Oh no,' I thought, as I eased out of the drive. 'It's like someone's father undoing one too many of his shirt buttons and trying to dance.'

But it isn't. The 2.4-litre i-VTEC engine doesn't spin quite so readily, or sound quite as fruity, as Honda's other sporty engines, and nor does it develop quite as much power as I was expecting. That said, it's a very good engine, which is coupled to a sublime gearbox. But both are overshadowed by the ride.

Not even the new Jaguar, with its air suspension, can cope with bumps as well as this Honda. Even when you're going quickly, and you won't be because you grew out of that sort of thing 40 years ago, there are no jars or shudders.

On the road I use to test this sort of thing, I was astonished. You feel the car rise as it crests a bump in the road and you tense, waiting for it to crash back down again. But the crash never comes. It settles gently, like it's a burly paramedic and you're on a stretcher.

Strangely, this doesn't seem to have affected the handling unduly. The steering's beautifully weighted. There's a good, seat-of-the-pants feel. The brakes are powerful and the seats hold you in place perfectly. This is all very clever. I've been saying for ages that I want a car that's fast and sporty, but not so that it breaks my spine in two every time I run over a badger. And that's what you get from the Accord Type S. Performance for the Past-It boys.

There's more, too, in the shape of a low £20,000 price tag and unburstable mechanicals. I found out the other day that in the past 13 years there has never been a single failure of Honda's VTEC system. Not one. Ever.

People talk about Volkswagens being reliable, and Mercs. But if I may liken reliability to the M1, the German cars are only at Milton Keynes. Toyota is outside Leicester, whereas Honda is already on the A1, going into Scotland.

I hope the tyres are reliable, too, because (as is increasingly becoming the norm these days) no spare wheel is supplied. It saves weight, say the car manufacturers. Yeah, right. And money.

You only get a puncture once every 150,000 miles, they counter. Sure, but when it happens it's nice to know you'll only be held up for 20 minutes, not two weeks while a replacement tyre is shipped from Yokohama.

And no, we're not fooled by the sealant and pump that are supplied. This may work if you discover a drawing pin in the tread when you come out of the house one morning. But they are of limited use if your tyre is in 578 small pieces all over the M20.

The only real upside to this penny-pinching is the extra space in the boot. Not that the Accord estate needs it. The rear end is almost Volvoesque in its vastness.

So, a pretty good effort then, all things considered. Except for one enormous detail. Look at the picture and tell me if you have ever, in all your life, seen anything quite so ugly.

If I may bring the M1 into it again, we have Gérard

Depardieu at Bedford and the new British Library at Sheffield South. But this is off the top of the map, up round the North Pole, alongside Ranulph Fiennes's frost-bitten fingers.

Why, for instance, does the rear window taper when the bodywork does not? And why does such a big car come with wheels like Smarties? I've seen more balance and cohesion at a stag party and more aesthetic merit in a Prague housing project. Did Sara Cox design it? Or was it drawn in the middle of a yardie shootout? In my Top 10 worst-ever looking cars, a list that currently features 145 different models, this is number one. Along with 38 others.

Sunday 19 October 2003

Bentley Continental GT

The man from Budleigh Salterton Council was adamant. 'Of course it'll be all right,' he said. 'People take their cars on to the beach all the time. Don't worry, it's surprisingly firm.'

Beaches are never surprisingly firm. If anything, I'd say they're surprisingly un-firm. It doesn't matter whether they're made of shale, shingle, grit, sand or big slabs of volcanic rock, they'll munch you up and hold you fast until the tide can come along to finish you off.

Over the years I've had to dig countless cars off various beaches around the world. A Corrado in South Wales. A Saab Turbo in St Tropez. And, most notably of all, a massive Lamborghini LM002 on Hayling Island.

But I never learn. So I drove the £110,000 Bentley Continental GT on to the shale at Budleigh Salterton, thinking that its four-wheel-drive system would get me off again. And with the words of the man from the council ringing in my ears: 'If it does get stuck, we've got a man with a tractor.'

Great. Except, when it did get bogged down, the man with the tractor had gone home.

Welcome, then, to the joys of filming for *Top Gear* which, incidentally, returns to your television tonight. Albeit without the Bentley, which – when I left the scene in the dead of night – was still buried in stones up to its axles.

Happily, however, before Mother Nature intervened, I did have plenty of wheel time with what is probably the most talked-about new car of the year. David Beckham is getting one. Elton John has bought one for his boyfriend. But I hear that the first to roll off the lines will go to Gordon Ramsay.

Bentley, then, will be supplying the wheels to the kind of people who get their diet from Atkins, their frocks from Versace, their Botox from Harley Street, their tans from Barbados and their friends from the pages of *Hello!*

So what kind of car is it? Well, the first thing you need to know is that it's fast in a wholly new and exciting way. Normally, a quick car introduces you to each one of its horsepowers and torques with a lot of shouting and growling.

Ferrari even invented a new type of exhaust that gets louder the faster you go, and now everyone's at it. Hit 3,000 rpm in an Aston Martin Vanquish, for instance, and a little valve diverts all the waste gases away from the catalytic converters and silencers and into what sounds like the room where God practises shouting.

People who claim in court that they drove a really fast car without realising just how fast they were going are either lying or stone deaf. Or they were in a Bentley Continental GT.

It's uncanny. You put your foot down, wait the tiniest of moments while the turbos gird their loins, and then the view goes all wobbly. There's no increase in noise, no increase in drama. You just have time to register the speedo needle climbing at what looks like a suicidal rate and then, with barely a whisper, you arrive at wherever it is you're going.

The secret to all this oomph is a 6-litre W12 engine which, for that little extra something, has been garnished with two turbochargers. The result is a set of figures that looks more like Swiss bank account numbers. And the result of that is a top speed of 198 mph. This is a very, very, very fast car.

It is also very, very heavy. In fact, it weighs very nearly the same as a Range Rover. So if your right foot fancies a workout, you'd better stand by for a wallet-shrivelling experience at the pumps. How does 10 mpg sound? Well, forget it. You'll only get that if you hop out and push.

The reasons it's so heavy are twofold. First of all, it is immensely well engineered. Shutting the door requires teamwork, and it comes with the biggest brakes ever fitted to a road car. And secondly, it has what appears to be a couple of oak chests and 16 dead cows lining the interior. It looks like Lord Kitchener's library in there.

Sort of. Instead of making its own dials out of ivory and fitting a nice Alan Turing-style computer with valves and ticker tape, Bentley has simply raided Volkswagen's parts bin. There's barely a knob or a read-out in there that hasn't been lifted straight from the Phaeton.

And there's more VW stuff behind the skin, too. The engine, for instance, and most of the floor and, worst of all, the layout.

As is the way with Volkswagens and Audis, the engine is mounted as far forward as possible without bits of it actually sticking out through the radiator grille, and the power is fed to all four wheels. It sounds like a recipe for terminal and dreary understeer.

But no. You arrive at the corner in complete silence, doing about 5,000 mph, dab the brakes, but not too hard because they're powerful enough to pull your head off, and then turn in. Every fibre of your body expects the nose to run wide and the peace to be shattered by the sound of a road-going Second World War bomber hitting a tree, but it just grips and grips.

If you go really fast – and I'm talking now about 'tired of living' fast – the back loses traction and you are presented with an easy-to-control power slide. How they have achieved this when the layout is so obviously wrong I simply do not understand.

But there's no doubt about it. This is not just a luxury barge, designed to whisk you and your third wife off to St Tropez for a weekend's bloating. It is a truly wonderful, jaw-slackeningly awesome driver's car. You could take it to a track day and spend the whole time punting Ferraris and 911s into the Armco. For a laugh.

Now shall we get to the bits that aren't so good. For something that's about the size of a football pitch, it is cramped in the front to the point of claustrophobia. And if the salesman tells you there's space in the back for any human life form, laugh openly in his face.

Also, I must say that while it has presence, it's not handsome or pretty or attractive. From the front it looks like a Rover 75, and from the back it looks like a car. But then it was designed by a Belgian.

Then there's the rear spoiler, which pops up at 70 mph – that should make the job of the traffic cops a little easier – and the satellite navigation, which, I think, was on a work-to-rule. It was still working out a route to Budleigh Salterton when it was already there and going no further.

In addition, the glovebox lid didn't shut properly, the armrests squeaked and the endless succession of warning bongs and beeps drove me mad before I was even out of Knightsbridge.

These, though, are niggles, and I'll find just as many in any car. Overall, there is no single reason why you should not buy or dream about buying this car. Unfortunately, there is also no single reason why you should.

With the new Phantom, BMW seems to have captured the essence of Rolls-Royce, but I have to say that VW has failed to pull off a similar trick with the Continental. Put simply, it feels like a big, fabulous, fast, well-engineered Volkswagen.

I couldn't help thinking, as it hauled me down the A303, that I'd have enjoyed the drive more in an Arnage. Oh, it would have been noisier and less fast and it would have fallen apart on the twisting lanes of Devon, if it had got that far without breaking in some way.

But the old Brit Bruiser has a grandeur that the Continental lacks somehow. There's no sense of occasion when you step inside. It's a car you can respect, but not love.

Let me put it this way: as I drove away from that beach

the other night, in a rented Nissan Primera, I wasn't saddened that I'd had to leave the Bentley behind. It had been, when all is said and done, just another car.

Sunday 26 October 2003

Porsche Cayenne Turbo

Last week it was disclosed that a company which once held shares in a firm that made the cyanide gas for the concentration camps is helping to build Germany's Holocaust memorial. And of course, there was much brouhaha.

I wonder how much longer this sort of thing will go on. Am I to be prevented from drinking Red Stripe because my great-great grandfather was bosun on one of the slave ships? Should you be ejected from your local curry house because your great-uncle's second cousin fired some of the shots at Amritsar?

If so, then it will be awfully difficult to buy a new car. Obviously a Volkswagen, BMW or Mercedes are right out because they powered the U-boats and built the tanks and made the planes that dropped the bombs.

So how about a Subaru Impreza, or a Mitsubishi of some kind. I'm sorry. Have you forgotten about the bridge over the River Kwai? Do you not recall Alec Guinness in that box?

And you can forget about a new Fiat. First, it comes from the country that gave the world Mussolini, and second, it will break down.

I'd like to say that you can have a Saab. But we can't pretend the story of Reeve Beaduheard didn't happen.

He met what he supposed was a fleet of Norse trading ships and directed the sailors to the nearby royal estate. For his troubles he was rewarded with an axe in the face. It's hard to forgive and forget that sort of thing.

And that's before we get to the muddy wartime history of Porsche. Although the founder of the company, Ferry Porsche, was cleared of any wrongdoings by everyone except the French, he was undoubtedly involved in the Nazi apparatus.

Having served as Archduke Ferdinand's chauffeur, a job with no future, Porsche met Hitler at a race meeting in the 1920s and the two became friends. His company made military vehicles, tanks and parts for V-1 rockets. And Porsche was an honorary SS officer. But if you're looking for a good reason not to buy one of the new Cayennes, you can do better.

It has been on the market for some time now and, to be honest, I haven't bothered reviewing it. I didn't see the point. People, I figured, will not dream about owning a car as ugly as this, and even if they are immune to its aesthetic forcefield they will be stumped by the £70,000 price tag.

What was Porsche thinking of? An SUV off-roader? That's like the board of directors at Lurpak deciding to branch out into video recorders. What's more, I keep reading stories in the specialist press about the problems Porsche is having. Demand, apparently, was massively overestimated, and now smaller-engined, cheaper alternatives are being rushed into production to take up the slack.

However, there's no getting away from the fact that the damn things are everywhere. They're jamming the back streets of London and littering the rugby club here in Chipping Norton. They're out-Ranging the Rover on the school run and doing a Ronin on the Shoguns on partridge drives from Inverness to Totnes.

So I swallowed my prejudice, called Porsche, and days later a twin-turbocharged V8 gargoyle was sitting on my drive.

It really is absolutely hideous. They've obviously spent much time and effort giving it the Porsche family nose, but this is like fitting Meg Ryan's conk on the front of a buffalo. And having completely messed up the sharp end, they didn't bother with the back at all.

You are not, ever, going to buy this car as an art form. And nor will you buy it for practical reasons. There is, for instance, no split folding tailgate, nor does a pair of seats rise up from the boot floor. What you get is space for five, just like you get in a Ford Mondeo.

I decided, then, that I had been right to ignore this big, ugly, impractical, overpriced piece of marketing origami from the company that brought you the V-1 rocket. And there was no point going for a drive because I'd already tested its sister, the Volkswagen Touareg, and that's about as bad as cars get.

Still, because it was sitting there with a full tank, there'd be no harm popping to the shops . . . and whoa . . . bloody hell, it's quick.

I don't mean quick for an off-roader, or quick for a car of this size and weight. It's quick by any standard you care to lay in its path. From 0 to 62, for instance, is dealt with in 5.6 seconds, and flat out you'll be going at 165 mph. To get some idea of what this feels like, imagine doing nearly 170 mph in a City Hoppa bus.

And it isn't just the straight-line speed that leaves your liver in the back seat. This is a high-riding, off-road car that corners like a normal, well-sorted sports saloon. And to get some idea of how hard this must have been to achieve in engineering terms, imagine skiing down a slalom on stilts.

Whenever I drive an off-road car down the motorway I'm always mildly terrified that I might have to swerve for something. This, I know for a fact, would result in many deaths because big, tall off-roaders don't slide. They roll over.

The Cayenne, however, does not. And as a result it is no more dangerous or unwieldy than, say, an Audi RS6.

Now you might argue at this point that a BMW X5 is similarly nimble and I would agree. But that is one of the most monumentally stupid cars ever to turn a wheel because it doesn't work off road. You pay all that extra money, and suffer at the pumps, too, for what's basically a slightly taller 5-series.

Unbelievably, the Cayenne manages to perform well on the road and still work properly when you decide to follow the crows home.

On one of the country's toughest off-road courses, I pointed it at a hill that, moments earlier, had defeated a Land Rover. And to make things more interesting I didn't bother reading the instruction manual first, choosing instead to prod away at some buttons until a selection of red warning lights illuminated.

Halfway up the slope, on mud and loose gravel, it stopped, and that's always a sign that you need to back down and start again. Not in the Cayenne it isn't. I simply kept my foot hard down and allowed the computer to work out which wheel wanted how much power at any given moment. Bit by bit and inch by inch it clawed its way to the top.

And once there I turned off the traction control and for a half an hour or so behaved like a contender in the World Rally Championship. I have never treated a car so roughly, not ever; and yet, despite this, all that fell off was one of the wheel weights.

Then, half an hour later, I was back on the motorway, flashing my lights at BMW M5s and AMG Mercs, trying to get past.

This might have had something to do with the Porsche's surfeit of power, but could also be down to its satellite navigation system. While Merc and BMW men are waiting for their sat navs to decide if there are any roads which go to London, the Porsche's has a route, and several back-ups, already figured out.

This, then, is a simply staggering engineering achievement, a car with the build quality of a volcano that will match anything from Land Rover on the rough and go home as though it's being fuelled with extra-hot horse-radish sauce. How it can be a sister to that godawful Touareg I just don't understand.

If ever a car could be said to suffer from ugly-bird

syndrome, this is it. It really does try harder. It gobbles up the miles and isn't all out of ideas once it's past 69.

But could you have one? Having found out just how good it was, I tried to look at it in a variety of new ways. Through a thin film of tracing paper. While wearing my wife's spectacles. Through the wrong end of a pair of binoculars. But it was hopeless.

For aesthetic reasons alone I'd plump for second best and buy a Range Rover. And ignore the fact that it's now made by Ford, whose founder thought Hitler was a pretty good bloke.

Sunday 2 November 2003

Porsche 911 GT3

In a normal year we can expect two or maybe three exceptionally good cars to come along. But 2003 has been extraordinary. The Rolls-Royce Phantom has not been much of a sales success, but then you don't find too many bottles of 1945 Château Petrus being served at your local Harvester. As a piece of engineering, though, it is undoubtedly exquisite. Put simply, the Phantom is the best car the world has ever seen. By miles.

Then we saw the Volvo XC90, which is a seven-seat people-carrier that isn't too mumsy and a chunky 4×4 that isn't too butch. It's also relatively inexpensive, without being cheap. It's small wonder, then, that the dealers have already sold their entire allocation for 2004.

There were big advances on the safety front, too, with Renault leading the charge: its Mégane became the first small family hatchback to get the full five stars in the respected Ecro NCAP safety performance test.

And just the other day Mercedes announced that it had finally produced an A-class that runs on hydrogen. It looks completely normal, can do 87 mph, and yet produces nothing but water from its exhaust pipe. The only drawback is the price: £300,000.

Of course, none of these cars offers much in the way of driving fun. Earlier this year I drove the new Rolls round a race track, and to understand what it felt like you must try to imagine Queen Victoria doing the 100-metre hurdles. Or, better still, A. A. Gill on a jet ski. In one corner, the traction control didn't just intervene, it blew a silent whistle on proceedings – and that was that.

With no fuss and no drama, and with my foot hard down on the throttle, the three-ton car just ground to a halt in a cloud of palpable incredulity. 'What in the name of all that's holy,' it seemed to be saying, 'do you think you're doing?'

You might think this to be a fair question. You look at all the speed humps and the cameras and the traffic and the price of petrol . . . and you think, well, what's the point of a razor-sharp, ice-cool, four-wheeled bullet like this one?

Cars like the Rolls and the Volvo (which plods around like a tractor) and the Mégane, which doesn't ever go fast enough to crash, are undoubtedly in tune with the times.

Maybe so. But despite this, the big news in 2003 was the sheer number of out-and-out fun cars that came on to the market in a flurry of spinning bow ties and clown shoes. There were so many, in fact, that I've made a video and a DVD about them. It's called *Shoot Out*, and I shall be forever in your debt if you go out tomorrow and buy it.

I shan't tell you here which car from the most fun year in the history of motoring I reckon is . . . the most fun. But to give you an idea of just how intense the competition was, I shall write instead about a car that didn't even make it to the final magnificent seven: the Porsche GT3.

The first thing you need to know about this is that Porsche is a difficult, arrogant, humourless company; and on the face of it, that's not a very good thing to be when you're in the business of making fun cars. A 911, you always sense, 'likes a laugh as much as the next man', which is probably another way of saying 'doesn't like a laugh at all'.

None of the truly great comedians are funny when you meet them in real life. Rowan Atkinson, Ben Elton, even Richard Curtis. For these people, you see, comedy is a science, which means it must be approached in a straight-forward, methodical fashion.

Creating a situation designed to make an audience fall off the backs of their seats is no different from creating a bridge or a chest of drawers. Seriously, folks. Tell Steve Coogan a funny story and he won't laugh; he'll probably say, 'That's funny,' but without a hint of a smile. Or, more usually, if he's listening to me: 'That's not funny.'

So it goes with the po-faced and utterly humourless 911. It's not a fun car. There's no *joie de vivre* in its styling and no sitcom at all in that dark and gloomy interior. But put it on the right stage and all that Teutonic fine tuning pays off, because then it starts to deliver fun, and by the skipload. That said, I've never much liked the whole 911 thing.

Yes, I'll pay to see a comedian strut his stuff in the theatre, but what's the point of socialising with a person who thinks that someone with a bad wig is 'a possible source of interesting material'? Am I disappearing up my own backside here? Whatever.

While I respect the ability of the modern Porsche 996 Turbo, I much prefer the madness of Ferrari and the sheer idiocy of Lamborghini. And there's another thing: life is way, way too short to try to get a handle on the depth and breadth of the 911 range, with its endless variations on a single theme.

All you need to know is that, over the years, the 911 has become increasingly soft core, with pixellated private parts and silicon breasts. But every so often Porsche produces an adult-rated version that harks back to the hard-core roots. Usually these cars bear the RS badge. But, as is the way with the 911, sometimes they don't.

Whatever the case, every single one of them has been horrid. There was an RS in the mid-1990s that was about as awful as anything I've ever driven. I bounced all the way from Balham in south London to Cadwell Park race circuit in Lincolnshire in one, imagining that when I got there I'd find some recompense for the simply dreadful ride and complete lack of creature comforts. But no. After I removed its lead and took off the muzzle, it spent the entire afternoon trying to bite my head off.

This was a car that understeered badly every time I went round one particular corner, and then – for no reason at all – would suddenly decide to oversteer. I hated it.

So I really wasn't expecting much from the GT3 which, for those of you who can be bothered to clutter up your heads with this sort of thing, is basically a Carrera 2. That means you don't get a turbocharger and you don't get four-wheel drive. And you don't get bulging wheel arches either, although you do get a bill for £73,000.

Inside it, despite the enormous bill, you don't get air-conditioning or much in the way of luxury, and instead of back seats there's some scaffolding which I suppose could also be used as a roll bar.

Now, you'd be happy about all this minimalism if the end result were flyaway and featherlight. But it isn't. Because the GT3 has the same body as the stiffer Carrera 4, it actually weighs more than the Carrera 2. I told you the 911 range was a muddle.

What isn't even remotely muddling, though, is the way this car goes. With 381 bhp pumping out of the 3.6-litre flat-six engine in a muscular and seemingly never-ending scream of pure ecstasy, it absolutely flies.

And not just in a straight line either. Like all 911s since the year dot, the heavy engine sits at the back and gives huge traction in a corner; but, unlike any 911 I've ever driven, there is no punch-in-the-face punchline if you overcook it.

In terms of grip and handling, I don't mind sticking my neck out here and saying that I've never, ever driven anything that gets even close to it. In terms of comedy, it's *Fawlty Towers* – honed to perfection.

Bring the new M3 CSL to the party if you like. Bring a 911 Turbo. Bring a 360 Ferrari. Bring anything you want and so long as it costs less than £150,000, I guarantee the GT3 will nuke it.

In a little race I staged with an immensely fast and wonderfully satisfying Aston Martin DB7 GT, the Porsche was a full 10 per cent faster round the lap. That's

10 per cent faster, as well as being 40 per cent cheaper and probably 98 per cent more reliable, too.

Yes, admittedly the GT3 is stiff and a bit jarring over the speed bumps, but it's (just) on the right side of bearable. Think of it as Stephen Fry: probably a little bit difficult to live with from time to time, but you'd put up with the hard edges for those moments when one bon mot tears your sides literally in half.

The GT3 is not the first 911 I've respected. And, if truth be told, it's not the first 911 I've liked. But, although it's only the eighth most entertaining car from 2003, it is also the first Porsche 911 that I've thought long and hard about buying.

Sunday 23 November 2003

BMW 530d SE

We read much these days about the benefits of modern diesel engines.

We hear about the new-found quietness, the relaxed gait on the motorway and, of course, the parsimonious appetite for fuel.

It all sounds jolly lovely, but when the school has just rung to say your daughter has fallen over and should really go to hospital, you don't want a relaxed cruise and, frankly, you don't give much of a stuff about fuel economy either.

It actually happened this week. A nurse at the school rang to say my nine-year-old had had a 'little' accident. Now in America that would mean she'd had a 'little' accident but here, in understatement central, it could be anything from a damaged hairstyle to total decapitation.

What I wanted for the mercy dash was a V8 the size of an office block. But, when news of my daughter's 'little' accident came through, I ran out of the house to be presented, and there's no other way of putting this, with a f****** diesel.

Much praise has been heaped on BMW's 3-litre oil-burner. It's been described as refined and quiet and unusually powerful. Some say it's actually better than BMW's petrol engines.

Certainly I have no doubt that as paraffin stoves go it's excellent, but can we be clear on something. Comparing it to anything fuelled with petrol is as stupid as comparing a typewriter to your computer. Yes, it's more environmentally friendly. Yes, it's cheaper to run. But you try downloading Gary Jules's 'Mad World' on to a Remington Atlantic.

They say that on a motorway it is not possible to say which fuel is being used. But that's codswallop. It's like saying you can't tell whether you're listening to a cassette or a CD.

Or whether you're eating fresh or frozen fish. You just know . . .

And puh-lease can we stop trying to pretend that the superior torque offered by a diesel engine in any way compensates for the lack of brake horsepower.

When you accelerate in a modern diesel there's a satisfying surge, for sure, but it's over in a moment. And there's no power to carry the momentum. Time and time again I put my foot down in that Beemer, pulled out to overtake the Rover, and then when I was on the wrong side of the road simply ran out of oomph.

A petrol engine will spin happily, in some cases to 8,000 or 9,000 revs per minute. The BMW diesel is revvier than most, but it's all out of ideas at just 5,000.

Of course, even when you drive like you're on fire, it will refuse to do less than 40 mpg and that makes for massive savings at the pumps. I'm talking about halving your fuel bills. But if saving money is so important, why not go the whole hog and use the bus? A diesel would work in a car that's not supposed to be fun, a big 4×4 for instance or a small Volkswagen. But in a BMW, or a Jaguar for that matter, it's daft.

These cars are supposed to be all about poise and balance and delicacy. They're supposed to be the ultimate driving machines and they're just not when you have a coal-fired power station under the bonnet. If you just want cheapness, why not save even more money and buy a Mondeo? Still, let's leave the absurd and ridiculous engine out of the equation, shall we. Assume you'll buy a petrol version and have a look at the rest of this remarkable car.

The new 5-series is very possibly the most talked-about new car of the year. Chiefly this is because the old one was just so utterly fabulous, easily the best car in its class when it came along seven years ago and, astonishingly, still the leader when they pulled the plug seven years later.

You didn't have to think when you were looking for a £30,000 four-door saloon. You bought the Beemer and you loved it. But you do have to think with the new one, because the styling is, how can I put this, a bit challenging.

I'm told that as time passes we will become accustomed to the looks, which manage to be sharp and bulbous at the same time. But that's like asking a seven-year-old to live on olives because he'll like them when he's an adult. In the here and now the 5 is truly gargoylian, a symphony of discords and stylistic infighting.

And it's no better on the inside, with acres of extraordinarily cheap-looking plastic moulded into a series of shapes that jar.

This then is going to be one of the trickiest road tests I've ever done. Because I've got to ignore the engine and the styling. And the views of my children, who claimed it made them feel sick because they couldn't see out. Even my wife didn't like it, because she can't understand why anyone chooses to buy a BMW and then doesn't go for the M3.

Surprisingly, the new 5 is not that far removed under the skin from the old one. They have the same multilink rear axle and the same quasi–MacPherson strut arrangement at the front. And both use electronics in the shape of stability and traction control instead of mechanicals like a limited slip diff.

The only real difference is weight. Although the new version is a couple of inches longer and comes with more kit as standard, it's 65 kg lighter. So it should be more nimble than the old one.

It isn't though. The balance is still there and the poise, and the ride is exceptionally good for a car which handles and grips so well. In these respects it's still far, far better than any Audi, Jaguar or Mercedes. But the steering is odd.

It's fine when you're moving at a lick, but it's devoid of feel at low speed. Maybe it'd be worth buying the new £800 active system, which changes the amount of wheel-twirling you have to do as the speed builds. So, at 10 mph, a quarter of a turn of the steering wheel moves the front wheels as much as a whole turn does at 100. It works well.

The trouble is that this is just one of about 1,000 extras

that can be fitted. There are seven different types of wheel, eight different types of front seat, endless stereos and a trim selection that puts the Farrow & Ball colour chart to shame. Mercedes, it must be said, doesn't give you enough choice when buying a car – 'you vill have ze grey' – but it could be argued BMW gives you too much.

If you go for the standard car it's pretty well equipped anyway and costs £30,950. But you won't, because you'll buy the 530 petrol which is just £5 more.

Or will you? Yes, the new 5-series is unpleasant to behold and yes, its steering is a bit weird, but what else can you buy for this sort of dosh? You can't have a Mercedes because it'll break down all the time and the dealer won't be able to fix it. The Audi A6 is on its last legs. The Saab 9–5 is mad. The Lexus is dull. You won't pay £30,000 for a Volkswagen. And I'm sorry but if you're worried about aesthetics you're hardly likely to go for an S-type Jaguar.

The BMW, then, is still out in front. But only because all the other cars are so far behind.

Footnote

I wonder what would have happened had I been caught speeding on my way to the hospital in the 5-series.

Had it been by one of the two speed cameras I drove past, I fear no amount of pleading would have worked. You can't argue with a box.

Whereas if we had real policing on the road, I feel sure

Plod would have been understanding. It's a small point, but one which is rarely raised in the speed camera debate.

My daughter incidentally turned out to be suffering from a small bruise. And a large dose of hypochondria.

Sunday 7 December 2003

MG SV

I have a fairly comprehensive, all-enveloping hatred of MGs. They may have been acceptable when Kenneth More was stepping out of his Spit and taking Susannah York to the saloon bar at the Downed German, but by the time I was old enough to notice they were absolutely horrid.

With their wheezing, asthmatic little engines, they were as sporty as a man in an iron lung. And with their botched suspension they cornered like a horse in wellingtons.

No, really. When the American safety wallahs announced in the early 1970s that every car's headlights must be a certain height above the road, all the car makers redesigned their cars' noses to comply with the new legislation.

Not MG, though. They simply stuck blocks in the suspension to raise the whole car a little higher off the ground. That's a bit like cutting out draughts by fitting uPVC windows. Effective, but dynamically and aesthetically unwise.

And I haven't even mentioned the sort of people who drive the damn things. They are not hairdressers. In fact, come to think of it, they wouldn't know what a hairdresser was, with their mad barnets and their huge, sprouting face-fuzz. And they are always dirty because they have to spend so much time under the car, mending it.

David Attenborough is currently putting the finishing touches to a six-part documentary about the life of bugs. Doubtless he has been to the ends of the earth in search of all the most rare and disgusting creepy-crawlies. But there was no need, because there's no insect that can't be found under an MG driver's fingernails.

These guys bathe in engine oil. They eat Swarfega. And they talk and talk and talk about nothing but their infernal, limp-wristed, boneless-handling, sloth-slow, pug-ugly cars that are so unreliable even the damn wheels need servicing every few hundred yards.

'It takes you back,' they always say. And I'm sure it does, to a time of diphtheria and demob suits. Frankly, I'd rather go forward, and that brings me slithering to a halt beside the car you see in the pictures this week: the new MG SV.

My God, it's a beast. There's nothing wheezing or asthmatic about the huge V8 that lives under its bonnet. Though it can muster a wonderful bronchial cough when you poke its throttle with a stick.

Honestly, when you hear this thing start, it feels like everything within a hundred yards of the air intakes, all the air, the birds and the flies, have been sucked into the cylinders.

It started out in life as one of the world's worst engines: the 4.6 that powers Ford's Mustang in America. But Rover have changed everything, even the block, to create a snarling, chesty monster that spits fire and havoc down those twin Scorpion exhaust vents.

Fuel consumption? Well, let me put it this way. Flat-out at 165 mph it's downing a kilo of unleaded every minute.

In standard tune you get 320 bhp, which, in a car that's made entirely from carbon fibre and weighs just 1,400 kg, is enough to get you from 0 to 60 mph in 5.3 seconds. The car I drove, however, had been tweaked to give 400 bhp. And you can buy a nitrous kit to take it up to 1,000 bhp.

Yes, 1,000 bhp – 200 more than Michael Schumacher used to win his last Grand Prix championship.

All we ever hear about Rover these days are the disaster stories. We've had the pension fund scandal, the losses, the deal with the Chinese to produce cars jointly – that fell through – and the tie-up with the Indians that has spawned the horrid little CityRover.

Even this new SV was born from a botch-up. Rover spent a couple of million buying an Italian company called Qvale that nobody had even heard of, and no one could pronounce.

I think they thought they might be able to cross the word Qvale out and put an MG badge on instead.

But in fact they ended up throwing pretty much the whole thing away.

I'm told that only its windscreen wiper motors have survived.

The new chassis of the SV is therefore being made in Italy by the same firm that makes the chassis for Ferrari and Lamborghini. The body is made on the Isle of Wight. The engine is American. And Rover's so short of money, it has to borrow trucks to bring all these pieces to Longbridge, where they're all nailed together. This does not bode well.

So I am genuinely delighted to report that the heart of the beast is wonderful. A bona fide masterpiece.

The handling's pretty good, too. There isn't as much grip as you might have been expecting, but when you overstep the mark it puts a huge, gleaming smile on your face as the rear steps out of line in a totally controlled power slide.

Whoever set up this chassis knew what he was doing and what the enthusiastic driver wants. He is one great engineer, and I hope he makes man-love with the man who did the engine. I hope too that they have many man-babies together and that they all go on to be engineers as well.

And oh, how I wish we could end it there. But we can't. There are many more inches of newsprint to fill and I'm afraid it's bad news all the way.

First of all, this car is not priced to compete with a TVR or a Ford Mustang. It is priced to compete with the Porsche GT3, and that means it arrives on the market with its Birmingham accent, sporting a price-tag of £75,000. And that's for the base model. The faster ones will be up there in six-figure la-la Lambo land.

Now this car is fast. Be in no doubt about that. But it simply isn't as fast as the German and Italian thorough-breds with which it must compete. It's not very well equipped either. There is no satellite navigation, no air bag, and the seats must be moved fore and aft manually.

More worryingly, it's not very well made. The day started with a dead instrument panel, which was a nuisance but not the end of the world. But pretty soon the anti-lock braking had also packed up, and that was more armageddonish.

Inside, there's nowhere to put your left leg, the windows don't go all the way down, the gearbox is awful, the wind noise at speed is terrible, the trim is woefully cheap, the seats don't offer enough lateral support, and it is very easy to bang your head on the door frame. I know. One minute I was going round a corner, the next the rear tyres found some grip and shortly afterwards there was much sickness and a handful of stars.

Some said this was mild concussion. But I thought it might have had something to do with the petrol fumes that leak into the cockpit when you're throwing it around a bit. Or maybe I thought it was petrol fumes because I was concussed. Or perhaps someone slipped me a tab of acid. God knows, but for 24 hours after driving this car I felt decidedly odd.

I feel odd now, and a bit cruel, because I wanted to like the SV. I think it is extremely good looking, a brutal symphony of testosterone and muscle, and I wish all cars sounded like it. At 150 mph it sounds . . . well, like rock'n'roll.

I really did hope that it would detonate the whole prissy wet weekend that is the MG experience by running off with your sister to a heroin den in east Africa. I wanted it to be bad. I wanted to take it to an MG owners' club event and blow all the bugs out of their beards. But alas . . .

Yes, it is exquisite to drive, but the attention to detail and the overall quality just isn't good enough for a £75,000 car.

And speaking of attention to detail, Happy Christmas to you all.

Sunday 21 December 2003

Fiat Panda

It has always been accepted that the car is the second most expensive thing you will ever buy, after a house. Really?

Anne Robinson admitted in her newspaper column last weekend that she has been bombing around in a Perodua Kelisa — a car built in a jungle clearing by people who go to work in shoes made from leaves.

Nonetheless, it costs just £5,000, so taking a family of four to the Caribbean for a summer holiday would be considerably more expensive.

There are other things which cost more, too, like a pair of binoculars I saw the other day in a shop window on Walton Street, or some kitchen cabinets, or a piece of jewellery from one of those shops on Bond Street. You could, if you were a mentalist, spend £5,000 on a suit or a cooker, or a set of speakers for your drawing room.

Getting married costs more than a Perodua Kelisa. Getting divorced costs more than two. And you'd need a fleet to pay for the cost of educating a child, or dying.

The thing is, though, that you don't want a Perodua Kelisa, because it sounds like a disease, only has three cylinders and takes a fortnight or so to accelerate from 0 to 60. You know that you can't have a real car, not a new one anyway, for much less than £9,000.

I would have concurred, but then, for reasons that

aren't exactly clear, someone brought a new Fiat Panda round to my house to test. The cheapest version costs £6,295 and I wouldn't be at all surprised to find that Elton John spent more than that on his hair.

I therefore wasn't expecting much. And to reinforce this view, I remember the old Fiat Panda well. Styled by someone who only had access to a ruler, it came with hammocks instead of seats, no interior trim and the top speed of a Galapagos turtle. It was fine for the walnut-faced peasantry of Italy but not really on for anywhere else.

I was therefore a little surprised to find that the cheapest new Panda comes as standard with electric windows, an adjustable steering column, remote central locking, pre-tensioning seat belts, two air bags, a stereo and power steering that can be made super-light in the city.

Much more is available. Air-conditioning, for instance, as well as a sunroof, a CD player, parking sensors and air bags for your testicles. But even if you go mad with the options list, it's still nowhere near the second most expensive thing you'll ever buy. I bet Barry Manilow spent more on his new nose. I bet Danniella Westbrook spent more powdering hers.

Hell, I bet you couldn't even buy a real panda for £6,300.

The first time I went out in it, it was raining. After half a mile the rain had turned to a sort of icy hail, and five minutes later it felt like I'd gone to another planet. Or maybe Canada. There was thunder, lightning and a blizzard of such ferocity that within moments the road was invisible under its new white blanket.

In front of me a Range Rover slithered to a halt,

bumping into the kerb, then sliding back down the hill. Ordinary cars had had it, their fat, sporty tyres utterly lost in the Arctic chill.

Yet my little Panda soldiered on, its skinny little rubber tyres cutting through the snow like four Stanley knives. Not once did it even give the impression of being in difficulty.

The next time I went out in it was Saturday night, and it had an even bigger surprise up its sleeve. The back was so roomy that it not only swallowed all three children but even gave them enough space in which to fight.

And then it was Sunday morning and time for mini-rugby. Now since Jonny Wilkinson punted that last-minute drop goal between the posts in Sydney, the number of people turning up with their offspring for training has swelled to the point where the car park looks like Bangkok at rush hour.

But this was no problem with the Panda, which slotted neatly between the posts of a croquet hoop on the bowling green. 'What the hell's that?' cried the dads, mocking my car's unusual appearance. 'Handy,' I replied, mocking the four-mile walk they'd had from the field where they'd parked their BMW X5s.

And there's another advantage the Panda has over its larger and more expensive siblings. Normally it takes three or four minutes for their big engines to heat the cabin. But the Fiat was amazing. Turn on the engine – I timed this – and in just 21 seconds soothing warmth was flowing through the heater vents. In fact, it goes from 0 to 60°C almost as fast as it goes from 0 to 60 mph.

The 1.1-litre version takes 15 seconds to cover this yardstick and that, in human terms, is 18 months. The 1.2 isn't much better, taking 14 seconds, although for some extraordinary reason it's more economical. It'll average more than 50 mpg.

However, I don't want you to be put off by the lack of performance because, being Italian, it never feels under-powered or lethargic. In fact, I have to say it feels like the fastest car I've ever driven.

After the snow had been blown away by the gales, and the roads returned to normal, I couldn't believe how much fun the Fiat was. Panda? Grizzly more like. You roar away from junctions in a cocoon of noise. 'Grrrrrr,' it goes up through first, and 'Grrrrr' again all the way through second.

You brake late for the corner, turn in, and so long as you have the steering in its 'normal' setting there's a huge amount of feedback from the road. It doesn't whisper or mumble; it shouts at you through a megaphone. I've driven sports cars that are less communicative.

This is a car that puts a huge grin on your face. It waves its arms about and shouts, much like a waiter in an Italian restaurant. And sticking with this metaphor for a moment, the food it serves up, with aplomb, is delicious and tasty too.

But the best thing is, you're rarely going faster than 24 mph. And this means you can have all the excitement of driving with almost none of the danger. If the brakes were to fail, for instance, you'd coast to a halt long before you hit the hedge.

And that, of course, brings me on to the biggest problem

with all Fiats. We assume the brakes will fail, and that the crankshaft will come off, and that the windows will start to play the hokey-cokey, while the central locking thinks it's the horn. Fiats feel flimsy.

And it's not just a perception either. In the recent *Top Gear* survey, Fiat had two cars in the bottom 10 and none at all above 93rd. Owners criticised quality, poor dealers and the high cost of spare parts. Nearly 72 per cent of Seicento drivers said they would not buy one again.

The Panda, however, breaks with tradition here. It feels much more robust than the Renault Mégane CC I wrote about two weeks ago, but then a bin liner would also have felt more robust. No, the Panda feels German. It feels like bits won't drop off. It feels good.

Of course, this is only a feeling. The car was launched just two weeks ago, so it's impossible to predict what will happen in the long run. But I will say it's worth more of a punt than a Punto.

Put simply, I loved it. When it was here, I drove nothing else. The Mercedes SL, the Volvo XC90, all the other test cars, they all just sat on the drive as I bombed hither and thither in my new best friend.

Quite apart from being a proper, grown-up car, it has two tricks up its sleeve that are hard to ignore. It has a wonderful personality and it costs less than an Aga.

Sunday 8 February 2004

Kia Rio

Under normal circumstances I know you're not very interested in cars like the Kia Rio. However, stick with me because you can buy it, brand new, for one pound. One pound is really very little for a full-size car. Actually, it's even very cheap for a two-inch model of a car. I'm not sure, but I bet you couldn't even buy a pair of shoes for a pound.

Plainly, there are going to be a few drawbacks with a car this cheap. And, sure enough, there are. You may have seen *The Fly II*, in which a scientist attempts to teleport a dog. In one of the most gruesome scenes I've seen in a film, it arrives at its destination completely inside out. Well the Rio is uglier than that.

Inside, things get worse. Yes, there is plenty of space for generously proportioned adults in the back but only because there's almost no space at all in the front. Those with long legs or a bit of a gut – and I have both – will find the driving position excruciating.

And you should see the quality of the interior trim. I've used many metaphors in the past to describe cheap-looking plastic, but none seems to work here. It's not like it was made from a melted Action Man. It's not like a video rental box. It's even worse than a Barnsley market trader's pakamac.

Now, I was going to explain at this point that such things could be overlooked in a car that costs a pound. But then I found that it's not a pound at all. The headline-grabbing sticker price is just a deposit. To secure the whole car you will end up paying seven thousand five hundred and seven more pounds. And that looks like one of the biggest jokes in automotive history.

This kind of money would get you a real car, a Fiat Panda with some change. Or a Nissan Micra. Bargain a bit and it would get you a Ford Fiesta 1.25 Finesse, a Renault Clio or a Volkswagen Lupo. In fact, the list of things I'd rather buy with £7,508 is endless. It even includes 750,800 penny chews.

I knew it wouldn't be much cop when the man from the importer asked, incredulously, why on earth I wanted to road-test it. And my expectations fell even further when he telephoned, just 24 hours after the car arrived, to see how I was getting on with it. Car firms rarely do this; it implies they have no confidence in the product.

But, sadly, his nerves didn't lower my expectations quite far enough, because the Rio was dreadful. Sure, with 1.3 litres under the bonnet you get more cubic capacity than you do from an equivalent Euro car, but as we chaps keep being reminded, size isn't important. It's what you do with it that matters. And what Kia does with its 1.3-litre pecker is nothing at all.

The actual performance figures don't look too bad if you're used to walking. From 0 to 62 mph takes 14.2 seconds and, in the absence of a headwind, it will crack 100 mph. But not on a hill. I have cycled into Chipping

Norton from my house – once – and didn't notice any gradient, but the Kia did. And in fifth gear it simply didn't have enough oomph to overcome gravity.

Then there's the quality of the power. It comes in lumps, as though the engine mapping were modelled on Monument Valley. One minute you're on a plateau, then for no obvious reason there's a burp of torque, followed by a hole the size of the Grand Canyon.

And the noise. Oh my God. You long for the moment when you can cut the din by going into fifth . . . but when you do, you find yourself on another hill, virtually grinding to a halt.

Mind you, the need to move around at 4 mph is useful because of the way the Rio goes round corners. I haven't driven a car so inert and with so much body roll since the 1970s. If you have a Hillman Hunter now, you will probably find this acceptable. If you don't, then you won't.

Small wonder Kia's importer in Britain is sponsoring the Pedestrian Association's Walking Bus scheme. The idea is that parents take it in turns to walk a group, or 'bus', of children to their school of a morning.

After three days of being transported in the Rio, my kids thought it was a brilliant idea to walk instead. Even though their school is 18 miles away and it was blowing a gale directly from the Canadian tundra.

So, why is the Kia so bad? Well, typically what happens in an emerging economy is that the government doesn't want to see its hard-earned cash being squandered on cars and trucks imported from elsewhere. So indigenous car firms are established and, to protect them, huge import duties are introduced.

Kia went bust when the tiger economies collapsed, and it had to be rescued by Hyundai. As a general rule, this protectionism causes these car firms to flourish. Then, when things are going well, they decide to earn foreign currency . . . so, hey presto, Kia and Daewoo, Hyundai and Proton – not to forget Perodua and Ssangyong – all end up in Britain. This would be fine; but here in the West our grandparents grew up with the car, whereas in Korea everyone's grandparents grew up on an ox. In their civil war, which started only 50 or so years ago, the army in the south faced the Russian T34 tanks on horses. As a result a car, any car, is still a novelty.

It's no surprise to find that over there the Rio is called the SF, which – I'm not joking – stands for Science Fiction. To them, it's probably as amazing as the Model T Ford was to the Americans 80 years ago.

Think about it. The people who designed the Rio got the wheels in the right place and knew how to fit electric windows, but they know nothing of engine refinement or suspension compromises. For Koreans, trying to make a world-class automobile is as hard as us trying to make dog-and-vinegar-flavoured crisps. We wouldn't know where to start.

So will Kia ever get it right? Well, today the western car firms are technologically advanced, but look where that's got them. General Motors makes more from financing cars than it does from making them. Fiat is in deep, deep dung, Chrysler has been swallowed up by

Daimler-Benz, and Rover, the last drop of Britain's once mighty car industry, is teetering on the edge of evaporation. Even Nissan had to merge with Renault, so there was no chance for Volvo, Jaguar, Land Rover and Aston Martin, all of whom are now under the Ford umbrella. Not that there's much respite under there, since Ford itself is perilously close to bankruptcy.

Maybe all the Korean firms will come together to form a sort of Korean Leyland. Maybe the whole thing will be brought to its knees by an oriental Led Lobbo. Maybe one day they will make a car every bit as refined and lusty as the Fiat Panda.

Or maybe, just maybe, the problem the western car firms are having is that their cars are just too good, too complicated. In the heat of competition they've accelerated their technology to a point that's way in advance of what the customer needs. I mean, electronic brake distribution; really? What's that all about then?

So maybe the Kia Rio is actually what the market wants these days: something that's not very good, but probably good enough.

Sunday 15 February 2004

BMW 645Ci

Mostly, people are bullied for a reason. In interviews, Gwyneth Paltrow has admitted she was bullied because she was gawky, Mel Gibson because he had an American accent at an Australian school, Michelle Pfeiffer because of her big lips, Whitney Houston because she was too white and Anthea Turner because she was too posh. But then she's from Stoke-on-Trent, and in the Potteries even Fred Dibnah would have similar problems.

I was bullied at school by a chap called Dave and it's really not hard to work out why. He was a bully and I was the nearest living being when he felt like a workout.

It is my fervent wish that the nurse who calls round to mash his food these days is also a bully. I hope she wees in his pudding.

Sometimes, though, people are bullied for no reason. A friend of mine was at the Edinburgh Festival once, which, so far as I can work out, involved sitting in a pub drinking lots of beer. This meant, inevitably, that pretty soon he rushed off to the lavatory to be sick.

Unfortunately, and I guess we've all been there, stomachular reversal is not an event which can be tamed and timed. So it all started to arrive before he made it to the stalls.

At the last moment he shoved the cubicle door open

and vomited extravagantly . . . all over some poor chap who was in there doing, and minding, his own business.

Without a word my friend slammed the door shut, and then he thought: 'Oh no. I have just been sick all over someone who is Scottish. He is bound to come out of there and pull my arms off.' So, confused by drink, he thought he'd better get the first punch in.

With that he opened the door again and, before running away, planted a huge fist in the man's startled face.

Now put yourself in the shoes of the man in the loo. What if he wasn't someone who eats piledrivers for relaxation? What if he was simply a poet, up in Edinburgh with his bookish girlfriend for the festival? How do you think he's going to feel, being punched by a man who's just vomited into the Y of his trousers and pants? To get some idea of the bewilderment and the sense of persecution, try driving around Britain in one of the new 6-series BMWs.

After a while you're forced to think: 'I am sitting here at a road junction with my indicator on and nobody is letting me out. Why does everyone hate me so?' I think we are genetically programmed to be fearful of BMW drivers in the same way that we are programmed to be just a little bit frightened of Scottish people in pub lavatories. We know that most people above the border are normal, but we've all seen *Trainspotting*. 'Glass' may have been turned into a verb by the youth of South Yorkshire, but it was turned into a pastime in the bars of Glasgow.

And so it goes on the road. You may be a very good

driver. You may be a caring father who runs a meals-on-wheels service for the old folks at weekends. But if you drive a BMW, you are tarred with the same brush as the berk in the 3-series who thinks the *Highway Code* stopping distances are measured in millimetres.

Two or three times in the 645Ci I was genuinely staggered at the belligerence of other road users when it swung into their peripheral vision. I don't think I could have had the door shut so firmly on me if I'd had www.kiddieporn.com emblazoned on the doors.

If you currently drive a Jaguar or a Mercedes – or any other type of car, actually – you will find this reasonless bullying hard to stomach, and for that reason alone I'd steer clear of the 645, which to everyone else is the 666.

But of course, if you are a BMW driver, right now you'll be used to the persecution and you'll be wanting to know what the new boy is like. So here goes.

First of all, it's a lot less than you might be expecting. I sort of assumed it was a replacement for the unloved 850i and would cost, ooh, I don't know, £75,000. But actually it's a whisker under £50,000, and that, for such a big, imposing car with such a big, imposing badge, is good value.

However, we can't ignore the looks. Most car designers are anonymous souls who labour away in a back room, trying their best to accommodate the wishes of engineers, marketing men and the boss's wife. Unlike people who design clothes or cook food, we don't know their names or where they live. Peter Horbury is not Coco Chanel. Walter de'Silva is not Nicole Farhi.

But Chris Bangle, the man who's reshaped BMW, is different. We know he is American. We know he has a beard. We know he hates journalists. And we know, because there was a story about it in the *Sunday Times* last week, that he has recently been 'promoted' and will no longer have his fingers in the pencil case.

He really has created some monsters in his time. The 7-series is weird and the 5 just plain ugly. With the 6 it's almost as though he was being overseen all the time by more conventional theorists. You can sense his flamboyance in every detail, every angle and every panel, but it's been suppressed.

Unfortunately, his minders obviously popped outside for a fag when he did the back end, because he went berserk. It's his maddest work yet, Prokofiev meets Munch in a discordant Munchen blaze of horror in B flat. Certainly, if you were to buy a 6-series, I recommend you select reverse when leaving friends' houses so they don't see its backside.

Inside, you sense the hand of Bangle in the quality of materials. Because he's from America, where Styrofoam is considered to be luxurious, everything has a coarseness to the touch. There is no wood, but if there were you get the impression it would be MDF.

Then there is the driving position. Despite the usual array of adjustments for the seat and the wheel, I never once found a sweet spot where I was truly comfortable. The wheel was either too high or I couldn't see the dials.

And you do need to keep an eye on your speed,

because, as you'd expect in a 4.4-litre two-door V8 coupé, it doesn't exactly hang around.

Now I want to make it absolutely plain at this point that the 645Ci is bloody good to drive. With its Vanos this and its variable that, the engine produces a seamless stream of power, and the dynamic-drive suspension teamed with fluctuating-rate steering means the handling is pin-sharp. You'd have to nit-pick to find any dynamic fault with the way this car goes.

And yet, despite everything, I'm afraid I didn't like it. The problem is that I had no idea what sort of car it's supposed to be.

In essence it's a two-door version of the 5-series. So you think coupé. Right. That must be sporty in some way. And it is, but not in the way I was expecting.

It could have been aurally sporty, producing a V8 bellow every time I put my foot down. But it didn't. The engine is almost completely inaudible 90 per cent of the time and gently hums when it's asked to work hard.

So perhaps it could be sporty in terms of interior trim. But no. You won't find body-hugging seats or splashes of carbon fibre in there. It's just the usual BMW blend of utter functionality, topped off with a satellite navigation system That Does Not Work. Again.

OK then, so it's a stylish car, a car with discreet good looks (ahem) in which none of the comfort or silence has been lost? No again. Because the ride is firm to the point where it's almost annoying.

This is silly. If they're going to give us a hard ride, then go the whole hog and give us exhausts like wheelie bins and deep Recaro seats. If, on the other hand, they're going to give us the acoustic signature of a nuclear submarine, then let's have a comfy ride.

Maybe a car without the optional dynamic-drive system would be better, but one thing's for sure, the model I tested fell between two stools, trying to play a ballad and thrash metal . . . at the same time.

If you want a thrilling drive from a car like this, buy a Porsche 911. If you want the last word in comfort, buy a Jaguar XKR. If you want to be abused by the dealer, buy a Mercedes of some sort. And that means the BMW is stuck out there with only one USP.

It's the automotive equivalent of ginger hair. You're going to be bullied.

Sunday 22 February 2004

Mazda3

I'd like to begin this morning with an apology. For the past few weeks I've been filling these pages with cars you might actually buy, rather than cars you dream about. It's been a drizzle of Golfs and Civics, rather than a scarlet blaze of Gallardos and Scagliettis.

I thought this would go down well. I thought you'd appreciate some time in the real world. But it seems not. Sure, the handful of letters I used to get complaining about my love of million-horsepower, two-seater supercars has dried up, but they've been replaced with a flood of missives from people asking me to get back where I belong.

'No more Hondas,' you say, as though you think I enjoy bumbling around in the pensioners' special. No more crummy Volkswagens. No more Fiat Pandas. It seems you're just not interested in the bread and butter; only the jam.

So you'll probably be jolly angry this morning to find I'm wasting your time with a 1.6-litre five-door family hatchback called the Mazda3. But look at it this way: I'm only wasting 10 of your minutes. It wasted a whole week for me.

I honestly thought it would be good. I thought it would stand head, shoulders and torso above all the competition and that we could draw a line under this hatchback malarkey once and for all. I thought I'd conclude by saying it's the best of them all, and then next week we could get back to the thin air out there beyond Mach 1.

Mazda has always been a left-field choice for those wanting a Jap-o-box. They were just as reliable as the equivalent Toyotas and Nissans, but somehow they were never quite as dreary. Maybe this is because they're made in Hiroshima. Maybe there's something in the water there.

Mazda may have been nothing more than a division of Ford for the past 25 years, but they're the only ones to have persevered with Wankel rotary engines. They were the ones who reintroduced the sports car in the shape of the still-marvellous MX-5, and they were responsible for what I think is the best-looking Japanese car of them all – the old RX-7.

In recent months, though, they've gone berserk. First of all there was the Mazda6, which is certainly the most handsome and possibly the best driving mid-range four-door saloon money can buy. Then there was the Mazda2, which I'm told is pretty good. And sitting above them all, like a golden halo, was the RX-8.

It's not perfect. It's not as powerful as the initial projections led us to believe, and the Wankel engine uses oil and petrol in equal measure. But you have to love those backward-opening rear doors, and the price, the smoothness and the perfect front-engine, rear-drive balance. And then there's the styling which, according to my daughter, is 'way cool'.

So all the evidence suggested the Mazda3 would be *les genoux de la bee*. And there's more good omen too, because it's based on the next-generation Ford Focus. Quite a pedigree when you remember the current Ford Focus is quite simply the best-handling hatchback of them all. The Mazda3, I figured, would be the biggest blast to come out of Hiroshima for nearly 60 years.

Well, it isn't. And that means I have to use the strongest word in the English language: 'disappointing'.

When I was younger, my bank manager would write from time to time saying he was 'saddened' to note that I hadn't done anything about my overdraft. This was no big deal. And nor would it have mattered if he'd said he was 'angry', 'livid' or 'incandescent with rage'.

He could have been whatever he liked, but it still wouldn't have altered the fact that I had three thousand of his bank's pounds and no intention of doing anything about it.

But then one day he wrote to say he was 'disappointed', and that changed everything.

That meant he'd had high hopes for me and that I had let him down. Suddenly it was all my fault.

Try this with your kids. Tell them you're really cross and I guarantee it won't make a ha'porth of difference. Tell them you're disappointed, and they'll immediately clean their room and take up the cello.

I'm no stranger to the concept of disappointment. There was Bob Seger's last album, for a kick-off. And then there's my yew hedge, which is six years old and still only six inches high. But the Mazda was something new. It's not just worse than I was expecting, it's worse than I'd have expected even if I wasn't expecting anything.

I mean, why, for instance, base a car on the Ford Focus – which has independent rear suspension – and then not fit independent rear suspension? Yes, Mazda saves a pound, but I end up disappointed.

And why do the brakes have to be operated with a switch? Sometimes you just want to slow down a bit, but the Mazda can't do that. You're either going along normally, or you're stationary with your face all squidged on the windscreen and blood pouring out of your ruined nose.

Yes, you get Electronic Brakeforce Distribution, Emergency Brake Assist and anti-lock, but I'd trade all of that for a bit of 'feel'.

It's the same deal with all the controls, actually. There's no finesse to the gearbox, the clutch or the steering. There's a sense, with everything, of pared-to-the-bone, penny-pinching, accountancy-driven engineering.

Then there's the styling. Mazda says that with its long wheelbase and aggressively flared fenders it has an assertive presence, even when viewed from a distance. What are they on about? A werewolf has an assertive presence. Nelson Mandela has an assertive presence. The USS *Nimitz* has an assertive presence . . . but the Mazda3 is no more assertive than soil.

It's especially unassertive at a distance because it would take such a long time to get from wherever it is to wherever you are. You can buy a 2-litre version, which is probably capable of movement, but I tried the 1.6, which isn't.

Mazda says the 1.4 is 'lively', and the 2-litre 'powerful', but is plainly stumped with the middle-order 1.6, which it describes as 'highly balanced'. 'Asthmatic' is perhaps more accurate. 'Strained' is good, too. 'Woefully short of oomph' works as well.

Strangely, it's not short of power. With 103 bhp on tap, it's right in the standard 1.6-litre ballpark, but somewhere between the engine and the road it all seems to escape.

Time and again I'd gird my loins for an overtaking manoeuvre on the A44 – it's never easy – and time and again I'd realise as I drew level with the Rover I was trying to pass, that I didn't have enough grunt. So I'd get on the brakes and then have to spend the rest of the journey picking bits of gristle and cartilage out of the heater vents.

As far as price and equipment levels are concerned, it's fine. My TS2 model costs £13,600 – about the same as a Focus 1.6 Ghia – and came with air-conditioning, curtain air bags, a CD player and traction control – a little more than you get on a Focus.

But this is not enough, I'm afraid, to swing the pendulum Mazda's way. Last week, in the *Good Car Bad Car Guide*, I said that those wanting a car of this type should choose between the Golf, the Focus and the Renault Mégane. Nothing's changed.

Well, one thing has. I've had enough of testing humdrum hatchbacks so I'm going to sign off now, ring Aston Martin and get my hands on a DB9.

Sunday 21 March 2004

Lotus Exige S2

I am growing bored with the Mitsubishi Evo. It may be the fastest road car money can buy, the cream of all things auto-motive in the Milky Way, and the great and wonderful grandson of the formidable Audi quattro, but we've had enough now, thanks.

Pretty well every day a new version comes along which is claimed by those of a downloading disposition to be better than the one before. But do you know what? It's just more of the same. Brilliant, but eventually you tire of lobster thermidor, especially if you're given it for breakfast.

I don't doubt that each tweak of the dampers and each fettle of the differentials makes life a shade faster on the world's rally stages, but shaving half a second off a 20-mile flat-out run through the Corsican hinterland is simply not noticeable when you're popping out to buy some Rawlplugs.

I tried the Evo VIII FQ300 last week and, as expected, it offered up scramjet performance within the world of internal combustion. But then I could have said pretty much the same of the normal VIII, which in turn felt about the same as the VII, the VI and even the V.

I could say the same of the Subaru Impreza. Every month we read in the car magazines of another new version. We've had the RB5, the PPP and the STi, and now we have the WRX STi Type RA Spec C Ltd. Why would anyone buy a car like that? To impress girls? I think not. So it must be to impress other men. I suppose this is logical: because as the car's power goes backwards and forwards you end up that way inclined too.

What's happened here is what happened to the world of rock'n'roll in the mid-1970s. Bands like Genesis and Yes started fiddling with simple concepts until they ended up with songs that lasted two weeks, presented in Roger Dean album covers with 42 gatefolds.

I liked *Seconds Out* and *Fragile*. But you need to take a deep breath before admitting to this kind of thing in public. And it's the same story with the Evo VIII and a specced-up Subaru. They have become 'progressive rock' cars. Lots of smoke and light and noise and an auditorium full of really, really ugly men who have told their wives and friends they're working late.

What's needed is a dose of punk, a retaliation to the clever-clogs synthesiser and the technically amazing half-hour drum solo. What's needed is something small, tight and angry. What's needed is the Lotus Exige.

This is a car that has no active yaw control and no active diff. It has no turbocharger and does not need to be told what sort of road it's on before setting off. If the Evo VIII, with its spray-jet intercooler, is Rick Wakeman's *Journey to the Centre of the Earth*, then the Exige is a spitting, strutting Sex Pistol.

It costs £30,000, which – give or take – means it's about the same as the Japanese toys, although you do get rather less for your money. For a start, there are no back doors, no back seats and, while there's a boot, it's really only big enough for an overnight bag.

Other things you don't get are air-conditioning, electric windows, carpets, air bags, traction control, satellite navigation . . . even sun visors. Yes, just about everything is an extra-cost option.

To understand this car, we need a bit of history. Lotus has enjoyed many years of success with its little Elise, but in the past 18 months or so sales have fallen sharply. This is partly due to the Vauxhall VX220, which is the same car built in the same factory but which is faster and better value. And partly it's because the Elise had become a bit yellow around the teeth.

Lotus decided that, to keep the factory busy, it would start to sell cars in America, but sadly the Rover K-series engine doesn't meet US legislation: apparently it smokes too much and likes a drink at lunchtime.

So Lotus decided to fit Toyota's 1.8. This is a teetotaller that lives in a gated community, stands up for the national anthem and cries in public. It's also a bloody good engine, with two camshafts – one for economy and then, after a little step at 5,000 rpm, another for power. Nice.

For some extraordinary reason, Lotus decided to keep going with the old Rover-engined cars here in Britain and, to make them more appealing, lopped £2,000 off the price. This went down well with my wife, who bought a 111S at the old price last year. 'The *******
*********,' she said. Anyway, the Toyota engine worked so well in the Elise they decided to do a hardtop, hardcore

version, and thus the Exige was born. If you see one, here's a tip: get out of its way.

Yes, the Toyota engine may produce only 189 bhp, which is about the same as you get from your Aga, but because it has no sun visors and no active yaw control it weighs less than a microwave oven. Put it like this: when Genesis went on tour, they needed 16 pantechnicons and a football stadium. With an Exige, you simply rock up and play.

Getting to the playground, however, can be unnerving. Because it's so tiny, you feel dwarfed, even by people in Peugeots. After a day in London I developed small-man syndrome, squealing away from the lights and cutting people up just to assert myself.

There are other problems with the size, too. Getting in, for instance, is not something that can be achieved with any dignity. Nor should it be attempted in a skirt. But once you're there, and you have your breath back, it's more spacious than you might imagine.

Better still, it's quite comfy. I was expecting a completely solid suspension set-up, but actually it's fairly soft, bumping over potholes with a jar that's noticeable rather than back-breaking. Don't be fooled, though. Don't think it's all pose and no go, because – trust me on this – you can bring whatever you like to the party, a Ferrari, a Lambo, an Evo . . . anything, and the Exige will leave you gasping and bewildered in its wake. You simply will not believe how fast this car goes.

Part of the secret is downforce. Pretty well all cars rise up on their suspension as the speed increases, but the

Exige, with its low, bumper-snapping front, its flat floor and that big spoiler on the back, generates F1-style downforce. In other words, the faster you go, the heavier it becomes. By the time you're up to 100 mph it's like you have a baby elephant sitting on the roof, pressing the tyres into the road.

Ah yes, those tyres. These are the real jewels in the armoury. Specially made for Lotus, they're as slick as the law allows. I'm told they can be used when it's raining, but I would advise extreme caution. Hold back, wait till it dries up, and then you will absolutely not believe the treat they have in store.

It's not so much the grip, which is prodigious, but the feel they provide when that grip is exceeded. You can sense the precise moment when they're about to let go, and you know exactly what to do about it. I have never driven a car which goes through corners as well as this one. Never.

At a stroke it makes the Elise feel like Bambi on that frozen lake, and any Italian supercar like a heffalump. It's as if you're driving a housefly: the agility and sheer ability to get out of harm's way beggar belief.

It's no slouch in a straight line either, getting from 0 to 60 mph in 4.9 seconds and hammering along till it's gone past 140 mph. By which time, I should imagine, it weighs more than the Flying Scotsman.

I want to give it five stars. As a driving experience it warrants about 47. I'm only held back by the price, which is steep, the looks, which are odd, and the noise, which is just that.

It can have four stars, though, and it can be content in the knowledge that it has swept away a tidal wave of excess weight and over-complication. It has brought a bit of anarchy to the UK.

Sunday 4 April 2004

Aston Martin DB9

For some time now I've been a worried man. It was obvious from the photographs that Aston Martin's new DB9 would be pretty, but would it be the epitome of Britishness? Would it be a steel-and-wooden fist in a leather glove? Would it be an Aston Martin?

The evidence didn't look good. The factory these days looks like a UN convention. It's owned by the Americans, the chief stylist is Danish, there's a Japanese peacekeeper, a token woman, and the big cheese is a German doctor called Ulrich Bez.

He popped round for coffee this morning to try to allay my fears but, to begin with, he did no such thing. For half an hour he talked in microscopic detail about how the car is built. I learned how everything, from the firewall backwards, is glued together using a Norwegian system, and how the front is held on with bolts. I learned about the composition of every single panel, and I thought, oh no. I'm going to be here until I die.

He wasn't finished. For the next half-hour I had a lecture on the gearbox. Unlike the 'Wankwish' – that's what he calls the Vanquish – the paddles behind the steering wheel operate an automatic box rather than a manual. This is better, he says, because with the Wankwish system you have to concentrate all the time on changing gear. If you do not, the gearbox breaks.

Then we got to the engine, and I needed more coffee to stay awake. It is the same 6-litre V12 that you get in the Wankwish, but the UN delegation from Botswana has fiddled with the on-board computer to make it a little more relaxed. Naturally, Bez gave me chapter and verse on all the hows and whys.

This is the problem with the Germans. They like to analyse, with flip charts, every single detail of every single part of the car. That's fine, but there is a downside, which is plain for all to see on the new 6-series BMW. It's as boring as hell.

Advertising men will tell you that when it comes to cars they need to attach a single word to the brand. So if you want a 'safe' car, you buy a Volvo. If you want a 'reliable' car, you buy a Volkswagen. And if you have a small 'penis', you buy a BMW.

It's not just brands, either. There are single words that describe the national characteristics of a car, too. A German car is 'engineered'. A French car is 'soft' and an Italian car is 'exuberant'.

I've always felt that a British car is 'traditional'. We, as a nation, don't like change. When the submarine was invented, for instance, the navy top brass dismissed it as 'underhand and ungentlemanly', and we see the same sort of thing with our cars. They all hark back to the Blower Bentley, which set the scene by being big, heavy, powerful and green.

Everything from the Bristol to the Allegro Vanden Plas

and from the old Aston Vantage to the Jaguar XJ6 looked like a Spitfire from the outside and a Harvester pub on the inside. Lots of dark colours, lots of heavy wood and very little natural light. Given half a chance, the British car designer would fit an open fire instead of a heater, and some horse brasses.

'Pah,' said Bez. 'Of course tourists still come here to see the Queen and the changing of the guard, but the country has changed. You've got the London Symphony Orchestra and Gieves & Hawkes. What they are doing now is not what they were doing 10 years ago.'

He says that the tradition in Britain is for discipline. 'You can see this with your armed forces' – he'd know – 'but discipline isn't enough now. Look at your football team. You can discipline them all you like, but you need creativity and flair as well. That's what David Beckham brings.' Again, after the 5–1 drubbing, he'd know about that, too.

But still I was alarmed. Because he was arguing that the DB9 should be like Tate Modern, which I think is as British as a coffee shop in Zurich. Pale woods, neat design and zinc are European, which is fine if you're making furniture, but it's not British. It's not spotted dick and big thick custard. It's not the library at Blenheim Palace. Heavy, dark, and a bit damp.

Eventually we ended the discussion and I was taken outside to see the car. It's not as pretty or as dainty as the old DB7, but even so it's still agonisingly, knee-tremblingly good-looking. Let me put it this way. The DB7 was like Liz Hurley. Classically good-looking in a feminine sort of way. The DB9 is more like George Clooney.

Then I opened the door, and relief washed over me like waves on a Caribbean shore. The dash, the carpets and the seats were finished in what can only be described as placenta red. It didn't go at all with the wood and the metal. Joy of joys. It was still like a pub in there, and not an airport departure lounge.

Better still, the controls for the electric seats look like I'd made them, and the power-steering pump juddered as I turned the wheel. Bez had a terribly British excuse for this. 'Oh, they all do that,' he said. But he said it in such a way that I suspect the man responsible has been shot.

He also suggested that there will be no judder on the cars people actually buy, and he pointed out that you don't have to have an interior the colour of an afterbirth.

So I turned the key, pressed the starter, pushed a button to engage drive, set off, and on the first corner knew, with absolute certainty, I was in an Aston.

When you turn the wheel in a Ferrari it communicates with the front tyres using telepathy. The whole car lets you know that it could flow from bend to bend whether you were there or not. In the DB9, however, you are made to feel like part of the equation. You have to man-handle the nose into the apex, so when you kiss it perfectly, and you will, because this car handles like a dream, you feel like it was all down to you. That makes you feel good.

Coming out of the corner you floor the throttle and

the exhaust makes a perfectly judged snarl as 450 bhp hits the gearbox, which is mounted at the back for better weight distribution. It's not so loud that it's wearing, but not so quiet that you think you've bought a washing machine by mistake.

The ride also strikes a perfect balance.

A 20-year-old would say it's too soft. A 70-year-old would say it's too hard. But for the fortysomethings who'll actually buy the thing, it steers a Radio 2 course right down the middle.

You can feel, when you push, the outside rear wheel scrabbling for grip – you really can feel it through your trousers – but when you fly over a crest on a British B-road, the nose does not smash into the tarmac with a sickening thud.

And boy oh boy, is it fast. The figures say it will go from 0 to 60 in 4.9 seconds and on to a top speed of 186 mph, but actually, as you snarl and roar through the countryside, it feels even faster than that.

Once, I was given the controls of a World War Two P-51 fighter. That thing danced and jinked like no machine I'd ever been in, and all the time there was a glorious roar from the Merlin engine. Well, that's what the DB9 feels like. Like a fighter. Like everything mankind knows about excitement and machinery and technology has finally come together in an orgasm of absolute, thrilling and total harmony.

And yet. Inside, you have a Volvo satellite navigation system that works, you have a stereo system which looks and sounds as good as anything from Quad, and you have space to move too. The back's a bit cramped, even if you're Douglas Bader, but the front is massive.

So Bez – may God smile on him and all his family – has done it. He's kept the traditional qualities of a British car, but blended them with German engineering, to create a party in the park. An old-fashioned setting, but a whole new sound.

As a result he's ended up with a car for which only one word will do. If you want a 'fast' car, buy a Ferrari. If you want a 'Volkswagen', buy a Bentley Continental GT.

If you want a 'perfect' car, you simply have to have a DB9.

Sunday 18 April 2004

Autodelta 147 GTA

Every week I find it jolly easy to be rude on these pages about the latest product from some large and faceless corporation. But because I'm fundamentally weak and spineless, I find it awfully difficult to be similarly critical about the heroic efforts of a mere one-man band.

Chances are, the one-man band in question will have laboured over the project, in his unheated shed, for years and years. He'll have ignored the needs of his wife and the education of his children because everything in his life will have been devoted to the creation of his new 'baby'. And as a result he'd take it badly if a reviewer peered into the pram and said: 'My God, that's ugly.'

Unfortunately, however, it will be ugly; and dangerous and impractical with it. That's because cars made in sheds on Black & Decker Workmates are rarely tested in Australian deserts or in the frozen Arctic wastes.

They aren't deliberately crashed to ensure they're safe for people to collide in, nor are they driven round a track for thousands of miles to make sure they're reliable. In fact they're rarely tested at all, and this is another reason that I avoid them. Because most are accidents that haven't yet happened.

Somehow, though, a specially tuned car did turn up at the house the other day. It was an Alfa Romeo that had been breathed on by a company called Autodelta, and since there was nothing else for me in the drive I swallowed my nerves and took it for a spin . . .

I suppose if any cars can be tuned, Alfas make ideal candidates, chiefly because Alfa Romeo itself is not allowed to tune them. Fiat, you see, owns just about all the car firms in Italy, and each is given a specific role.

Ferrari: your job is to win the Formula 1 world championship until the end of time. Maserati: your job is to make Ferraris that are a little softer and a little more practical for the middle-aged businessman who wants bespoke engineering on an everyday basis. Fiat: your job is to make cars for the walnut-faced peasantry. And Lancia: your job is to make Fiats for the more successful and style-orientated motorist.

Job done, and a car in there for everyone. But unfortunately that leaves Alfa Romeo with nothing to do. They aren't allowed to compete with any of the others and that means they have to try making cars that aren't too fast, or sporty, or luxurious, or stylish, or cheap. In other words, it's in their remit to be deliberately average.

Happily, they're not very good at it. I drove a 166 to Wakefield last week and must say that, on paper, it's complete rubbish. It's slower than the equivalent 5-series BMW, thirstier than a solid rocket booster and equipped with . . . well, almost nothing at all. It doesn't even come with a cupholder and the depreciation has to be experienced to be believed. Buy one tomorrow for £29,900 and in one year it will be worth just £13,000. That's £17,000 gone down the pan. Small wonder, I reasoned, as I plodded along, that they've only managed to sell two in Britain this year.

And yet, beneath the politically inspired ordinariness, you can sense it has been designed and thought out by people who really do care. It had a soul, that car . . . a real, genuine character that somehow managed to turn every mile of the journey into a heart-warming event.

If I were to be in the market for a large four-door saloon, I wouldn't hesitate for a second. I'd hang the cost and get myself a 166.

Imagine, though, if you could combine this sense of being with some genuinely exciting performance. Imagine if you could free Alfa from its Fiat shackles and untie the engineers' arms. And now stop imagining, because such a car is here, in the shape of the Autodelta 147 GTA.

The heart of the machine is the engine, which is a bored-out version of the renowned Alfa V6. So you get 3.7 litres, which, thanks to specially made stainless-steel exhausts, a Ferrari throttle system and a remapped computer, means an almost unbelievable 328 bhp is to hand.

Now, that's all well and good, but the standard car cannot cope with the power from its 3.2-litre, 247-bhp engine. If you even think about going near the throttle, its front wheels light up like Catherine wheels and you go nowhere in a cloud of expensive Pirelli smoke.

The trick is to trickle away from the lights, wondering why you didn't simply buy the 1.6-litre version, and then floor it. But even then you need to be careful, because torque steer will put you straight into the nearest tree.

The fact is that you cannot put large power outputs through the front wheels alone. They've got their work cut out doing the steering and the last thing they need is to be distracted from the job with all those angry Italian horsepowers.

Engineers at Saab once told me that the most power you could realistically entrust to a front-wheel-drive car is 220 bhp. A point they proved recently by launching an unwieldy 250-bhp front-driver called the Hot Aero.

And yet here's Autodelta putting 328 bhp through those front wheels. Are they mad? Do they want to kill only their customers, or are they after people coming the other way as well? Driving a front-wheel-drive hatchback with 328 bhp is like playing Russian roulette with a fully loaded gun. It's like trying to fly a helicopter gunship while drunk: you're going to crash, and you're going to die.

To try to get round the problem, they've fitted a limited-slip differential, and that started the alarm bells ringing even more stridently. Ford fitted such a thing to its Focus RS and turned what might have been quite a nice car into a complete liability. On anything other than a smooth track it would suddenly turn sharp left for no reason. And you couldn't prepare yourself, because sometimes it would suddenly turn sharp right. Limited-slip diffs in front-wheel-drive cars, I deduced after a sweaty, terrifying drive through Wales in the RS, Do Not Work.

I was therefore decidedly nervous as I tippy-toed out of my drive in Autodelta's passport to the next life. I'd said a tearful goodbye to my wife, and hugged the kids: Daddy wasn't coming back.

The accident, I knew within moments, was going to be a big one, because this car isn't ferociously fast. It's much quicker than that. Ferrari throttle? Forget it. When you stamp on the accelerator it's like you've hit the Millennium Falcon's hyperdrive. Suddenly all the stars are fluorescent tubes.

In bald English, 0–60 mph takes 5 seconds. Flat out you'll be doing 175 mph, and therefore there has never been a hatchback this hot before.

A corner was coming. And then it was a distant speck in my rear-view mirror. I vaguely remember turning the wheel and I have a dim recollection of being astounded by the grip . . . and then the moment was gone.

No, really, the damn thing's a barnacle. Normally, in a tight bend, a front-drive car will spin the inside wheel uselessly, which means the one on the outside suddenly has to do all the steering and power-handling. But obviously it can't and you understeer off the road. But with that diff, the inside wheel doesn't spin, it grips and grips and then it grips some more.

Yes, bumps will cause some violent tugging at the wheel, and yes, it graunches horribly while reversing at slow speed, but the upside is a whole new chapter written into the laws of physics.

I'd love to stop at this point and give the man who made this car a nice warm feeling in the pit of his tummy. But I'm duty bound to point out one or two shortcomings.

First, the body kit was awful, but worse than this was the ride. The car I drove belonged to a 22-year-old – I'd love to see his insurance bill – and he'd set it up completely wrong. It had the compliancy of an RSJ and the comfort of sitting down sharply on the sharp end of a piledriver.

But, I see from the brochure, you don't need to fit springs and dampers made from oak and iron. You can have more conventional stuff if that's what you fancy – and take it from me, you do. You can leave the body kit off the options list as well.

This has an effect on price. As tested, my car cost £40,000, which, considering the speed and grip, has to be the bargain of the century. But if you just stick to the engine, the diff and some tasty tyres, it's going to cost a lot less.

Better still, you can have all the important modifications that can be fitted to any Alfa: the 166, the 156 and the GTV. And that's a tempting prospect. It means you can have an Alfa Romeo. Not just a Fiat with an Alfa Romeo badge.

Sunday 25 April 2004

Subaru Legacy Outback

Ask anyone who is truly, properly famous and they'll tell you that the single greatest gift God gave to man was anonymity. The ability to walk into a restaurant without being pointed at. The comfort blanket of being able to make a phone call safe in the knowledge that nobody else is listening – because nobody else cares about what you have to say.

Anonymity? Ask Harrison Ford, or Madonna, or John Ketley, and they'll tell you that it's more precious than two functioning lungs.

Oh, you see all those silly, half-naked soap stars desperately trying to attract the attention of the paparazzi outside two-bit PR puff parties. But if they were to really make it, if they really were to become a household name with a household face and a household love life, if we really were to find out what they have for their elevenses and where they are every minute of every single day, and what text messages are stored on their mobile phone, they'd go absolutely mental.

I'm not famous, but I do appear on the television from time to time, and that's enough to make my life difficult on occasion. Chiefly because sometimes I forget myself and I think I *am* famous.

Last year I was shown to my hotel room in Dubai by

a porter who, when he'd shown me how the door worked and explained what the bath was for, asked: 'Do you think I could have your signature?'

'Sure,' I replied, with a huge grin. So, snatching up a piece of hotel notepaper, I wrote: 'To Ahmed, with lots of love, from Jeremy Clarkson.'

'No,' he said, with a puzzled face. 'I mean, do you think I could please have your signature on the registration form.'

This year, the same sort of thing happened again. I was lying on a sun lounger, generally taking in some Caribbean rays, when I noticed the telltale glint of a paparazzi lens in the bushes. Angrily, I threw down my book and stomped over to express my displeasure.

Sadly, it was a wasted journey, because when I'd finished shouting the poor guy explained he hadn't a clue who I was and had been photographing someone called Alex Best, whose bikini top had slipped down a little.

And there you have it. This girl was apparently married to a footballer and then lived in a jungle. And that's enough to make the positioning of her swimsuit interesting. Can she possibly have been ready for that?

Can any one of these Madonna wannabes imagine what it would be like to be photographed every single time they walk out of the house, and how they would cope when the assistant in the local knicker shop telephones the newspapers to tell them what colour bra they've just bought?

Only last week I was having a serious heart-to-heart with a friend when, quite out of the blue, a brassy woman with metal hair marched up to me and asked what I thought of the Honda CRV. And, like I said, I'm not famous.

If you want a sense of how it feels to be well known, try walking into your local bistro naked. Or go to work tomorrow dressed as a trout. Or, better still, buy yourself a Porsche 911 GT3RS.

It's finished in Human League white and has red wheels. It says GT3RS in foot-high letters down the door. And it has a spoiler the size of a hospital stretcher.

As a result, everyone tries to come alongside so they can point and stare. And, worse, complete strangers stroll over in petrol stations, and won't go away even when you put the nozzle down their trousers and produce a match.

There are many reasons why you wouldn't want this car. A steering wheel that has nothing to do with your direction of travel. A roll cage where the back seats should be. And a ride quality that . . . well, put it this way – I doubt it would make a suitable platform for disarming a nuclear weapon. Or getting a tattoo. But the worst thing about it is the never-ending attention it draws.

Which brings me on to the world's best antidote to fame – the £26,500 Subaru Legacy Outback Estate. Russell Crowe could drive through the middle of Pontefract in this car and nobody would notice, even if he were naked at the wheel. You could impale Uma Thurman's head on the radio aerial, and that wouldn't do the trick either.

It's so invisible that you could almost certainly drive it into the vault at the Bank of England and steal all the gold. And speed cameras? Help yourself, because the Outback makes the F-117 stealth fighter look like a pterodactyl.

Then there's the quality. In the past couple of years I've noticed a distinct downturn in the robustness of virtually all cars. Mercedes used to be a byword for dur-ability but now it's a byword for being on the hard shoulder at four in the morning with steam coming out of the bonnet. And Volkswagen has suffered, too, coming near the bottom in the *Top Gear* customer satisfaction survey. Toyota used to employ a man to ensure the switches all made the right sort of click when you pushed them, but, judging by my recent experiences, I think he may have left. And then there's the new Volvo V50, which feels like it's running on suspension made from tinfoil.

The Outback, though, is different. When you shut the door, it makes exactly the same noise as a dead pheasant hitting the ground at 40 mph, a sort of muffled, autumnal 'bumph' sound. And the quality of the material used on the dashboard is up there with Sabatier.

Of course, in recent years Subarus have become famous for going through woods at high speed, spewing stones into the faces of men in bobble hats.

The Legacy, however, is far removed from all of this. The top-of-the-range 3-litre version does 0–60 in a whisper-quiet but rather pedestrian 8.1 seconds and is all out of ideas at a near-silent 139 mph.

This, then, is more a Subaru of the old school. Let's not forget that when these funny cars with their flat-four engines and four-wheel drive started arriving in Britain, they weren't sold through plate-glass and rubber-plant dealerships. No, they were sold to country folk by agri-cultural supply centres.

That's why on the Legacy's door panel there is a sticker explaining its four-wheel-drive layout. To remind you that under the invisible, Teflon-tough skin, it's still a tractor.

There's been a rash of new estate cars in the past few months. Jaguar has whacked a greenhouse on to the back of its X-type, Volvo has the aforementioned V50, and we mustn't forget the old hands from Mercedes-Benz, Audi and BMW.

Think of this lot as holiday destinations. You've got all the obvious ones, such as Minorca and Florida, plus a couple of new choices, like Costa Rica and Rwanda. Well, the Subaru is like Croatia, you see: you wouldn't normally even consider it, but those who do so keep returning there, year after year.

I must say I was deeply impressed. It was smooth, quiet, dignified, and it had quite the largest sunshine roof I've ever seen. Certainly, if you ever tire of it as a car, you could use it as a hangar for your helicopter.

More than this, however, I enjoyed the way it dealt so easily with any kind of road surface. The slightly raised suspension meant that the car's underside was high enough to miss the boulders on rutted lanes, but not so high that on twisting A-roads it felt like I was in a boat.

I really was enjoying this car, right up to the moment when I completely lost it in the long-term car park at Birmingham airport.

This was one of those times when anonymity doesn't work for you. Another, of course, is when you want a table at the Ivy.

Sunday 9 May 2004

Mercedes-Benz CL65 AMG

This week I have been reading mostly about the battle of the north Atlantic, and just how terrifying and terrible life must have been for Britain's merchant seamen.

The seasickness, the bone-numbing cold, smoking with cupped hands so Fritz couldn't see the glow through his periscope, and then, when (not if) you were torpedoed, being plunged into the oggin, where your head was cooked by the burning fuel oil and your body frozen by the icy waters. Sausages suffer a better fate on the barbecue.

But they had to keep going out there because Britain needed 55 million tons of imported commodities each year in order to survive and, by 1941, thanks entirely to the U-boats, the amount coming in had been nearly halved. We barely had suffcient raw materials to build ships to replace the ones being lost.

Consider the maths. The U-boats were sinking more than a hundred ships every month. In 1942 alone, 7.75 million tons of Britain's merchant fleet went to the bottom. To make matters worse, for every seven ships sunk, the Royal Navy was getting one U-boat. So you might deduce from all this that we were getting our stiff upper lips kicked in.

But no. Churchill once said that he considered U-boats to be the biggest threat to our survival, and as a result a huge amount of time, money and manpower was diverted to thinking of ways they might be neutered.

This set in motion perhaps the most astonishing techno-race in human history. We developed sonar, the Germans had to think of a way to get round it; we fitted aircraft with radar, the Germans gave the subs radar detectors so they could dive when a plane was on its way. We broke their codes. They broke ours. We built fast frigates. They built faster U-boats. We invented forward-firing depth charges, the Germans built better pressure hulls to go deep; and when we introduced four engined Liberator bombers that could cover the whole Atlantic, the Germans developed engines that ran on hydrogen peroxide and breathed through snorkels so they never needed to surface. And all of this happened in just four years.

Now, whenever a scientist or an engineer says something might be possible, it's always claimed that no working model will be ready for 30 years. What good's that, if it's a cure for cancer? Back then, they were having ideas, testing them, building prototypes and getting the damn thing into production in weeks.

Of course, war is a great motivator. A point that's being made obvious by the horsepower race we're seeing at the moment.

Since the Germans aren't allowed to fight other countries any more, they've decided to fight themselves with

Audi, Volkswagen, Mercedes and BMW all engaged in a full-on scrap to see who can extract the most power from a road-going engine.

It all started, I suppose, when BMW announced the M5 would have 400 bhp. That seemed like a colossal achievement and I remember remarking at the time that Jackie Stewart had had less when he won the world championship. But pretty soon Bee Em's 400-bhp V8 was made to look like a paraffin stove.

Mercedes came along with a supercharged 5.5 litre that got perilously close to 500. Then Volkswagen announced it was working on a Bugatti supercar that would offer drivers a nice round 1,000. And to show they were serious, they built a twin-turbo W12 for the Bentley Continental with 552 bhp.

BMW immediately scuttled back to its drawing board and began work on a V10 for the next M5, while Mercedes pointed the eeking machine at its 6-litre V12. This was deemed a 'bit light on the throttle', so they enlarged it to 6.5 litres and added a couple of turbos. The result was 612 bhp. A few supercars claimed marginally more, but when it came to torque, this engine was way out in front with 738 lb per foot. In short, it was the most powerful road-going engine ever made . . . and now they've gone and put it in a car.

Putting 738 lb per foot of torque on the road is like putting a full-scale avalanche in a snow shaker. It's like lighting your sitting-room fire with Mount Etna: 738 lb per foot of torque is insane.

Maybe, just maybe, and this is an argument that hangs

by a silvery thread, Ferrari could get away with such a move. The car would need to be carefully designed by people who understood aerodynamics and traction, and it would almost certainly not resemble any car we've ever seen. Who knows, to contain and harness that much power it may have to look like a Saturn 5 launcher, or an oil rig. Or a pepper grinder.

But no. Mercedes has simply slotted its amazing new power plant into the ordinary CL. Oh, they say they've beefed up the drive shafts and fitted bigger brakes, but that's like saying, 'Yes, we've employed Satan to teach Form IVb this year, but it's OK because we've confiscated his cape.' You can't put 738 lb per foot of torque in a standard coupé . . . or can you?

I knew it was an ordinary Mercedes straight away because, even though it had been carefully prepared as a press demonstrator, it arrived at my house with one headlamp not working and a driver's seat backrest that wouldn't lock. Standard Mercedes build quality, then.

But there was nothing standard about its simply astonishing acceleration. My wife drove it first. Normally she will avoid anything big, heavy or with suspension, but her Lotus was away, being fitted with more power, so she climbed into the Mercedes, thinking it was just another hateful squidgemobile. She came home later that day and could only squeak.

I now know why. It is hysterically fast. From 60 to 130 it goes like a rocket, but, unlike any similarly speedy supercar, it makes no noise in the process. At 150 it sounds like a gentle breeze.

And, better still, it's comfortable, too. Amazingly, Merc's engineers have not felt the need to fit suspension made from brass and oak to try to keep the body in check. So you just glide from place to place, in sepulchral silence, at Mach 4. It's almost eerie.

They haven't fiddled with the exterior styling either, which means other road users have absolutely no clue about the nuke under the bonnet. I know you're too grown up to be interested in this sort of thing, but on one trip a bloke in a Porsche Boxster came up behind and flashed his lights, trying to get past.

By the time his girlfriend looked up to see what was in the way, I was already at home reading the children a bedtime story. I would dearly love to have seen his face. 'No, really, darling, there was a car there – I promise – and then it disappeared.'

You could have an extramarital affair with a car like this, popping out for hanky-panky and popping back before anyone knew you'd gone.

Of course there are some drawbacks to all this grunt, like you need to remember that half an inch of throttle movement in an ordinary car increases the torque reaching the wheels by no more than 10 lb per foot. Half an inch of movement in the Merc's throttle, and you've added probably 200 lb per foot. This has an effect on grip.

No, really, any brutality – no matter how minor – will light up the rear tyres, which are not made from kryptonite or dilithium crystals. They're just rubber, and rubber has a finite level of traction.

If you're exuberant, you're going to go off the road

backwards. But what a way to go. Germany is still after world domination, but being killed by its attempts this time around might actually be called fun.

Sunday 16 May 2004

Mitsubishi Warrior

Last weekend the skies turned blue, literally and meta-phorically, when Richard Littlejohn, the roly-poly pro-war columnist for the *Sun*, came for lunch. Over the years Richard and I have established that we share wildly different views on America, Israel, the Arab world, Yasser Arafat and what might be done to solve the 50-year war. So, instead of arguing, we have put the whole Middle East into a demilitarised, no-go zone and we simply don't go there any more.

Unfortunately, we spent so much time toasting the demise of Piers Morgan that by six in the evening we had both forgotten the golden rule.

Giddy from the merlot, I pointed out that Britain cannot afford to run its armed forces, a National Health Service and a welfare state and that Europe, no matter how unpalatable and difficult it may be, must become a cohesive, unified forsh.

'Nonshensh,' thundered Littlejohn, who began to outline his vision of an Anglified world in which Britain, Ireland, Canada and Australia join forces to back the US, which, he says, is the last beacon of hope for this troubled and violent world.

Littlejohn, you need to know, spends a deal of time in a gated community in Florida. Much of his family lives in Detroit. He really thinks America is the land of the free and the home of the brave. If you cut him in half . . . I'd be grateful.

I, on the other hand, feel more at home in a Zurich tram station than I do in the bar of a Ritz-Carlton hotel. And I have more in common with my dog than I do with the immigration officers at an American airport.

It's the little things that baffle me most of all. The way every coffee shop plays Pachelbel's *Canon in D* on the Muzak system, the way the middle classes don't wear socks, the way they address one another in such loud voices across the hotel swimming pool, the inability they all have to locate themselves, or anyone else, on a map of the world, the love affair with country music, the mullets, the television ad breaks, the way they don't offer you a cup of coffee or a drink when you go to their houses. I always feel like a civilised human being at a garden party for very rich apes.

The strangest thing about America, though, is that half the cars sold there every year are not cars at all. They're SUVs. And the best-selling car of them all is the Ford F-150, which is a pick-up truck.

The car makers love this because a car is quite expensive to make. It needs to be safe, quiet, fast, spacious, economical and comfortable. And by the time you've shoehorned a list of requirements like that into a vehicle, the profit margins are tiny.

A pick-up truck, on the other hand, is made by nailing a couple of slabs of pig iron on to a chassis that would be recognisable to the makers of any nineteenth-century covered wagon. Then you simply add leather seats to make it feel like a premium product, and charge whatever you like.

Those in the know reckon that on a $12,000 pick-up truck, Ford will make $3,000–4,000 more than it would from selling a $12,000 car.

Well, $4,000 dollars might not sound like much. But you need to remember that Ford has sold 800,000 F-series pick-up trucks every year for the past five years. They account for a quarter of all its sales and half its profits. They bring in $20 billion a year, which means that if the F-150 pick-up truck were a corporation, it would be in the *Fortune* 100 list. It is, quite simply, a machine for making unimaginable lumps of money.

Do the American customers feel cheated by this? I should cocoa. Gas-guzzling cars are all but outlawed these days, but a pick-up is classified as a truck so it's exempt from swingeing legislation on fuel economy. That means it quenches your thirst for a V8, and it gives other road users the impression that you are Charlton Heston.

When you have a pick-up, you are not an IT engineer from Intel.corp. You are a frontiersman who likes his beer cold, his deer raw and his music country-style. You can go to the woods at weekends with your other pick-up-driving friends and dream up plans to rid Washington of its coloureds. You have the military-style wheels. You have the military-style haircut. You have the guns. You even have the uncomfortable shirts.

Imagine my horror when my wife casually announced the other day she'd like a pick-up. 'What,' I exclaimed, 'in the name of all that's holy, do we want one of those for?' We're European. We were sipping tea while the Americans were shooting Indians. We've had 2,000 years to get used to civilisation, not 20 minutes. We're advanced, we're slim, we're at the cutting edge of evolution. We think that shooting bears is daft. Budweiser gives us a headache and we think George Bush is an arse. So why in God's name do we want to drive around in a car made from a hen house and two bits of railway track?

Apparently we need one for taking wounded chickens to the vets and picking up trees and donkey feed (life on the wild western frontiers of Chipping Norton can be tough).

I argued that if we must have a Ku Klux Klan mobile, it'd have to be Japanese, because at least they are built to withstand just about anything. 'Look,' I said, pointing at the news from Somalia/Iraq/Sudan/the Balkans, 'I don't see those freedom-fighter Johnnies turning up for the battle in a Land Rover or a Dodge Ram. They've all got Japanese pick-ups because, along with the cockroach and the AK-47, they're the most indestructible things on earth.'

Without further ado, I called Mitsubishi and asked if I could borrow one of its L200 double-cab Warriors, which account for nearly half of all pick-up-truck sales in Britain. Sales of which, worryingly, have been growing at the rate of 40 per cent per year.

It arrived, sporting lights on the roof, chrome roll bars and chunky wheels. And it lasted three days before a hose fell off and, in a cloud of black smoke, it ground to a halt.

Sadly, they sent another and I took it for a drive. Where do we start? The ride was more uncomfortable than the Cresta run. There was no performance at all. Space in the back part of the double cab was a joke. And it's all very well pointing at the undeniably large boot, but you can't put anything in that because every time you pulled up at a set of lights, passers-by would simply help themselves.

There's another problem, too. In his last budget, Gordon Brown decided that too many people were using tax-deductible vans and pick-ups as family cars at the weekend. And as a result, from 2007, those that do will be clobbered.

As a tax-avoidance scheme, then, the pick-up's days are numbered, which means it must be judged as a vehicle. And I have to say it's one of the worst I've ever driven. Yes, there's a ruggedness to the undersides, and yes there is four-wheel drive. But why? We have no wolves and the only arms we're allowed to bear have hands on the end.

If you really do want a work tool, buy a van. The only reason for buying a pick-up is because you want to look American. But there's an easier way of doing that. Eat lots of chocolate and lose your atlas. Or get Richard Littlejohn over for lunch. You could even sit on him – it's a lot more comfortable than sitting on a pick-up truck, trust me.

Sunday 30 May 2004

Ford Sportka

I've managed to completely forget how to drive. And since that was a split infinitive, it seems I've completely forgotten how to write as well. The driving thing is more of a worry. In the past couple of days I've pulled out on to roundabouts even though I could see perfectly well that a car was coming. I've jumped red lights. I've parallel-parked like I was using the force, and then yesterday, while reversing up a one-way street to shout at a bus driver, I backed, with a sickening crunch, into some poor chap's Volvo.

My progress from the wilds of Huddersfield to the confines of Sloane Square has been set against a tuneless cacophony of blaring horns, furious parking sensor alerts, squealing tyres, rending metal and hurled abuse.

We see this kind of thing in sportsmen. They train, reach a peak of physical fitness and then, one day, for no obvious reason, they're unable to perform properly. Of course, this doesn't matter. It means only that they'll lose the game. But on the road, the consequences can be far more serious. So why does it happen?

I've checked my horoscopes and none warns me to stay off the roads until the moon rises up out of Venus. I have no money or family worries. The job trundles on. And yet I can't drive. So I've been forced to revisit an issue that last reared its head about 20 years ago. Biorhythms.

It is said that the ancient Greeks first attempted to explain mood swings 3,000 years ago but it wasn't until around 1900 that a psychologist and a doctor worked out why people in perfect physical health with no worries could sometimes feel unhappy. They reckoned that from birth we go through intellectual, physical and emotional cycles. Each works on a different time-frame, but there are occasions when all three are at a low ebb. This makes us muddle-headed and depressed and unable to park a Range Rover properly.

Back in the early 1980s the *Daily Mail* got hold of the story and for a while everyone was talking about it. Except me. I thought it was just another load of ley line, tarot card, Area 51, weird-beard twaddle. And I uncovered further evidence to support this scepticism the other day when I consulted an internet biorhythm planner to find that my ideal partners – people with exactly the same 'waves' – are Uma Thurman (good) and Kim Jong-il (not so good).

However, I fed my birth date into the system and, bugger me, for the past three days all three of my charts have been bumping along the bottom. In essence, I've been driving up and down the M1 in a two-ton Range Rover even though I have been a weeping, slobbering wreck with the co-ordination of a half-set jelly.

I was, at this point, going to bring up Carole Caplin and some conjecture on what she might do to solve the problem. On an ordinary day it would have been shrewd and incisive, but today, with my head full of wallpaper paste, I can't seem to make any worthwhile link.

So I shall move on to the practical and cheap Ford Ka. Even though it looks like a teapot, it's been a huge success in Britain, taking nearly half of all the sales in its class.

Recently it was improved with the fitting of an electronic milometer, a low-fuel warning light, and, on luxury models, a rev counter and a wash wipe facility for the windscreen. This does beg a question: what the hell did it come with before?

There's a similar issue under the bonnet. The new engine will get you from 0 to 62 mph in 13.7 seconds, which is so slow you could start off on a biorhythm high and, by the time you were going past 40, be convinced you are no good at your job and that everyone hates you. Also, if this is the best the new engine can do, how gutless was the old one?

You might think that a solution to these shortfalls can be found with the Sportka (pronounced Sport Ka), but I'm afraid not. Despite the big alloy wheels, the fat 195 tyres and sports suspension, this comes with nothing more groovy than a 1.6 that has eight valves, just like a Triumph Herald, and a single overhead camshaft, just like your grandad's old Hoover.

The result is 0–62 mph in 9.7 seconds and a cheek-rippling top speed of 108. In other words, it's noticeably slower than the old 1.6-litre Golf GTi from nearly 30 years ago.

The Sportka has been around for a few months now, but I really couldn't see the point of driving one. I mean, who wants a tweaked teapot? Who wants a hot hatch that isn't even lukewarm? And what about that name: Sportka?

If they wanted something that sounds like a fast fish, why not go for a Turbo T?

I changed my mind because of Ford's new viral advertising campaign. Every day, millions of people send millions of other people e-pictures of people sitting on the lavatory. They take half an hour to download and are never funny. But it doesn't stop the recipients sending them on to millions of other people until, by the end of the day, everyone from the Falkland Islands to Falkirk is looking at the same picture of the same man on the bog.

Ford tapped into this, making a film that got on to the web. Bingo. An ad everyone would see, because downloading something from a friend is always more interesting than doing some work. What made the Ford ad stand out was that it was funny. What made it memorable was Ford's insistence that it reached the internet by accident. What? You went to all the trouble of filming a cat having its head chopped off by the electric sunroof in a Sportka . . . for fun? Yeah, right.

The ad really is worth a watch and can be found by typing 'Ford', 'Sport', 'Ka' and 'cat' into your Google. Then, when you've done that, you will see the car in a different light. I did, so a couple of weeks ago, before I forgot how to drive, I borrowed one and went for a spin.

It's not fast, but for £11,120 the SE version is well equipped with air-conditioning and anti-lock brakes provided as standard. There are lots of extras available, too, including a 'smokers' pack' for £15. I wonder what that is. Seems a lot for a packet of fags. Maybe they throw in a nice lighter and an onyx ashtray as well.

I doubt it, though, because the interior is not what you'd call luxurious. The glovebox is like a £4.99 swing-top bin from Argos, and there are acres of painted metal.

But boy, oh boy, is it fun. Because you have to work the gearbox like you're beating eggs to get any sort of go from the strangulated 1950s engine, you feel like you're part of the performance package, like you're the organic part of a machine. That means you feel involved.

And you are. This car has fabulous, wheel-at-each-corner unflappability, which makes spirited progress an absolute hoot. The steering is weighted just so, and the handling is truly joyful.

Remember the old Mini and how it could always put a smile on your face, even if you were used to a Ferrari or a Bentley? Well, the little Ka is just the same. It's like a Pitts biplane compared with a jumbo jet. And I know which most 747 pilots would prefer to fly. More importantly, it can defeat the black dog. For 3,000 years man has been trying to explain the reason why we have bad moods. Now, Ford has come up with a way to make them go away.

Sunday 4 July 2004

Toyota Corolla Verso

A new type of disfigurement has come to Britain's towns and villages. It's worse than illegal fly-tipping, and worse than those Styrofoam takeaway containers that carpet every provincial city centre at three in the morning. It's even worse than stone cladding. And it's all the fault of your local authority.

Many years ago I remember taking a mock advanced driving test, during which the examiner asked, out of the blue, if I could describe the last road sign I'd passed. It was easy then . . . but not any more, because now you go past a road sign every 1.3 seconds.

I first noticed it last week, coming into London on the A3, and now it's driving me to distraction. Every lamp post, every telegraph pole and every branch in every tree is festooned with instructions about what the motorist may or may not do at that particular moment.

You're on a red route so you have a sign, then another, and then another explaining exactly what that means. But you know what it means, and you know you're on a red route because there, at the side of the road, painted clearly on the orange of the bus lane, or the green of the cycle path, are two red lines.

If there's a bus lane, then there will be signs telling you what that means too. And then things really start to get stupid. You're told that the central London congestion-charging zone is five miles away. Why? Lots of things are five miles away. You're also told that there's a speed camera ahead, that there are bus lane cameras, that you're near a library, that there's no left turn into Acacia Grove . . . and what's this? Oh, that you're entering a 'drinking controlled zone'.

It's got to the point now where there are so many signs that they blur into a background hiss of white noise. It's a bit like the warnings you get before a film on television. In the olden days, when the announcer said in a solemn BBC-ish tone that the film about to start contained violence, you knew you were in for a 90-minute bloodbath with many severed heads. And so you sat a little more upright in your Parker Knoll Recliner.

But now, when they say the film contains mild violence and strong nipples, you just go into a trance. Yeah, yeah, yeah. And then you're surprised and horrified when the movie starts with a shot of Al Pacino having his arms sawn off.

This is what's happening on the roads. They can put up a sign saying there are speed bumps ahead, and even if it isn't blocked by another sign saying the road to the left has children running around on it, it really doesn't register. So you hit the sleeping policeman doing about 80 mph. And your back snaps.

The reason, of course, for all the signs is . . . lawyers. After your back has been broken the council can send its legal team round to the quadriplegic department of the local hospital to explain to your relatives that, unfortunately, no claim for damages can be made because there was a sign warning motorists that there were humps ahead.

That's why you get those idiotic messages on the motorway matrix boards these days; if they tell you it's windy, you can't sue anyone for being blown into a bridge parapet. And you won't be able to argue, of course, partly because they're right and partly because you'll have lots of tubes coming out of your nose.

The upshot is that every single street is now a Technicolor blaze of legal disclaimers and nonsense. Not only is this ugly, but it's dangerous too, because not that long ago, when you ran off the road, the chances of hitting a sign were slim. Now, though, you're almost certain to hit something thanking you for driving carefully through the village.

Sadly, I can only imagine that things will get worse, because soon the sign advising you that you're entering a nuclear-free zone will have to be translated into 14 languages, and there will have to be some sort of mushroom-cloud pictogram as well, for the educationally challenged.

Then, of course, there will be signs telling you not to smoke within 250 yards of any inhabitable structure, and more signs explaining that the town centre you're entering is off limits to off-road vehicles.

I can smell this one coming. There is such a palpable sense of hate and bile among ordinary road users that if big 4×4s were to be banned from built-up areas the roads would doubtless immediately unjam themselves. I agree with you all. I too think these school-run mums in automotive leviathans should be horse-whipped to within an inch of their lives. And I'm speaking as someone who actually owns one.

But the trouble is that 4 × 4s are like nuclear weapons. Because you've got one, I can't put my kids in a normal hatchback, because if we were to crash into one another yours would survive and mine wouldn't. So I have to have one too.

The only solution is for the bosses of GM and Ford and Toyota to meet in Reykjavik and come up with a Salt treaty of their own.

But then what will we do? We've become accustomed to the rough-and-tumble interiors and the vast acreage of space. So how could we go back to a simple Golf after that? Happily, there's no need, because while you weren't looking the car makers introduced a new breed of car that is no bigger than a normal saloon, so it won't clog up the roads like the fat in David Bowie's artery, and yet inside there are seven proper seats with seven proper seat belts.

Vauxhall was first out of the trap with its Zafira – which I've written about many times before. It's rather good, and now it has been joined by the Renault Grand Scénic – which is ugly and made from tracing paper – by the Volkswagen Touran – which is like the Black Hole of Calcutta – and by the Toyota Corolla Verso, which is excellent.

I know, I know. You can't conceive of the insanity that would have to blow through your head before you'd consider changing your Range Rover for a Toyota Corolla, but bear with me here.

According to the boffins at Euro NCAP, the independent body that tests cars for safety, the Corolla has a top-notch five-star rating, whereas the Range Rover has to make do with just four. Yes, in a head-on accident between the two, you'd be better off in the off-roader, but if you run into an enormous warning sign, amazingly, you'd be better off in the little Toyota. What's more, if you go for the Corolla, it means your sex life can be more carefree.

You see, with those seats that pop up out of the boot floor, you don't need to worry about condoms, or intra-uterine devices, or going into reverse at the last moment. Thrash away. If the resultant baby paste hits the bull's eye and you end up with another child, at least you won't have to buy a new car.

The best thing about the Corolla Verso, though, is the quality. There's a robustness which you simply don't find in any of its rivals. This car looks like it was designed by someone who actually knows how destructive children can be.

Kids never understand that their feet are going to be further away than they were the week before. So they break stuff. Mine smashed a Renault Scénic to pieces the other day in about 15 minutes.

I have to say at this point that the Corolla is not that pleasant to drive, with roly-poly handling and a cement mixer of an engine, but come on: with the possible exception of the Porsche Cayenne, your average off-roader isn't exactly a Ferrari, is it? Finally there's the question of money. A top-of-the-range 1.8-litre Verso is £18,795, a little more than its main rivals, but three times less than you're asked to pay for a less practical, less safe and more antisocial Range Rover.

I'd like to think, then, that this review is a signpost to a better and less congested future. But unlike the council signposts it doesn't mess with the view, and if you don't agree with what it says you can at least use it to light the barbecue.

Sunday 18 July 2004

Mitsubishi Evo VIII

It's a new day, so obviously we have a new version of Mitsubishi's turbocharged road rocket to slobber over. This one's the Lancer Evo VIII MR FQ-340, and don't worry, my dog hasn't just walked across the computer's keyboard. That really is its name.

Let me try to decipher it for you. Evo VIII means this is the eighth evolution on an original theme. Comparing this, then, to the first high-performance Lancer is a bit like comparing Stephen Fry to Judy, the chimp in *Daktari*. It's much, much cleverer.

MR stands for Mitsubishi Racing, which signifies that it's had a hand in its development, and FQ for f★★★★★★ quick. But then it would be because 340 is how many horse powers the 2-litre engine develops.

This is remarkable. Not even 15 years have elapsed since Daihatsu put a turbocharged 1-litre engine in its little Charade and in so doing created the first road car to offer up 100 bhp per litre. Today the Ferrari 360 CS produces 116 bhp per litre and that's staggering. So what's to be made of the Evo, which churns out a mind-boggling 170 bhp per litre?

Of course, you may ask why they've gone to so much trouble. Why not simply fit a bigger engine?

Well, the problem is that the Evo is built primarily as a

machine to compete in international rallying, and the rules of the sport stipulate that 2,000 cc is the max. The big worry I have is that while a 2-litre engine could be coaxed into handing over a thousand horsepower if that's what you wanted, it would do 0 to 60 . . . once. Then it would explode.

You have to trade power for longevity, and I suspect that 340 bhp is right on the edge of everyday practicality. I note with some surprise that the engine still comes with Mitsubishi's three-year warranty, but then I see also that it must be serviced once every 10 minutes or so.

I'm tempted therefore to steer you away from this top-of-the-range machine and into something a little more sensible. Obviously we can ignore the 260 version, because, while it's just £24,000, it takes about two years to get from 0 to 60. But can we ignore the FQ-300 for £28,000 or the £30,000 FQ-320? These are very nearly as fast as the £33,000, full-blooded 340 but are almost certain to last a little longer.

The simple answer, after no thought at all, is yes, of course we can ignore the less powerful options. Going for a 320 is like going all the way to Paris and staying in the outskirts. It's like getting into bed with Uma Thurman and falling asleep. Buying a 320 is a sign that you're sensible and grown up and worried about practicalities, in which case why don't you buy a canal boat and go away.

If you're going to buy a road-going rally car, you have to have the best, you have to have the fastest. And that's the 340.

It's not just faster than the other Evos, either. It's also faster than its Subaru rival.

In fact I'm struggling to think of anything that could keep up.

Off the line, even the best four-wheel-drive cars bog down as the wheels refuse to spin, but not the VIII. You give it a bellyful of revs, dump the clutch, and there's no lag, no chasm. You're off like you've been fired at the horizon by one of Dick Dastardly's cartoon catapults.

A mere 4.4 seconds later you're past 60 mph and that means all but the most exotic rivals are left far behind. This car – and remember, it only costs £33,000 – can be mentioned in the same breath as the Porsche Carrera GT and the McLaren Mercedes.

Mitsubishi says it's limited the top speed to 157 mph, but why? I can hardly see Officer Brunstrom or Jonathon Porritt nodding sagely at their public-spiritedness. I suspect the real reason is that at 158 the sit-up-and-beg front-end styling would lose its war with the air and the car would run out of puff anyway.

So, yes, the world's supercars would take it on a long straight, but come on. What long straight? Are you going to take your Ferrari up to 180 on the M27 to make a point? I don't think so.

And anyway, eventually you'd get off the motorway and the Evo would catch you up again. This is because, when it comes to the business of going round corners, the Evo is quite simply in a class of its own.

You turn in and immediately a bewildering array of acronyms awaken from their electronic slumber to get you round the bend at a pace that will leave you reeling.

On the previous generation of Evo VIII the all-wheel control (AWC) gave priority at all times to the anti-lock braking system (super-ABS) which meant that under heavy braking the active centre differential (ACD) and the active yaw control (AYC) were disengaged.

Not any more. Now you can set the attitude of the car under braking, and still the yaw moment will be controlled.

Mumbo-jumbo? Not from behind the wheel it isn't. You fly through corners thinking how in God's name is this possible. You're being flung out of the supremely supportive seat, everything that isn't bolted down is being thrown round the interior, and yet the tyres, which are still just rubber, are hanging on.

All Evos are good at this, but the MR FQ-340, perhaps because of the reprogramming or perhaps because it has an aluminium roof to lower the centre of gravity, can make you seriously cross-eyed.

I urge you with all my heart to beg, steal or borrow one of these things and take it to a quiet road you know well. It will completely redefine your concept of what driving's all about.

In the hands of a Formula 1 racing driver, a Porsche Carrera GT would be faster. But if the world's future depended on me getting from here to Stow-on-the Wold in less than 10 minutes, I'd take the Mitsubishi every time. It inspires such extraordinary confidence and there's always the sense that, no matter how fast you ask it to go round a corner, it has plenty of grip left in reserve. It is magical.

What I really love, and I do hope the people who edit this page have shown this in the pictures, is the way its muscles seem to be growing out of all those ducts in the front. You get the impression that the machinery is barely contained within the body and that it's torn great holes in the metal, in the same way that the Incredible Hulk messed up his shirt whenever he became angry.

That said, however, this is far from a good-looking car. Underneath all the visual froth, it really is a cup of instant coffee, an extremely dull, four-door Japanese saloon car. And that spoiler doesn't help. Imagine Huw Edwards with a big bling signet ring and you get the idea.

You curl up like a foetus with embarrassment every time you park it in a built-up area, because you know everyone's looking and everyone's thinking, 'What a prat.'

Still, because it is a four-door saloon it is reasonably practical. I mean it has a boot and so on, and it does come with such niceties as air-conditioning and electric windows. It also has one of those stereos that slide out of the dash and beep a lot. However, not being 12, I couldn't make it work.

It wasn't the end of the world, though, because once I was up past, ooh about three, the din coming out of the Matrix-Churchill supergun at the back would have drowned out even Danny Baker. It's a rich, deep baritone that rattled every single window in my house whenever it started.

What I liked even more, though, was the ride. Yes, the body is as stiff as a teenager but, unlike previous Evos, this one can actually run over manhole covers without snapping the people inside.

It isn't even on nodding terms with 'comfortable' but it's not bad. And I like to think that by giving the suspension more bounce, the new lightweight wheels are in contact with the road more often, giving even more grip.

This, I know, has been a furiously technical and deeply insightful look at a car and if you were hoping for 1,000 words on satsumas, followed by 30 on the car, I apologise. Normal service will be resumed next week.

In the meantime, those of you who love cars, and love driving, go and try the Evo. After a mile you'll be vomiting superlatives too.

Sunday 25 July 2004

Land Rover Discovery

Damn it. I had some plans to introduce foxhunting in cars when the more traditional equine variety is banned, but now the government has announced it is deciding whether four-wheel-drive vehicles should be banned from Britain's ancient rights of way.

At the moment, you can drive any car down any so-called green lane providing you can prove that it was once used as a road. Those of a rambling disposition – and remember the Ramblers'Association began its life as an offshoot of the communist movement – say this is pre-posterous. You shouldn't be able to drive a Range Rover down the Ridgeway just because it was once used by a bullock cart in 1628.

Now I agree, people who spend their weekends in combat trousers pushing one another's Land Rovers out of muddy puddles are probably mental. I certainly wouldn't use one as a babysitter, that's for sure. But if they want to spend their free time driving their Isuzu Troopers into a lake, that's their business. And anyway, only 5 per cent of the nation's enormous network of country paths are available to off-roaders, so taking that small piece of the pie away does seem a bit unfair.

Fairness, however, doesn't really bother eco-twerps. They had a speed limit on all waterways in the Lake

District, except a tiny part of Windermere on which normal people could water-ski and ride jet bikes. Now, however, thanks to the communists, even this little piece is about to be taken away and given back to Bill Oddie.

If off-road cars are banned from the countryside, we may have a problem, because there are also whisperings in the rectory of power that they may also be banned from town centres. Everyone, apparently, is getting fed up with mums in their Chelsea tractors taking up too much space and generally bashing into everything.

So all in all then, not an especially good time for Land Rover to stick its neck above the battlements and announce the arrival of a new Discovery. A car that cannot be used in town . . . or out of it.

Now I should make it crystal clear at the outset that I absolutely loathed the last Disco. It used the old Range Rover's chassis, which means it was rooted in the late 1960s, and boy, could you tell on the road. You could have given one to an asylum seeker as a sort of welcome-to-Britain gift and he'd have gone straight back home again.

And it had the most awful image problem, because it was driven either by mums or by murderers. Mums liked the seven seats. Murderers liked the early models, at least, with proper locking differentials, which were very good off-road. This meant they could drive far into the woods to bury their victims' heads.

The new car is a completely different animal. The raised rear roof line remains for those who have a pet giraffe, and the doors seem to have come from a different

car but, overall, there's no doubt that it's a looker. A sort
of Matra Rancho for the twenty-first century if you like.

Underneath, you get a separate chassis and a mono-
coque, so you have the toughness to deal with the green
lanes you won't be driving on and plenty of refinement
in towns, where you won't be driving either.

It is a hugely comfortable car to drive: quiet, not too
roly-poly in the bends and blessed with an extraordinarily
delicate throttle pedal that makes parallel parking – even
on a steep hill – a complete doddle. The only thing I
really didn't like about the new Disco driving experience
was the parking sensors that beeped pretty much constantly and went hysterical when I was still miles from the
car behind.

What good is 2 feet in a modern city-centre parking
slot? They should be set to go berserk when you're
2 millimetres from impact, not 2 feet.

This is especially annoying, because the latest Disco is
so big that you're always 2 feet from everything. You
could be in Paris and still be only 2 feet from your own
front door. Mind you, at least this does mean that there's
now a small boot to be found behind the third row of
seats.

Under the bonnet you get a 4.4-litre version of Jaguar's
4.2-litre V8. This could uproot trees with its torque and
it surprises you with its power. And if you don't fancy
mpg figures in the low teens, you can have a diesel that
uses the stunning twin turbo from Jaguar's S-type.

Inside, while you don't get the style or flair of a Range
Rover, you do get a sense of utilitarian toughness. You

could certainly detonate a small – let's say one-kiloton – bomb in there, and nothing would break. Prices haven't been announced yet, but expect the base models to start at less than £30,000 and the more expensive, HSE petrol versions to nudge £50,000.

The Discovery is likely to be better off-road than its big brother, the Range Rover. It is also bigger, more powerful, more torquey, faster, more practical – thanks to the seven seats – more economical and considerably cheaper.

On this basis it would be easy to sign off by saying the Disco is better than one of the best cars in the world. But I'm afraid we're far from the end of the story. You see, the Range Rover is actually a five-seater executive car that happens to have four-wheel drive. Its rivals are the Mercedes S-class and the Jaguar XJ8.

The Discovery is the other way round. It is supposed to be an off-road car that you can use on the road. Its rivals are the John Deere tractor and the wellington boot. This is why the new version worries me. I have not yet had a chance to take it off-road, but I know I'll miss having a selection of levers that make an almighty clunking noise when you pull them, as solid chunks of pig iron interlock with other solid chunks of pig iron.

Instead, you get a rotary knob that you use to tell the car what sort of surface you're on: grass, gravel, a muddy track, sand or the M1. The onboard computer then changes the settings to optimise the diffs and the ride height and the throttle sensitivity.

In theory it sounds amazing, and in practice it'll

probably work beautifully. But if I were in the middle of the Kalahari, I'd rather have two chunks of pig iron than some silicon chips that were designed and developed by four blokes in Banbury. Of course, you may argue, the Discovery will not be used in the Kalahari or even the Lake District, so why worry about how it will perform there?

Oh, come on. That's like saying a nuclear missile will never be fired, so why worry whether it will fly. It's nice to know it can.

Whatever, one day soon I'll do something mad and adventurous with the new car to see if it can handle the rough stuff and then I'll report back.

In the meantime, I do have some concerns. The man from Land Rover could lift and tilt the middle row of seats easily, but that's because he was built like a supertanker's anchor and had arms like slabs of ham.

I struggled, and I suspect a mum with a screaming child under one arm would be completely flummoxed. The Volvo XC90, which is also made by Ford, remember, is a much more practical and marginally more spacious proposition – and cheaper, too, it must be said.

I also noted that each occupant in the rear is given controls to change the radio station. This sounds fine in theory, but do you let your kids choose what they listen to when you're driving? I don't. And if they had the wherewithal to override my decision and switch to Radio 1, I'd take a hammer to them – and their control panels – within the first three miles.

Here's the big one, then. Would I swap my Volvo for

a Disco? The Land Rover's certainly nicer to drive. It feels more substantial, too, as though you're getting more 'stuff'. It also has better engines and undoubtedly more ability off-road. However, I mainly need a device for moving children to and from school, so the answer is 'no'.

As a car for mums, the Disco is narrowly beaten. But at the first possible opportunity I'll take one off-road and we'll see just how it shapes up as a car for murderers.

Sunday 22 August 2004

Corvette C6

There is a great deal in the news these days about the forthcoming election in America, in which an incoherent man with eyes that are suspiciously close together is up against a man with an enormous chin. Why? We aren't treated to daily updates from the elections in Lesser Micronesia, or Holland, so why are we inundated with every last utterance from these super-buffoons?

A cynic might say that the newspapers and television stations maintain permanent offices in America and need to keep the staff employed with something. A more rational person would explain that this is more than a national election. It's a plebiscite to decide who becomes leader of the free world.

OK, well if this is the case: if he really will be my leader, why can't I have a vote? Why should I leave the choice to a bunch of tobacco-chewing backwoodsmen who aren't even bright enough to mark the voting papers properly?

I mean it. If the president of the United States really does think he's the leader of the free world, then the free world should have a say in who gets the job. That's me, you, every Indian, every Russian, every German. And yes, every Iraqi, too. All of us.

But no; our fate is in the hands of a people whose IQ is

generally smaller than their waistbands. A people who've trawled their 263 million citizens and come up with Bush and super-chin as the alternatives. A people whose soldiers wear sunglasses while trying to defuse trouble on the streets of Baghdad. You're not Jean-Claude Van Damme, you idiots. Take them off. Let them see your eyes. Or are you like the president? Do you only have one?

As a sort of protest about everything, but the sunglasses thing most of all, my wife recently decided to purge everything American from the house.

At first, I suspected this would be a long and painful task that would send us back to the Dark Ages, but do you know what? Most of the electrical equipment is from Japan, or Germany. The furniture is largely Italian or British. And pretty well everything else was made in China.

All I could find that bore the legend 'Made in America' was my toothbrush, which makes you wonder what they're all doing over there, apart from cleaning their teeth.

Computer software seems to be the answer. Because, so far as I can tell, my laptop's brain is just about the only American-made household product that I simply couldn't do without.

Out in the drive, however, it's a different story. We have a Ford Focus, which is American, a Volvo XC90, which is American, and next March I will take delivery of a Ford GT, which has a British steering rack, a British gearbox and Italian brakes. But I know I'm fooling myself. That's American, too. And so is the subject of this week's column. The new Corvette C6.

It's billed, like all previous Vettes, as a sports car to rival the best from Europe, and I hope you don't mind if I snigger politely at this point.

America has never really made a sports car, because while we were hanging it out to dry on Welsh moorland roads or Alpine passes, they were racing between the lights on Telegraph Road. And for that you don't need a pin-sharp turn-in. You need muscle.

And that, contrary to what you may have been told, is what the Vette's always been about: it's a car so pumped up on steroids, it would be unable to make it to a drugs test without falling off its motorcycle. It's a car with arms like Schwarzenegger but a penis like a shrivelled-up little acorn.

I once spun an early incarnation of the previous Corvette off the road while charging round the only bend in Arizona. But no ticket was forthcoming from the attending police officer because, in his words, 'These things spin so damn easy, you could park one outside a store, and when you came out it'd be facing the other way.'

People were nevertheless fooled into thinking the Vette was a sports car because it's made from plastic in Kentucky, far from the powerhouse muscle pumping station that is Detroit. And what's more, because it has always been fitted with massive tyres and no discernible suspension, it has always had a surfeit of grip. I think I am right in saying that the late-1980s Vette was the first road car ever to generate I G in a bend.

But really, the car's major appeal has always been its

respectable go from its massive V8 engine and its jaw-dropping looks. The 1960s Stingray is one of the world's truly ground-breaking pieces of car design. As much of a jaw-dropper as the Lamborghini Countach.

And so we arrive at the C6, expecting more of the same. It's still plastic. It's still made in Kentucky. It still has the big V8. And – stop laughing at the back – it still comes with exactly the same sort of suspension that you get on a Silvercross pram. Yup. It has leaf springs, which means it still rides like it's running on wooden tyres.

Of course, fourteenth-century suspension has no bearing on the way the car goes. What does have a bearing is the gearbox.

Put your foot down and, after a hint of wheelspin – and with tyres the width of a tennis court, it is only a hint – the bruiser launches off the line with what might fairly be termed much gusto. And then, at around 30, everything goes horribly wrong because you have to select second.

There are levers at the National Coal Mining Museum that move with more smoothness than the gear shifter in a C6 Vette. To get to second from third, you really need a second elbow.

Happily, you're distracted from this most of the time by the HUD. I'm not joking. This car has a head-up display, just like you get in an F-16 fighter.

It's fantastic. Whole bus queues are hidden behind the digital speed read-out, which is going to make for some wonderful insurance claims: 'The old lady was behind my rev counter so I never saw her until she'd already bounced over the roof.'

There is lots of other good stuff, too. It is very, very fast, it makes a wonderful muted roar when you floor it, and even I have to admit that it's eye-poppingly pretty.

So, you might be thinking, it's just the same as all the other Vettes. But hang on a minute because it's 5 inches shorter than the previous model and, thanks to lots of aluminium under the plastic body, it's lighter, too. Can you believe that? As European cars, which are supposed to be sporty, get heavier and heavier, the car from the Land of the Stomach is actually losing weight.

In fact, the new Corvette weighs 128 kg less than a BMW M3, and this shows. I had a few laps of the *Top Gear* test track in an example with tyres that had been modelled on Kojak's head and, whisper this, I loved it. Yes, the gearbox was a serious nuisance and it didn't have quite the subtlety of a Porsche or a Beemer. It squirmed quite a bit under braking, for instance. But the steering was sharp, the grip was mighty and the speed was always intoxicating.

This gave me a problem when I climbed out and gave the keys back to the man from Chevrolet.

'What did you think?' he asked.

'Oh,' I scoffed. 'Left-hand drive, vulgar, plastic rubbish.'

But actually it isn't. It is an extremely likeable car, and you can easily forget the railway junction gearbox and the jiggly ride and the cigarette-paper quality when you examine the price tag. It's likely to be about £45,000.

So there we are. The only thing that would stop me buying one is my wife. But since you're not married to her, I'd go right ahead.

Sunday 29 August 2004

MG ZT 260

When the announcement came through that TVR had been sold to a 12-year-old Russian boy, there was a sense in the land that Britain's motor industry was no longer coughing up blood. It was dead.

But aren't we forgetting something? Ooh, it's on the tip of my tongue. I know there's something . . . Why yes, of course. Rover! The still-intact tailfin of the crashed airliner that is British Leyland.

Oh, it may have been stripped of the Mini and Land Rover, and the rights to use names such as Riley and Wolseley, which BMW now owns. But it still has Longbridge. It still has thousands of employees. It is still a player.

But only by the skinny skin skin of its teeth. Sales are in free-fall, with the number of Rovers sold this year down by 19 per cent and the number of MGs down by 6 per cent.

The problem is that the line-up of cars on sale is now even older than the people who buy them. The 45, for instance, was launched when Rameses III was on the throne, and the MGTF is still painted with woad. And while MG Rover has so far spent £100 million developing a new mid-range car, which looks rather good, that's only one-tenth of what's really needed these days.

The company already had one tie-up with the Indians

to produce the truly ghastly and massively overpriced CityRover, and now details are emerging of a new co-production deal with the Chinese. There's even some speculation that the romantically handled Shanghai Auto-motive Industry Corporation (SAIC) might buy Rover, though God knows why.

As SAIC already has tie-ups with Volkswagen and General Motors, this would be a bit like Chelsea signing George Best. If the Chinese want British engineering skills, they could simply employ some British engineers. And if they want a base in the European Union, why buy Longbridge, which is in Birmingham and has a main road running through the middle of it? Why not simply build a brand new factory in, oh I don't know, St Tropez?

Of course, I don't own a short-sleeved shirt, or a set of golf clubs, or a freemason's robe, or a blue British Airways loyalty card, and this means I don't know anything about business. I'm here only to talk about the cars Rover makes, which brings me to the driver's door of its latest offering: the MG Nutter Bastard Head-Butt Sister Shagger.

It's a familiar-looking door because it's exactly the same as the one you'll find on a Rover 75. In fact, apart from a bit of tweakery here and a bit of chicken wire there, it is pure 75 – a car named for the average age of the people who buy it.

Inside, it's much the same story. You have that familiar and enormous steering wheel and a sense that you've somehow found yourself in a Harvester theme pub. It's all mock-Tudor this and half-timbered that.

At this point you will probably climb out again and

buy an Audi instead. But I urge you to persevere, because beneath the Radio 4 exterior beats a heavy metal heart in the shape of a 4.6-litre Ford Mustang V8.

With two valves per cylinder, it's far from being the most sophisticated engine in the world, and nor is it the most powerful, nor the most economical. But Rover's engineers have had it in the shed, and I must say it sounds and feels pretty good in a muted, throbby sort of way.

Think of it as the Merlin they used to put in P-51 fighters, an Anglo-American joint effort that is in no way as sophisticated as the creamy-smooth jets fitted to the German opposition, but a whole lot more charismatic and lovable nonetheless.

And now we get to the really good bit, because, instead of sending its power to the front wheels, which would be a recipe for torque steer followed by some hedge trimming, the oomph is fed down a prop shaft to the back wheels. So there you are. Beneath the Frank Finlay exterior, you get what, in essence, is a V8 muscle car with rear-wheel drive.

Rear-wheel drive matters. It matters so much, BMW is using it as the sole marketing thrust behind the new 1-series hatchback. The people at BMW know, unless they're blind mad, that this new car is horrid to behold and as practical as a curly ruler, but that's all OK because it's rear-drive.

MG Rover has a similar philosophy. It didn't bother changing the body, or the seats or the steering wheel on the 75. It spent every penny it had – all £4.50 of it – turning it into a rear-driver.

This is because, in the far, extreme corners of the

petrolhead's domain, we all know that no car can be really good unless drive goes to the back. It is a given, the central pillar of all we hold dear. In a front-wheel-drive car, the front wheels have to do the steering and provide the propulsion, and this never quite works. Never. Even if you fit female front wheels that can multitask, there's always the sense that both the power and the steering are being corrupted. It's not pure. It's not right.

In a rear-drive car, the jobs are split evenly around all four corners of the car, and while this isn't a guarantee of success it is at least the right sort of bedrock.

In the MG NBHBSS, it does work. Brilliantly. If you're going really, really fast, the whole machine assimilates you into its core, and you become one. The steering, unencumbered with power delivery, doesn't send back any muddled messages about what the front of the car is doing, so I had the confidence to push harder. And the harder I pushed, the better it felt.

It's not a razor-sharp handler. Think of it as a destroyer rather than a speedboat, but *in extremis*, trust me on this, it's very good.

Twice, in the last run of *Top Gear*, I took this car on to the track simply to wake myself up, ready for the show. It got the adrenalin pumping and served as a reminder about why I fell in love with cars in the first place.

So would I buy one? Well, no, actually. Partly this is because there are many faults, like there's nowhere to put your left foot, and partly because it could do with another 50 horsepower.

Also, I'd steer clear because I'd always have a nagging

doubt about the future of Rover itself. I'd worry that my expensive new toy would be stripped of its warranty and service back-up five minutes after I got it home.

Mostly, though, the reason why I'd steer well clear is that all those imbeciles who used to wobble about the middle of the road in their enormous Volvos have now got Rovers. Whenever I'm stuck in a huge tailback on the way into Oxford, it's always a 216 at the front, endlessly indicating right and never actually doing so.

There's a double mini-roundabout in my local town and I can pretty much guarantee that if I went down there now, there'd be a 416 in the middle of the junction, its driver glued solid by a wave of serotonin and fear. This is not a club I wish to join.

I therefore have an idea for the bosses at Rover. Forget these half-arsed tie-ups with engineering conglomerates in the emerging world. Make a pledge to go it alone, to fight back, to repair the damage done over the years by Red Robbo and the useless management and BMW. Adopt a Churchillian pose and speak to the workforce about fighting them on the beaches.

And then start the new dawn by publicly banning anyone from buying a Rover if they own a hat.

As I said earlier, I'm not a businessman and it might not be a sound business plan. But you've tried everything else, for God's sake.

Sunday 5 September 2004

Ariel Atom

Back in April I drove the new Aston Martin DB9 all the way to Monte Carlo and decided it was perfect. I loved every single part of every single detail, so I wrote a rave review, gave it five stars and toyed with the idea of actually buying one. But then along came a car magazine whose findings were rather different. They drove the DB9 on mountain roads, where they claimed it felt 'leaden' and 'floaty'. They said it flexed and crashed over bumps and speculated that it had been rushed into production before it was actually finished.

To make matters worse, this was *Evo* magazine, whose road testers are talented and manly. So, alarmed that perhaps I'd missed something on my 900-mile motorway jaunt, I decided to put a DB9 on the track and see what's what when you really let rip.

I began with the traction control device turned on, and almost immediately I could see that the chaps at *Evo* had a point. The whole car seemed to squirm in the corners. There was no poise, no delicacy, and, with the back end tied down by an electronic straitjacket, the front was all over the shop.

But traction control always does this to a car, so I pushed the button to turn it off . . . and nothing happened. So I pushed it again, a bit harder, and with a slight sucking noise the whole caboodle disappeared into the dashboard.

This was annoying, but worse was to come, because, having fished it out with a handy pair of artery forceps, I couldn't believe my eyes. Instead of it being a simple switch, a device that connects two wires when you push it and disengages them when you push it again, there was a whole circuit board in there and two locating stubs the size of human hairs. It looked like the kind of thing you might find in an ECG machine, or a space probe. So, with a lot of a harrumphing, I left the job of reassembling it with an assistant and climbed into the car – the Ariel Atom.

None of the buttons could possibly go wrong in this car because – apart from the one used to start it – it doesn't have any. Mind you, it has no bodywork either. Those tubes you see are its chassis, so what we have here is the world's first exoskeletal car. A sort of beetle-cum-Pompidou Centre. What we have here is also a lesson in how cars work, because as you drive along you can actually see the mechanical parts moving around.

From the driver's seat you can see the steering system, the brakes, the inside of the wheels and the double-wishbone suspension absorbing the bumps. What you cannot see are the wasps and bees, until you smash into them at 90 mph. Also, because there is no mirror, you can't see yourself, which means you have no idea what the hurricane is doing to your face. As you can see from the pictures, it's doing quite a lot. After only a few minutes my normally florid complexion had begun to resemble

Florida. And you know what? I didn't care, because this car – if you can call it that – is motoring nirvana.

Because there is no bodywork (actually, because there is no anything) it weighs less than 500 kg, which in automotive terms is an ounce. It makes a Lotus Elise look like Terry Wogan. You could fit such a thing with the engine from a motorised pepper grinder and it would go like Apollo 8; but in fact it uses the VTEC motor from a Honda Civic. And not the weedy 190-bhp unit from the Type R either, but a full Japanese-spec version with 220 bhp. So that means you're getting 440 bhp per tonne, and that's about 100 more than you get from a Lamborghini Murciélago.

Obviously it has lousy aerodynamics, so the top speed is around 135 mph, but the time it takes to achieve this is simply mind-boggling: 0–60 mph, for instance, is dealt with in just 3.5 seconds.

If that sounds scary, they're working on a supercharged version that won't ripple your face so much as tear it off.

We're talking motorbike performance here, and real motorbike thrills. But because the Atom has four wheels it won't fall over when you leave it alone, you don't have to wear a helmet, and rubber fetish clothes are not de rigueur.

Of course, when I first drove the Atom it was a lovely sunny day. The thermometer was nudging 80°F and I was on a track, kissing the apexes perfectly because I could actually see the point where the wheel touches the road, and holding power slides until I was bored with them.

Honestly, I felt like a toddler who's just seen his first zoo animal.

But the acid test would come on the road, so I tweaked the suspension to make it a bit softer – you only need a spanner – and ventured into the real world.

Because the Atom looks like a racing car, it seems at home on the track, but in a village it causes people to drop their shopping. And out in the countryside it is every bit as much fun as the photographs suggest. It is Absolut motoring at its frenzied best.

Maybe the front's a little bit floaty, and maybe the brakes could be a touch more powerful. And maybe I should have put on a full-face helmet, because running into a cloud of dust kicked up by a passing juggernaut at 60 mph really hurts. But with the engine air intake trying to suck my left ear off, and the wind wreaking Jamaica-style havoc with my hair, I kept bursting into spontaneous laughter. You would, too.

Of course you wouldn't want to have a crash, because this car has never had any impact tests carried out. Thanks to Britain's unique Single Vehicle Approval system, small-car firms can bypass all the European Union regulations, and that's why we have so many such firms in this country.

Ariel is one of the smallest. Started up in Somerset four years ago by a former teacher, it has only seven employees, who make just 30 cars a year.

Don't worry, though, about buying a car from something that isn't even big enough to be labelled a cottage industry. The engine and gearbox come straight from

Honda and are bolted in place, so it's extremely unlikely they'll go wrong. And you can't worry about the trim falling off or squeaking, because there isn't any.

It really is just a chassis, an engine, four wheels and a surprisingly comfortable plastic seat. Oh, and a front-mounted boot that is easily big enough for a small bread roll. The only really complex part, it seems, is the adjustable suspension. But as it's supplied by Bilstein, you don't have to worry about that either.

I think the best thing about this car, though, is the way it looks. It's as cool as a Philippe Starck juicer, as tempting as any of the brushed-aluminium toys you find in an airport gadget shop. But unlike rechargeable underwater currency converters, I doubt you'd ever be bored with what it can do.

In terms of sheer thrills, the Atom is easily a match for the Porsche Carrera GT, and that makes its £19,999 starting price (for the 160-bhp version) look almost ludicrously low. That's yet another reason why I have no hesitation in giving the Atom five stars.

Which brings me back to the DB9, one of the few others to have been awarded this accolade. With its computerised traction control switch repaired using Blu-tack and gaffer tape, I turned off the electronic nanny and set off once again.

Compared with the Atom, it felt huge and stodgy, but against other leather-lined luxury expresses it was magical. I honestly do not know what *Evo* is on about, because with the back end freed up it was transformed into a growling, balanced, grand-touring wonder car.

I still think it's perfect, but after my introduction to one-cal motoring, I do wish it was just a little bit simpler.

Sunday 19 September 2004

Dodge Viper

God, I hate being English sometimes. Latin people don't seem to care when they tread on a social landmine, while Americans just open their arms in a heartfelt gesture of apology. Us, though? We come over all hot and spluttery, stuttering our way out of the gaffe with a series of Hugh Grant-style crikeys and goshes.

Just last week a fresh-faced young man from the press offce at Chrysler wondered why I hadn't written about the Voyager people-carrier I'd borrowed in July. 'Gosh,' I said. 'Crikey.'

The truth is that I'd completely forgotten about it, but being English it was impossible to say so. That would be like admitting you couldn't remember someone's name. Or mistaking their baby boy for a baby girl. Stuff like this is the first commandment for the middle classes here – way, way above 'Thou shalt not kill' and 'Thou shalt not hunt foxy woxy'.

To compound the problem, I can never remember anyone when they're out of context. I once introduced myself to a chap at a dinner party in London. 'Yes,' he said. 'I know who you are because we've been on the same shoot all day.' If I meet the man who comes to murder our moles in the pub, he may as well be from the moon. Once I met my dad by coincidence in the

Imperial War Museum and it took me a moment to place him.

But this Voyager business: it's the first time I've ever forgotten a car. I vaguely recall now that it was too big to fit in a standard British parking slot, and that its sliding rear doors opened electrically, which I thought was pretty cool. But the engine, the layout of the seats and the performance? A complete mystery.

Happily, I'm unlikely to forget the subject of this morning's story for some considerable time because it's the new Dodge Viper, one of the worst cars I've ever had the misfortune to drive. And one of the best.

The old Viper was created during one of Chrysler's seemingly endless financial crises. So the whole process was done by just 17 men, for $50 million – one-twentieth of what it usually costs to design a car. The cost cutting did show in certain areas, such as the complete absence of windows, and the roof, which had all the sturdiness and weather protection of a bin liner.

Under the bonnet there was the 8-litre V10 engine from a truck and a chassis made from melted-down tramp steamers. It was as sophisticated as a Russian hammer, but you had to love the simplicity; the honest-to-God recipe of big, big power and four big, big wheels.

I have an even bigger reason to love it. You see, Chrysler provided one to take my wife and me from the church to the reception on our wedding day. The church had seen some devilment in its time – it was where Patrick Troughton had been pierced by a lightning conductor in

The Omen – but that was nothing compared with the noise of hell I made leaving the graveyard.

What was it like to drive? Well, if you've ever tried one on your Gran Turismo game, you'll know. It's like trying to wrestle with a tiger in an out-of-control nuclear power station.

I'd been hearing stories about the new Viper for some time, and they were not good. Word was that Chrysler, now owned by those dour Germans from Mercedes-Benz, was trying to civilise the concept. It was trying to make the beast a bit more mainstream, a bit more usable.

And at first glance it looks like Chrysler has succeeded. It has a proper canvas roof that stows away, albeit manually, in a neat recess behind the seats. It has windows that go up and down, and, horror of horrors, it has pedals that can be adjusted electrically to suit your shoe size. This is like giving Lucifer a side parting and a cardigan.

But don't worry. Chrysler may have sprinkled the surface with a veneer of twenty-first-century living, along with a million safety notices advising you to 'drive carefully', but underneath beats a heart that's still as cold and as unforgiving as stone.

The engine is no longer an 8-litre V10. Now you get 8,300 cc, which means the brake horsepower has shot up from 400 to 500. That's pathetic by European standards, but because the weight of the car hasn't gone up it means the Viper, to be called the Dodge SRT-10 when it's sold here early next year, goes from 0 to 60 mph in 3.9 seconds and on to a top speed on the wild side of 190. It is an idiotic engine that uses fuel like it's coming from a fire hydrant, but the torque is sensational, and the noise coming out of the side exhausts sounds like Beelzebub barking.

It's not all mouth, though. Put your foot down and, when the wheels have stopped spinning, on Tuesday, it lunges off towards the horizon, not so much like a rabbit as like a wrecking ball. The build-up of speed is not electric, but it is relentless. And then you get to a corner. There is masses of grip from tyres that are so wide they could roll a cricket pitch in one pass, but when the grip is gone so are you. All is well – and then, in the blink of an eye, you're going backwards in £1,500 worth of thick, cloying tyre smoke.

Then there's the gearbox, which works with all the fluidity of a Victorian signal box, and the steering, which has a full centimetre of play around the straight ahead. And now you're going backwards again, desperately looking for the traction control switch, which isn't there. The devil doesn't do traction control.

You could compare the new Viper with any Porsche, Ferrari, BMW or Mercedes. You could even compare it with the new Corvette, and it would lose badly. As a driving tool it is just as wayward and just as hopeless as its predecessor.

The windscreen seems designed to push as much air as possible into your face, the dash seems to have been made for £4.50, it's cramped, and the £80,000 price-tag seems awfully steep.

Also, it is catastrophically vulgar. Maybe, just maybe,

David Beckham and his boyfriends in Britain's footballing elite could get away with such a thing, and possibly it will find favour with 28p and his fellow rappers. But with that ludicrous bonnet and those bling chrome wheels, even Cheshire would deem it too ostentatious.

You know what, though? I don't care. It's as fabulous as an epic piece of weather – a huge thunderstorm or a hurricane, perhaps. If I may liken the Euro cars to Dire Straits and Phil Collins – technically perfect and beautifully produced – the Viper is like George Thorogood and the Destroyers: loud, proud and bad to the bone.

If it were available with right-hand drive I'd love to have one. It would set me out as someone who won't conform to the English norm, someone who can forget who you are and not give a damn. It is the concept of hedonism made real.

Sunday 26 September 2004

Audi S4 Cabriolet

Educating your children in the olden days used to be so much easier. You packed them off to whichever boarding school was furthest from where you lived, with some simple advice: 'See you in five years, son, and try not to get sodomised too much.'

Public schools back then had to prepare boys for a life that would see them squatting in a muddy trench being shot at, or dying of diphtheria in some far-flung corner of the empire. So the school had to be as uncomfortable and as sadistic as was technically possible. There needed to be 10-mile runs through minefields and executions for those caught, as John Cleese put it, 'rubbing linseed oil into the school cormorant'.

You may have read a short story by Roald Dahl called 'Galloping Foxley'. It chronicled Dahl's time at school: the bullying, the sub-zero humiliation and the terror. Well, I was in the same house at the same establishment 50 years later, and I endured much the same sort of thing.

I was flung into unheated plunge pools in the middle of February and used as a goalpost in games of bicycle hockey. Younger boys were made to do all the cleaning and those who failed to do it properly were beaten with whips, strangled, stabbed, sodomised and drowned. Once I forgot to empty the bins and was eaten.

Then, as a real preparation for the astonishing unfairness of life, when I reached the sixth form and was licking my chops at the promise of being able to kill and eat a young Canadian boy for having an annoying whiney accent, fagging, bullying and murder were banned.

It was the start of the slippery slope down which it seems all public schools have now tumbled. Today you don't prepare boys for a life of misery. You have to prepare them for a life of 24-channel, hot-and-cold-running luxury, and as a result the great and the famous educational establishments seem to be competing, not for which can be the most brutal, but which can most closely resemble Claridge's.

I looked round a couple of the big ones last week and couldn't believe the metamorphosis. There were cleaners doing the cleaning and exotic Thai dishes on the menu – the menu, for God's sake. There were carpets, and fire extinguishers that worked. The lavatories had doors. There were trout lakes, and the mattresses on the beds were stuffed with feathers rather than horse fur and dead fags. Most of all, though, some of the boys wore skirts and had breasts.

One thing hadn't changed, though. Parents (i.e., me) are still turning up in expensive cars they've borrowed for the day.

When I was at school we had the local bobby check the registration plates on all the visitors' cars and you wouldn't believe how many were from rental companies. On one speech day we calculated that a full 25 per cent of the motors had been hired by mums and dads who obviously felt their own wheels were too downmarket.

They probably felt good stepping out of the Avis Cadillac or Hertz Jag, but the elation rarely lasted since, as a punishment, we liked to fling their sons from the top of the church tower. One father arrived at the end of term in a chartered helicopter, which we thought was so obscene we took his son round the back of the cricket pavilion and set fire to him.

Public schools were, and always will be, anti-chav. They are bling-free zones where uniforms must be secondhand, watches must be broken, stereos must be wooden and cars, ideally, must be Subaru Legacies.

All of this came flooding back last week as I nosed into the genteel quadrangle of a traditional school, which shall remain nameless, in an egg-yellow Porsche 911. That wasn't mine.

You could see the sneers on the pupils' faces. You could see them making a mental note that when my child starts there he will be made to pay. I doubt, in these softer times, that he will be murdered but they may well chop up his teddy bear. And it's all my fault. A Porsche 911 is bad enough. But an egg-yellow Porsche 911 with 'Porsche GB Press Fleet' written below the terrifyingly personalised number plate. That, quite simply, is as low as you can go.

Or so I thought. The next day, to get to another school, I inadvertently climbed into a Mini Convertible with stripes on the bonnet. This would have been like turning up at a black-tie cocktail party dressed as a 6-foot banana, so I parked it in the next village and walked.

What's desperately annoying is that I had the perfect

public school parent car parked in the drive at home. It wasn't a Subaru but a silvery grey Audi S4 Cabriolet. One of the most tasteful, unassuming and beautifully made cars money can buy. Yes, with four-wheel drive and a V8 engine, it's as lively as an Ibiza discotheque, but from the outside it's no more ostentatious than a Regency town house in Bath.

This car really is very fast. There's no V8 burble, no vulgar-sonic Route 66 soundtrack to attract attention, just a relentless whine to accompany a blurring of both the hedgerows and the speedometer needle. And then, before you know it and with seemingly no effort, you're doing an indicated 155 mph and being prevented from going any faster by the electronic limiter, put there to keep the Green Party happy. Even at high speeds the electric roof doesn't lift or flap and nothing rattles. And with it down there's space for a family of four to enjoy a buffet-free cruise. In so very many ways, then, this is a great car. Practical, well made, fast, silent, stylish and cool. There are very few cars that do quite so much quite so well. So why, you may be wondering, did I not use it?

Well, behind the veneer of sophistication and brilliance it is badly flawed. First of all, I couldn't get comfortable. If I arranged the seat so my legs could reach the pedals the steering wheel was too far away, and if I sorted out my arms I could only go a mile before cramp started to solidify my right calf. I've never noticed this in an Audi before, but my cameraman, who's also long, says he suffers from exactly the same thing in his A3.

And it's not just the driving position that makes life

miserable. I know I'm starting to sound like a stuck record but Audi has absolutely no idea how to tailor a car to accommodate the sloppiness of Britain's roadworker Johnnies.

Where an S-type Jaguar glides and floats over potholes and ridges the Audi crashes and judders. The ride comfort is simply appalling. On one dip, where the A40 joins the M40 just outside Oxford, I really thought it was going to take off.

On a smooth track the hardtop S4 handles beautifully, and I have no doubt the cabrio would be similarly impressive, but the price you pay for this is too high and not necessary. BMWs handle without being uncomfortable. So do Jags and Mercs. So Audi must find the people responsible for this shortfall and, at the earliest possible opportunity, throw them in an unheated lake.

The people who did the satellite navigation system should go, too. It's very clever, shoehorning the screen in between the speedo and rev counter, but with no map it doesn't work. With no map you can't tell how far off the route you are until you're in Snowdonia.

Over the course of a week, this car drove me mad. Think of it as a shepherd's pie that's too salty, or a wonderful holiday resort that's full of German taxi drivers. It was so close to perfection and yet so very, very far away.

That's why I left it at home and that's why I went in the Porsche, and that's why my children are going to spend five years at school with no teddy bear.

Mercedes-Benz SLK350

What, exactly, is the point of the M1? In the early 1960s, for sure, it was a technical and sociological masterpiece, a concrete intranet connecting Britain's provincial muscle with the financial brain in London.

When my grandfather first started driving from Doncaster to London in the early 1950s, he had to break the 150-mile journey with an overnight stay at the George in Stamford. The M1 changed all that. The M1 meant he could, and did, pop to Simpson's on Piccadilly simply to buy a pair of socks.

Now, though, things are very different. We read all the time about the migration of people from the north to the south-east and how five million new homes will have to be built in the home counties to accommodate the new boys.

But it's not migration at all. It's simply a load of people who came to London for a day's shopping and can't get back. They're waiting for a moment when the traffic reports say the M1 is running smoothly, but it never comes because it is no longer an intranet. It's a permanently clogged artery.

And it's not like there's any kind of alternative. Every train that leaves King's Cross or Euston only gets 30 miles before one of the day trippers, heartbroken by the enforced separation from his family up north, leaps in front of it, bringing the entire network to a halt.

The A1 is no good either because every time you stop for petrol or a snack in one of those eastern county flatland service stations, you are murdered by a lorry driver.

Last week, as I set out for Yorkshire, the woman on Johnnie Walker's afternoon radio show said Britain's spinal cord was jammed pretty much all the way from junctions 22 to 32. As a result, I averaged 32 mph over the 170-mile journey. Some people can run faster than that.

I had time, as I sat behind a big van for hour after interminable hour, to speculate on what needs to be done. And it's really very simple.

When the M1 was completed, 45 years ago, there were 2.8 million cars in Britain. Today there are 27.5 million. This means we need not one motorway linking the north with the south. We need 10. No arguments. No public inquiries. The government has to ring Costain and say: 'Go out, tomorrow morning, and build nine more motorways from London to Leeds.'

Sadly, I had this worked out by junction 23, which meant I had another nine junctions, still behind the van, to think about something else. So I started weighing up the car I was in – the new Mercedes SLK 350.

This was more complicated, because it costs £36,110, which is about a third of what you're asked to pay for my car, its big brother, the SL 55.

You'd expect, of course, that this saving would be immediately apparent, but I was buggered if I could find it. Like the big car, the smaller one has two seats, a metal roof that folds electrically into the boot, heated this and electrically movable that.

In fact, if anything, the little car does slightly better on the gadget front because it has a seven-speed automatic gearbox and, joy of joys, heater vents in the headrests. This 'air scarf' means that as you drive along with the roof down your head is cocooned in a pillow of warm air. Mmmmm.

I think the SLK looks better than the SL, too. Yes, the front, which nods at the world of Formula 1, is faintly ludicrous, but the overall proportions are better somehow. And because the SLK has normal suspension, rather than air, it has a more predictable ride, too.

Power? Well, the SL55 with its supercharged V8 will get you from 0 to 62 in 4.7 seconds and on to a top speed of 155. The new SLK with a 3.5-litre unsupercharged V6 takes 5.5 seconds to get from 0 to 62, and will also reach 155. So the only difference is 0.8 of a second in the zero-to-62 dash which, on a journey that was taking half a lifetime, didn't seem all that much.

Because the cars are so similar, it's hard to work out what's going on. Is Mercedes making an indecent profit on the £100,000 SL or is it selling the £35,000 SLK at a catastrophic loss?

By junction 25 I had the answer. Everything in the SL feels substantial, whereas everything in the SLK feels like it was made by a satellite channel's version of *Blue Peter*. I'll take one example: the sun visors. They're hard, brittle, nasty to the touch and feel like they'll break in less than a month.

Magnify the cost savings here across the whole car, and it explains why the SLK is so damn cheap.

And now things get really complicated. Is that a good thing? Should we dismiss the SLK for being flimsy and thin, or should we rejoice in the fact we can buy such a fast, well-equipped and good-looking car for such a small amount of money?

I ummed and aahed all the way past Nottingham and decided, as I finally reached the M18, that we should rejoice. So long as the main components have some Mercedes unburstability, who cares if some of the trim pieces have come from Mattel's reject bin?

And now, with a clear run up to the Wolds, there was an even bigger question to answer. What's this SLK like?

The old one was a pretty, well-made thing that had the sporting credentials of a small occasional table. As a result it became the transport of choice for everyone with a tanning salon, all female television presenters, and Nicole Kidman – although hers, it must be said, had a 6.5-litre V8 under the bonnet.

The SLK was girlie central, bought only as an accessory to make your hair look good rather than rip it out in lumps by the roots.

The new one is completely different. Obviously, with that 3.5-litre V6, it's much faster, but it's harder too, and more poised. Even the old farmyard-style steering system has been junked to make way for something more precise and with more feel. This, as I discovered on the single-track roads of East Yorkshire, is a serious, proper, grown-up sports car.

You can make good, safe and very fast progress, and what's more you can have an enormous amount of fun in the process, even if it's wet, there's mud on the road and you've just spent four hours in a traffic jam.

It's not perfect, though. The traction control and the anti-lock brakes both cut in far too early. It's like driving along with an extremely overenthusiastic health-and-safety man in the dashboard.

And then there's that infernal seven-speed gearbox. Jesus. Who thought this was a good idea? With so many ratios to choose from, the onboard computer can never really make up its mind, so when you put your foot down it selects third and then thinks, 'Ooh no, hang on a minute, let's have second. No wait. Third was good . . . or what about fourth?'

And because the exhaust note verges on the irritating at the best of times, the car begins to sound like a field full of frightened cows mooing their way through a tuneless song.

When I finally arrived at journey's end, I decided that, despite Merc's almost hysterically awful reputation with manual boxes, I'd definitely go for a six-speed self-shifter over that stupid auto, which comes close to ruining the whole car.

I have to say, though, that despite these shortfalls the SLK is actually a better car than its big brother. It's more fun, and less golf-clubby too.

But what about its peers? Well, I haven't driven the Nissan 350Z convertible, which looks interesting, nor have I tried the drop-head Chrysler Crossfire, which doesn't – chiefly because it's actually based around the dreary old SLK.

That leaves us with the BMW Z4, which is one of Chris Bangle's more successful styling efforts. Mind you, that's a bit like saying Milton Keynes is one of Britain's more successful new towns. It's still weird-looking. And it does have an unforgivably hard ride, and a sat nav with the IQ of a chaffinch.

Choosing between this and the SLK is tricky. For sitting on the M1 in a jam, the SLK is a more satisfying place to be. It looks good, there are many toys and that air scarf is the brainchild of a genius.

But if you want to avoid the motorway and use back roads instead, the slightly more cohesive Z4 gets the nod.

Sunday 31 October 2004

BMW 1 series

One of the things I used to admire about BMW was the focus shown by its designers and engineers. They were the snipers of the car industry, lying in wait while the enemy blundered about with smoking tanks and faulty machine guns, and then, boomf, delivering a killer shot that never missed.

Once the company had stopped fiddling about with three-wheelers and converted Post Office vans, it developed a recipe that served it well for nigh on 30 years. All its cars had double headlamps at the front, a straight-six engine in the middle, and rear-wheel drive at the back.

There were, in essence, three body styles, five engines and a range of options, so the customer could indulge in a spot of pick'n'mix.

You could have a small car with a big engine and no equipment. Or you could have a large car with a small engine and electric everything. But whatever you chose, there was a rightness to the feel of the thing. A sense that the company had put driving pleasure above everything else.

Then it did a Coca-Cola. The sniper decided he didn't want to be a sniper any more and changed the damn recipe. So we ended up with four-wheel-drive cars that were made in America, and two-seater convertibles, and a wide range of diesel engines. And then it put a chap called Chris Bangle in charge of design.

Before Bangle, most BMWs adhered to the same set of rules. They had a lean-forward shark's nose, they had the double-kidney grille, they had grey paint and then there was that little kink on the rear pillar. It's called the Hofmeister kink, after the man who invented it, and it gives the car an aggressive, lean-forward stance.

Now, though, all of these design cues have been lost in a sea of planes and creases that probably play well in design circles. But in the real world they don't look modern or sharp. They look daft.

Still, at least the BMW badge continued to count for something. Apart from dipping their toe into the mass market with the truly awful 3-series Compact, Beemers were always a cut above norm. They were what you bought to demonstrate that life was treating you well.

Only now, with the launch of the 1-series, this last bastion of BMWishness has gone. Because the 1-series, like a Focus or an Astra or a Golf, is a five-door family hatchback.

For now, of course, this is great. It means a large number of people who could never afford a BMW in the past can put that blue-and-white badge on their drive. The neighbours will be impressed. The curtains will twitch. Men will offer their daughters to your sons.

But how long will it be, I wonder, before the 1-series does for BMW what Freddie Laker did for air travel? Turns something glamorous and exciting into a 'win free save!' orgy of packaged mass transportation.

In the early 1970s, if you went to Florida for your holidays you were seen as pretty cool. But now you're seen as a rather stupid oik.

The 1-series will be the ruination of the BMW brand. Of that I have no doubt. But at the moment, despite the lost vision and the appointment of Bangle, that ruination has not yet got into its stride. For now you can still buy a Beemer and survive the experience with your dignity intact. The question is, should you? And to answer that, we have to work out if the 1-series is any good.

The advertisements tell us, endlessly, that unlike any other family hatchback on the market it has rear-wheel drive. And that's great. Rear-wheel drive is a significant part of BMW's DNA.

In a front-wheel-drive car the front wheels have to deal with the steering and the delivery of the engine's power to the road. It's a tough job and, in most cases, for the purist at least, the end result is deeply unsatisfying. With rear-wheel drive, the back wheels do the power delivery, leaving those at the front to get on with steering. It's a much more expensive option, but the result is balance. And balance is a building block on which something spectacular can be created.

You can feel the benefits, immediately, in the 1-series. Even at normal, trundling-about speeds it feels more together than even the Focus, king of the front-drivers.

There's more, too. In the Beemer you have a thick steering wheel, a short-throw gear-change, and an anti-lock braking system that cuts in when you're in real trouble and not because it can't be bothered to work out when that moment might be. There is absolutely no doubt in my mind that, as a driving machine, this is a significant cut above the hatchback norm.

And now, here comes the but, galloping over the hills with news of many, many problems that will leave you wishing, with all your heart, that you'd bought something else.

First of all there's the styling. Now I know that, when it comes to hatchbacks, familiarity breeds indifference. The new Astra is a truly stunning piece of design but, like pylons, you see so many you simply don't notice the grace and cleverness. The BMW, however, is just plain ugly. It may have the double headlamps and the kidney grille and the Hofmeister kink, but viewed as a whole it looks like a van.

So what about the engine? Well, the petrol version will get you from 0 to 60 in about two hours, so if you want any poke at all, and surely that's the reason why you're buying a BMW, you have to go for the diesel. It's not a bad diesel by any standards, but come on. Where's the fun in a car that sounds like a canal boat? So it's slow and ugly, and now things really go downhill because, thanks to the prop shaft and all the other rear-wheel-drive gubbins, there is no space in the back. And I don't mean that legroom is limited. I mean there is absolutely none at all.

Even BMW says this car will sell to young people with no children, but this is silly. If you have no children, why buy a family hatchback? Because you want a big boot? Well, forget that as well, because in the 1-series it's tiny.

And then there's the ride which, thanks to the fitment

of run-flat tyres, is intolerable on anything but a kitchen work surface, and the quality of some trim pieces, which will disappoint those who may have expected granite rather than plasticine.

But the worst thing about the 1-series is the prices. In the past, BMWs were expensive because they were demonstrably better, and more exciting, than all of their rivals But the 1-series, as we've seen, is demonstrably worse.

And yet for the top-of-the-range diesel you are asked to pay £20,700, and anything up to £32,000 if you go berserk with the options list. Even if you show some self-restraint you'd be lucky to put a car like this on the road for less than £23,000, and I'm sorry, but you can have two hatchbacks for that.

Park one of these on your drive and the neighbours will not think, 'Hmm, that's an expensive car. He must be doing well.' They'll think, 'Hmm, that's an expensive car. He must be off his rocker.' You can have a Golf GTI for less, and that, in almost every single way, is a better car.

So if you want a hatchback, buy a Focus. If you want a hatchback with some go, buy the VW. If you just want some action and you don't care about space in the back, or a hard ride, or the price, buy a sports car. A Honda S2000 would be fine.

I have been accused, in recent years, of having it in for BMW. There was even some talk, after my recent review of the dreadful X3, that I would not be allowed any more press demonstrators. And this is why I've devoted the entire column this week to a test of the 1-series rather than tagging it on to the end of a rant about cheese.

And it's why I'm choosing the words for my conclusion with even more care than usual. So here goes. The 1-series is crap.

Sunday 12 December 2004

Bentley Arnage

It's a no-brainer really. If you want to spend a very great deal of money on a nice car, you have to buy an Aston Martin DB9, which looks and sounds better than anything else on the road.

I suppose, maybe, that if you wanted to spend a very great deal of money and then another £70,000 on top, you could have a Ferrari 612 Scaglietti which, as *Top Gear* has just proved, can get from Surrey to Verbier faster than a plane.

Either way, there's certainly no need to go off and buy that enormous Volkswagen they call the Bentley Continental GT. Yes, it's quiet and, yes, it's beautifully made, but it's not that pretty, not that fast and really not that spacious. What's more, Ryan Giggs has one.

Not just Ryan Giggs either, but also Kieron Dyer, Rio Ferdinand, Gary Neville, Nicky Butt and the Middlesbrough striker, Jimmy Floyd Hasselbaink. Do you want people to think you are a footballer? Really? Well, why not have your brains sucked out through your ears and move to Cheshire and have some friends over this evening to roast your cleaning lady? (Not that the aforementioned players would, of course.)

You may point out at this stage that the Continental is not only sold to footballers, and that Dale Winton also has one. But I wouldn't if I were you. What I would do, if I had set my heart on owning the world's fastest lorry, is ignore the GT coupé and instead take a closer look at its four-door stablemate, the Arnage.

I've just spent a week with this leviathan and was fascinated by the meat cleaver that it took to Britain's increasingly blurred class system. The security guards at the BBC nodded a reverential nod and, for the first time in 15 years, waved me on to the premises without even looking at their clipboards. It was the same story on a shoot with Lord This and Your Grace That. Here, at the other end of the social scale, the Bentley was also much admired.

But in the centre ground things were rather different. At one party filled with blonde stick insects and men in loafers, it was universally agreed that the Arnage was as vulgar as Wayne Rooney's lounge carpet. Interesting, that. It seems the middle classes have no interest in the Bentley brand, and for that reason alone it's worth ploughing on.

And ploughing's the right word, because when you climb inside an Arnage and close the door, you'll think you've gone back about 200 years. Today's car designers are extraordinarily adept at eking out the very last cubic inch of space from even the tiniest body. But the Bentley was from a time when they didn't bother, and as a result it's microscopic in there.

At first you imagine the seat is not all the way back, so you start to hunt for the button that will engage the motor. Half an hour later, after you've pushed everything that can be pushed and prodded everything that can be prodded, you will locate the seat controls in a cubbyhole beneath the centre armrests. And at that point you'll find, to your horror, that you are as far back as you're ever going to go anyway.

So then you'll try to start the engine. You'll turn the key and nothing will happen. 'My,' you'll exclaim to yourself, 'this is quiet.' But there's a very good reason for this silence, which will become apparent after you've spent 10 minutes jiggling the gear lever into Drive and hunting down the parking brake release.

You press the throttle, which mercifully is where you expect it to be; and you'll go nowhere. This is because you haven't actually turned the engine on until you've pushed a button marked Start. This is to be found in the very last place you look.

It's so confusing in there, and so small, that the button to engage the satellite navigation system is in the roof. Push it and the screen slides out of the dash. But all the screen gives you is a health-and-safety message about keeping your eyes on the road. You need to press a button marked Okay to absolve VW from all responsibility should you drive into a tree while inputting the address of your destination.

Actually, you are more likely to crash into a tree while looking for the button marked Okay. Go on. Guess where it is. No. No. Ha, you're not even warm. It is, in fact, on a remote-control device in a leather pocket next to the foot-operated parking brake.

So what about life in the back of the Arnage? Well, here you get lots of room for lounging around, and lots of toys, including a DVD player and television system. This, however, is so fiddly and impossible to operate that even my eight-year-old son was stumped.

At this stage in your test drive, you'll probably want to turn round and go back to the dealership, fairly sure that this is not the car for you. But you won't be able to turn round because, unfortunately, the Arnage is bigger than most fields. You don't measure it in feet so much as in acres.

I took it to watch my son play rugby at the Oxford ground last weekend and I parked in a spot reserved for the chairman. And because it was so big it spilled over and completely filled the spaces reserved for the president and secretary as well. You try turning something that enormous round in anything smaller than Heathrow. You'd struggle even if you had the whole of Canada to play with.

To make matters worse, it has a throttle pedal cunningly contrived to keep all of Bentley's bodyshops in business for the rest of time. You press it gently, because you only want to dribble forward, and you don't go anywhere at all. So you press it harder and you become aware that the turbocharged 6.75-litre V8 is starting to work. But you still don't go anywhere. So you give it a big shove. And rocket forward at the speed of light into the car in front of you.

There's a similar problem with the brake pedal. Push it gently, and your speed remains unchanged. Push it firmly, and still the speed of your three-ton automobile is unaffected. So then you stamp on it like you're stamping on an angry scorpion, and BANG. Your nose breaks as it smashes into the steering wheel.

'Still,' you're thinking, 'all of this is a small price to pay for the privilege of being in one of the most comfortable cars that money can buy.' You probably have visions of sinking into a duck-down seat and being floated from place to place on a suspension system made from double cream and silk.

Well, sorry, but actually the seats are not that soft, and instead of an adjustable lumbar support all you get are two buttons – where you can't find them – that make whirring noises. But don't in fact do anything.

Then there's the suspension, which is actually made from the back hoe loader from an old JCB. I have driven small Fiats that are more comfortable than an Arnage. Falling over is more comfortable than an Arnage. Everything is more comfortable, come to think of it. Even being stabbed.

At this point I'd love to tell you about the fuel consumption, but the only way this can be tested is by brimming the tank, using the contents, and then brimming it again. I could not afford to fill it even once, I'm afraid. One time I put twenty quid's worth of fuel in there but it didn't move the needle at all.

On every rational level, then, this £160,000 car is junk. A throwback to the days when Britain was on a slippery slide to industrial death.

And yet . . .

If you push through the tricky town-driving characteristics, and the madness of the dashboard and the harsh ride, and you can afford the fuel needed for such things, you will find the Arnage shifts like a scalded elephant. It has much more oomph than you could reasonably expect from such a monster. And it handles like an absolute dream.

But the best thing about this car – the one thing that oozes from every weld and every handmade stitch and that overwhelms all the faults – is the unparalleled sense of occasion it affords. When you climb aboard, it's a bit like climbing into your dinner jacket. It's uncomfortable and stupid, but there's a sense that you're about to do something very special.

And for this pomp alone I would buy the Bentley Arnage like a shot. Because, with the exception of the new Rolls-Royce, which (don't forget) is nearly twice the price and even bigger, no other car made today has 'it' in such sheer abundance. No other car makes you feel so damn good.

Sunday 19 December 2004

Hyundai Accent

I've always thought that being a motoring journalist is a bit like being Prince Andrew. Hugely good fun but, in the big scheme of things, not very important.

Two recent events, however, changed my mind. First of all I drove a Hyundai Accent with a three-cylinder diesel engine. And then I went, as a paying punter, to the London Boat Show.

You see, I recently bought a small cottage by the seaside and thought it might be fun to have a boat of some kind, something that could tow a waterskier and be used for setting lobster pots. So I parcelled the kids into the car and set off for ExCeL, the huge exhibition centre that is so far to the east of London it really ought to have a Norwegian postcode.

All I know about boats is that they use up all your money and turn the person at the wheel into Hitler, so I felt the boat show would be full of experts who could help me make a reasoned and rational decision. It was not to be.

Because I've worked at many motor shows in the past, I know why. These events, you see, are not designed for the punter. They're designed principally so the people manning the stands can spend a few days away from home, getting sloshed and doing their very best to sleep with all the agency girls.

So when I rocked up, bright and breezy, on Sunday morning, most of the salesmen had had at best 20 minutes' sleep. Some seemed not to know what a boat was, leave alone which might have the best hull for dealing with choppy coastal waters.

After two hours my six-year-old was bored and crabby and I'd narrowed the choice down to either a speedboat or a rib. Those selling ribs explained that speedboats were very uncomfortable, and those selling speedboats said ribs lose all of their value in about 20 minutes.

What I wanted, apparently, is a tall freeboard and a deep V. 'Absolutely,' I said, nodding sagely.

Even the names of the boat makers were meaningless. I'd heard of Riva, but their only offering – a small speed-boat – cost £275,000. And I vaguely remember John Noakes careering around the North Sea in a Zodiac.

But does that make it a good thing? Or is it a sort of aquatic Rover? We found several boats that looked just like the Riva but cost a tenth of the price. Why should that be so?

I'd love to give you an answer, but the owners wouldn't let us on board in shoes and the ever-helpful Health and Safety people wouldn't let us take them off.

Engines? Well, I managed to discover that the absolute best were from Honda, Suzuki, Yamaha and Volvo, and that petrol was the way forward, or diesel. Inboard is vastly superior to outboard, outboard is vastly superior to inboard, stern drives knock rudders into a cocked hat and rudders are way better than stern drives.

Then we came across the Seadoo stand, where my

six-year-old had a tantrum and we learned that, in fact, what we wanted was a jet engine because it works in shallow water and has no propeller to sever your kids' legs.

'A jet!' howled one of the rib boys with derision. 'A jet is usheless. It gets shand in the impeller and is ruined, and who's going to service a shupercharged Rotax motor in the middle of the Irish Sea? Hic.'

I never did find the answer because by this stage the six-year-old was lying in one of the aisles banging her fists into the floor and saying she'd never been so bored in her life, the eight-year-old was lost and the ten-year-old was busy ordering a 115-foot Pershing.

I began to think it might be easier simply to buy lobsters from the market, but nevertheless we came home weighed down with, oh, about 400 brochures for a wide range of boats, all of which seemed to be suitable.

I shall probably end up buying the cheapest, and that's what started me thinking. Is it like this when people who know very little about cars go to a motor show? Do they come away drenched in salesman beer-fumes, clutching lots of shiny pictures of lots of cars? And then end up buying the Hyundai Accent because you seem to get so much for your money? I can understand the reasoning. On the face of it, the Hyundai Accent appears to be the same sort of size and shape as a Volkswagen Golf. If you'd heard of neither, you'd look at the Hyundai's £9,400 price tag and almost certainly wonder why the Golf costs £3,000 more.

The salesmen, if they were sober enough to remember,

would rattle on about torque and CO_2 emissions and all sorts of stuff you never knew mattered, and you'd end up as bewildered as I was by all the talk of deep V hulls and roller trailers.

This then is where motoring journalism starts to make sense. Because having driven all the family hatchbacks you might be considering, I can tell you with absolute certainty that You Should Not Buy A Hyundai Accent.

First of all, there's the obvious stuff. The Accent takes 14 seconds to get from rest to 60 mph, and I know people who can accelerate faster than that. If you buy this car, you will not be able to overtake anything, not even a tractor, or a horse, and that means you'll have to spend your entire motoring life only going as fast as the slowest person in the world.

The only good thing about the sedentary progress is that you'll never know what a rotten handler your Accent is. But you will notice the ride, especially when you get the bill from your osteopath for a new spine.

Dynamically, the Accent is possibly the worst new car on the market today. In every single respect every other car on the road goes, stops, steers and rides with more aplomb.

On its own, however, I know this is not enough of a deterrent. I was told that the cheapest speedboat wouldn't have enough grunt to pull a set of waterskis, even if they had nobody on them, and that it couldn't handle a ripple. But I kept looking at the price-tag and thinking, 'Yes, but . . .'

Well, try this for size. Hyundai is not selling the Accent

for less than £10,000 out of the goodness of its heart. It is cheap for the same reason that a cow's eyeballs cost less than its fillet.

Korean labour rates are the same as those in Europe. The tax burden is just as enormous, too, and you have just as many middlemen taking their slice of the pie. Which leads us to the inevitable conclusion that Hyundais cost less to make than VWs.

Do not think, however, that because the Hyundai is made from cheaper parts they'll be cheaper to buy when something goes wrong. I did a bit of research on this, and it turns out that Korean clutches, headlamp units and door mirrors are often more expensive to buy in the UK than equivalent parts from European makers.

And if that's not enough to dissuade you, consider the implications of depreciation.

The pipe smokers' bible, known as *Which?*, recently found that some Korean and Malaysian cars lose 77 per cent of their value in the first three years, compared with a 50 per cent loss on various European alternatives. So the initial £3,000 saving is wiped out.

There's something I've found out as well. If you buy a Hyundai, or any car from that part of the world, you will be seen as a bore. Invitations will dry up, your kids will refuse to speak to you, your wife will sleep with your friends and you may end up committing suicide.

If you want a five-door family hatchback, buy a used Ford Focus, and if you want something new, a new Ford Focus. A Golf is lovely, but you're paying what the market will stand rather than what the car is worth.

I do hope that my column this morning has been as helpful as the boat journalist I met as I left the show. You might think that writing about boats for a living was an even bigger waste of time than writing about cars. But he listened to what I wanted, and where it would be kept, and then he told me what to buy.

On that basis I found him to be more important and worthwhile than the new president of the Palestinian Authority.

Sunday 16 January 2005

Subaru Forester

News from the north. Apparently there are too many middle-class white people in the Lake District, and from now on they must all be banned.

It seems the vast majority of visitors who turn up to ramble around on the fells, pointing at heather, are called Toby and Caroline, and this does not sit well with a government that wants poor, miserable and downtrodden people to point at heather instead.

So the free guided walks run by more than 100 volunteers are to be scrapped while the National Parks' authority works out how the right sort of deprived urban youngsters can be persuaded to come. Maybe they could open shops in the fells where crisps and other fatty foods could be stolen. Just a thought.

This, of course, is yet another example of Tony's class war. He introduced the right to roam, which allows Janet Street-Porter to come and jump up and down in my flowerbeds whenever the mood takes her; and then his henchmen forced through a bill that prevents people from using their dogs to chase foxes.

On top of this we have idiotic European legislation that means you can't bleed a veal calf to death on your kitchen table. Instead, you must put it in a lorry and drive it hundreds of miles to a licensed abattoir, where it can install its diseases in the food chain.

Meanwhile, deer are eating all the trees, reinvigorated sparrowhawks are devouring all the songbirds, and small-holdings are going out of business. In short, the country-side is changing, and changing fast.

Who's to blame for all this? Well, Tony obviously, and all his meddlesome boyfriends in Whitehall. Then you have Neil Kinnock in Europe, and Bill Oddie in his tree house. But most of all, I'm afraid, it's me.

When I moved out of London eight years ago, a typical farm shop sold mud and bark, not vacherin cheese at £15 a pop, and geometrically perfect tomatoes. And then there's my local agricultural supply warehouse which, so far as I can see, no longer sells ploughs and other stuff for removing hands and arms, but gas-powered barbecue sets and radio-controlled lawnmowers that follow under-ground wires while you luxuriate in your split-level jacuzzi.

This metamorphosis has happened because, while I'm happy to embrace country living, I like it to be wrapped up in a duck-down duvet of urban comfort. I want to be able to buy Thai spices in the market town and I want my local electrical shop to sell 500 different types of low-voltage bulbs. Also, I want my friends from town to have second homes in the area so that I can see them more easily at weekends.

I even found myself the other day asking the local farmer if he could grow linseed in the field that backs on to my garden because the colour goes well with my pool house. How Islington is that? Yes, I have an Aga, but it's powered by gas, not coal. And I have stone floors, but they're heated from underneath so they're not chilly on my tootsies of a morning. In every way, then, I live in Notting Hill, except that I don't actually live in Notting Hill.

Of course, this means I want to drive a country car. I want it to blend and be a bit upright. I want it to look like the wagon in Constable's *Haywain* but I don't want it to be made from rocks and straw. And this brings me neatly to the Subaru Forester.

In the olden days the Forester was wilfully rural. When Subaru first came to Britain, the company had no dealer network so the cars were sold alongside horse blankets and combine harvesters by farm supply companies.

The cars weren't cars at all, really. They were mostly pick-up trucks with corrugated-iron covers on the back and a breast-feeding pig in the passenger seat. They smelled of manure and would run on anything that was liquid. Petrol, diesel, vinegar, your fat wife's cider brandy. Even a pint of pig urine, if times were hard.

You never used to see a Subaru estate car of any sort with a Kensington and Chelsea parking permit outside your local pub. It was a mud-brown mobile billboard for the Countryside Alliance. Carpeted with blood and feathers, it was the equivalent of a Le Chameau wellington, footwear for country folk who knew how to make black pudding. If it could speak, it would tell you that it had no clue what was meant by the word 'metrosexual', and then it would invite you round for a game of Aunt Sally.

Now, though, the car is changing to suit the new

face of rural Britain. The new Forester has carpets and air-conditioning. The car I drove over Christmas even had a huge electric sunshine roof and satellite navigation. It was a sort of Fired Earth kitchen-flooring car. Seemingly countrified but somehow not countrified at all.

Oh, it still looks rural because it's boxy and plain and as practical as a cowshed, and it still has four-wheel drive and a mildly raised driving position. You couldn't drive one over the Lake District, partly because it has no locking diffs and no low-range gearbox, and partly because you're called Toby so you're banned, but you could get one up the track to your second home in Norfolk.

What's more, it's still phenomenally reliable. The Forester has always been built like the countryside, and as a result it's a virtually permanent fixture in the top five of every customer satisfaction survey, anywhere in the world. Apparently they never go wrong, ever.

In the not-too-distant past this was because there was nothing to go wrong. You got four wheels and a seat, and that was about it. But the new cars come with an interior that could almost be classed as stylish. And a bag of electronic trickery underneath to send power to whichever wheel needs it most.

Think, then, of the new Forester as a paddock. It started out all rough and practical, but now it's been mowed and rolled so that it's still a paddock. But it's as smooth and well manicured as a croquet lawn. If that's a hard concept, think of it as a barn conversion.

And now stop thinking of it as a croquet lawn or a barn conversion, because while you can still have a paraffin stove under the bonnet, the top model, the £25,000 version I drove, has a new turbocharged, 2.5-litre flat four that develops 208 bhp. That equates to a top speed of 140 mph and an ability to get from 0 to 60 mph in 6 seconds. This, then, is more like a Le Chameau training shoe.

It really is an extraordinary car, because it looks like the sort of thing you find lying around in a barn, it's decked out in the sort of kit Poggenpohl would be pleased to sell in Knightsbridge, and it goes like its little brother, the Impreza Turbo.

Recently I suggested that no car does quite so much, quite so well as the new Volkswagen Golf GTi. But after a couple of weeks with the Forester I'm forced to think again. It's built as well as the Golf, goes as well as the Golf, it's more practical than the Golf and it isn't going to be stopped, should we have a cold snap.

Of course, despite the limited slip differentials, it isn't as much fun to drive as a Golf – it's too tall for that – but, even so, it is the perfect bridge between Chelsea and the more rugged bits of outlying Cheltenham. And that makes it pretty much the perfect car for the townie who wants to blend in with the green bits.

There is, in fact, only one thing that stops it from getting a rare and exclusive five-star rating. For some extraordinary reason, the car that does everything won't change gear on your behalf. It's not available as an automatic, and that means it's a bit like a barn conversion with an outside bog.

Sunday 23 January 2005

Citroën C4

I have some donkeys. The small one that looks like a cow is called Eddie. The quiet grey one that doesn't do much, except bite the hand that feeds it, is called Geoffrey, after the chancellor that did for Mrs Thatcher. And then there's the beautiful one: she's called Kristin Scott Donkey.

I've always had a bit of a soft spot for Ms Scott Thomas. I've seen *The English Patient* 20 times, except for the bathroom scene of course. I've seen that so often the DVD's got a hole in it.

As I'm sure we all know, Kristin lost both her father and her stepfather in air crashes. She went to Paris to study drama and still lives there today with her obstetrician husband, François Olivennes – a man for whom I've felt nothing but hatred. Until now. Because the crush is over.

In a recent newspaper interview Kristin laid into Britain, saying it was stuck in the 1950s, that everyone who goes to hospital dies, and that we're all fat, acquisitive television addicts.

Now, I'm sorry, but no one ever emigrates because of the success they've enjoyed at home. No one ever says: 'Well, I have a happy home life, I'm rich and I have many friends . . . so I'm off.' The only reason anyone has for going to live in another country is because they've cocked everything up in their own. So their views are bound to be jaundiced.

Everyone you see planting olive groves on those endless 'new life abroad' programmes is inevitably a sad and lonely individual who thinks their homeland is to blame for everything that's gone wrong in their empty, shallow, friend-free, halitosis-ridden lives.

This is why Australians are all such chippy bastards. Because every single one of them is descended from someone who, at some point, made a complete and utter hash of their entire life. This means they all have a failure gene in their make-up.

Of course, I also think that Britain is a nation of inarticulate, pugilistic slobs. I agree with Kristin, completely, but I'm allowed to say this because I live here. I'm also allowed to say that I much prefer France. I like France so much, in fact, that I'd like to demonstrate the point publicly, by buying a French car.

Of course, a French car is built by disgruntled and uninterested Algerians in a factory with a floor made out of mud, so it's not going to last very long. But then it's a statement more than a car really. I mean, a French car shows other road users that you loathe Tony Blair, that you disapprove of his stance in Iraq and that you prefer a quail's egg to a burger any day of the week.

The problem is that while the French are very good at mushrooms and shooting pigs, they've been in an automotive oxbow lake since about 1959. Now, though, we have the Citroën C4.

You'll no doubt have seen this on your television,

turning into a robot and dancing. Well, in real life the car can't do that. But it can do pretty well everything else. It may be the same size as a Ford Focus or Vauxhall Astra but it costs less, and it can do far, far more.

For instance, if you nod off while driving down the motorway, sensors under the front bumper will detect the moment when you stray into another lane and set off a vibrator in the seat to wake you up. My wife liked this feature so much she drove all the way to London last week on the hard shoulder.

Then there's the steering wheel. The rim turns but the middle bit stays still so all the buttons are always in the same place, and my, what a lot of buttons there are. You can set the sat nav, organise the cruise control, change the radio station, adjust the volume and answer the phone. There are so many buttons, in fact, that you'll almost certainly stray out of your lane while trying to find the right one.

Don't worry, though, because if you don't want a Meg Ryan moment there's even a button to turn the Rabbit off.

Now. Have you ever inadvertently pulled the bonnet catch while driving along? No, neither have I, but that hasn't stopped Citroën fitting a flap to make sure you can't, unless the passenger door is wide open.

I bet you have worried, however, that your car will be broken into. Well the C4 has an alarm and an immobiliser as you'd expect, but in addition its side windows are made from laminated glass. It's not bulletproof, but it's the next best thing.

Next up, we have the air-conditioning system, which

comes with a little flap into which you can insert a tailor-made capsule full of your favourite air freshener. That beats hanging a Christmas tree that smells of lavatory cleaner from your rear-view mirror. At this point I should draw your attention to the digital speedometer that is designed to ensure it's readable even in bright sunlight, the double door seals to cut wind noise, the nine speakers, the six airbags and the 280-watt amplifier. And then there's the electronic brakeforce distribution, the anti-lock brakes, the electronic stability control and the emergency-braking assistance, all of which have helped the C4 get a five-star Euro NCAP safety rating.

I should remind you at this point that I'm not reviewing a £100,000 S-class Mercedes. I'm writing about a normal, everyday family hatchback; a family hatchback that's an orgasmatron with swivelly headlamps. Yup, when you turn the bit of the wheel that does actually turn, the searchlight-bright xenon bulbs turn, too, illuminating bits of the road that would otherwise be hidden.

Of course, the old DS had this feature about 200 years ago, but it didn't have front and rear parking sensors, or wipers that come on when it rains, or lights that come on when it's dark, or tyres that let you know when they have developed a leak.

It's not often that I'm stunned by any car, leave alone a family hatchback. But the C4's equipment package genuinely had me reeling in open-mouthed disbelief.

And now you're expecting the but. The moment when the whole pack of *cartes* comes crashing down.

Well, sorry, but the five-door version is elegant and the

three-door is properly striking. And I must say the 2-litre VTS coupé I drove went, handled and stopped with much aplomb and vigour. It wasn't as much fun as a Golf GTI because it felt heavy. But then it would, with all that stuff weighing it down.

If you don't fancy the hot version, don't despair, because there are 22 models on offer, including four trim levels, five different petrol engines and a choice of three diesels. You've got to be able to find something you like in there.

You'll certainly be able to find something you can afford because even the VTS rocket ship is listed at £17,195. That's a full £2,000 less than a Golf GTI and that on its own is a good enough reason to ignore the VW. But then you have the £1,100 cashback deal that Citroën is offering at the moment. Factor that in and the price falls to just £16,095. And that . . . that is truly incredible value.

Of course, I can pretty much guarantee that your C4 will break down every 15 minutes. Citroëns just do, and I'm not fooled by the three-year warranty on this one. Having the fault fixed for free in no way compensates for being stuck on the hard shoulder at three in the morning. Although, if you leave the lane sensor on, you will at least have a nice time waiting for the tow truck.

Certainly, I would expect Kristin Scott Thomas, with her love of the French, to have a C4. But in fact it turns out she has a Volvo estate. How English is that? You can do better. You can be English and have a French car.

Sunday 30 January 2005

Maserati Quattroporte

Have you driven a modern-day Ferrari? Because it doesn't matter what you drive now, you would stumble from the experience, reeling in slack-jawed, wide-eyed astonishment at just how good it had been.

In a current Ferrari you have a oneness with the machine that you simply don't get from any other car. You feel connected, you feel assimilated. The steering, the brakes and the throttle don't feel like a collection of metal and wires and carbon fibre. They feel like they're organic extensions of your fingers and your toes.

This means you have no sense of manhandling the beast, of taming the monster. And because everything you do feels as natural and as instinctive as breathing, you can go much, much faster than you dreamed possible.

I was, at this point, going to liken Ferrari to Manchester United. But the simile doesn't quite work because in the world of football there are Chelsea and Arsenal who, on the day, are capable of beating the big boy. But in the world of cars no one gets even close.

When you climb out of an Aston Martin Vanquish and into a 575, it is like climbing out of the eleventh century and on to the bridge of the *Starship Enterprise*. Emotionally, both cars tug your heart strings with equal force, but mechanically the Ferrari is hundreds of years ahead.

We see the same sort of thing higher up the scale, too. Porsche was undoubtedly proud of its Carrera GT, and no doubt Mercedes had a warm, gooey sense of contentment when its McLaren SLR went on sale. I drove both, and they were magical. And then I drove Ferrari's rival, the Enzo, which, as a speed machine, was just miles better.

From this we can draw a sad but inescapable conclusion. Having the money to buy a Ferrari and then buying something else means you are going home with second best. You are buying south of the river, a Henman, a Bolton Wanderer.

So why do we do it? Why have I ordered a Ford GT when I could have had a technically superior 430 from Ferrari? Why are we tripping over Bentley Continentals when their owners could have had a 575 or a 612? Why is the DB9 one of the world's most sought-after cars when on any playing field, against any Ferrari, it would lose about 6–0?

Well, of course, the problem is very simple. Ferraris are just a little bit disgusting, with a dash of Beckham and a hint of Ferdinand. A Ferrari just won't go with your Fired Earth flooring and your BBC2 viewing habits. A Ferrari is sculpted vulgarity, which means we must turn our attention now to its bastard son. The Maserati Quattroporte.

I'm aware, of course, that the comedian Jimmy Carr reviewed this car when I was away, and I'm aware that he liked it very much. But then, what was the editor expecting? Asking a man who replaced a Rover 75 with another Rover 75 to review a car like the Maserati is a bit like asking a refugee from Chad to review the Ivy. He's going to be overwhelmed.

I wasn't. I've been watching Maserati's endless attempts to crack the nut for nearly 20 years now, and they've all been completely hopeless. Everything, from the wheezing Biturbo through the old Quattroporte to the 3200GT, was nothing more than a great badge from the 1950s nailed to a car that had all the grace and aesthetic appeal of Hattie Jacques.

The company was owned by Citroën, the Italian government, and then an Argentine playboy who sold bits of it to Chrysler, which couldn't manage and offloaded the whole thing to Fiat, who eventually fobbed it off to Ferrari, who joined forces with Volkswagen and turned the horrid 3200GT into the 4200, which wasn't very nice either.

At this point the powers that be in Italy decided I had it in for their useless bits of half-arsed engineering and banned me from driving all of their press demonstrators. So, last year, when they launched the new Quattroporte, I was in Coventry.

No big deal, I figured. Coventry's exactly the place to be when you have £70,000 in your pocket and a burning need to buy a large, fast, four-door saloon car. There was, I convinced myself, no way that the big Maserati could possibly hold a candle to the supercharged Jag.

I was still thinking along the same lines as the spat with Maserati ended and they said I could borrow a Quattroporte after the man from the *Welsh Pig Breeders' Gazette* had had a go. And so, last week, what looked like a swollen Vauxhall Cresta rumbled up my drive.

I stepped inside and, after a bit of fumbling among a dizzying array of buttons, found the switch that slides the seat backwards. It didn't work. At first I assumed this might be because it was Italian, and therefore broken, but in fact the seat was as far back as it would go. Which wasn't far enough.

That night, however, I wedged myself into the 'Cresta' and set off for dinner with the local lord. It was dark and sort of drizzling, so I constantly needed to flick the wipers on, and dip the headlights as I met cars coming the other way.

This was unusually hard to do because the 'Cresta' has a stupid, flappy paddle gearbox that is operated by levers right next to the headlamp and wiper stalks. So every time I met a car coming the other way I changed into fourth.

You can solve this by pushing a button that makes the gearbox an automatic. But then the changes are so ham-fisted that you will feel like you've moved back 200 years. And the ride's pretty sudden as well.

We arrived at the big house and I pressed the central locking button, which illuminated a light on the underside of the passenger-side door mirror. Hmmm. Was this some kind of feature, a time-delay device to light the path to the door? Or was it a faulty piece of wiring?

I waited to see if it would go out. And then I waited some more. I was just about to give up waiting when I thought that most people with Maseratis would have a long walk to the house, so maybe it would stay on a while yet. So I waited a little longer.

And then, when I was very wet and cold, I unlocked

the car, which illuminated all the lights except the one under the door mirror on the passenger's side, which went out. So I locked up again, and it came back on again.

At this point I thought of an expression that rhymes with bucket and went inside for dinner. Or pudding as it had become by then.

So, the 'Cresta'? It looks like a Vauxhall from the 1970s, it's cramped, the gearbox is stupid, the ride is too hard and its wiring is as cockeyed as the leaning tower of Pisa. And yet, despite all this, I absolutely loved it.

First of all, there's the name. Despite the efforts of everyone who's owned the company over the past 30 years, it still has a ring. 'Shall we take the Maserati tonight, darling?' That sounds good. And then there's the way it goes. The 4.2-litre V8 develops 400 brake horsepower, which is a hundred down on the German benchmark these days. But, unlike the German rivals, there's no electronic limiter, so when the AMG Benz is on the buffers at 155, you'll be able to keep on going. All the way to 170.

Then there's the noise. Mostly, it's quiet and serene in the super-tasteful cabin, but when you put your foot down, there's a faraway, dreamy peal of thunder. It's great.

What's more, on a dry, clear day when you don't have to worry about wipers and dipping the lights, even the gearbox becomes manageable. Not nice, you understand, and nowhere near as good as a proper manual. But usable nevertheless.

The best thing about this car, though, is the 'feel'. At no point do you have a sense that you're in a large four-seater saloon. It turns and grips and brakes with a fluidity and a sense of purpose that you just don't get from any big Jag, Audi, Mercedes or BMW.

I'll tell you what it feels like. It feels like a Ferrari – and, technically speaking, that's the highest praise there is. But, of course, the Maserati is not a Ferrari. And that makes it even better.

It's less brash than a Ferrari, more refined than a Ferrari, more practical than a Ferrari and, at £70,000, less expensive than a Ferrari as well.

Sunday 6 February 2005

Renault Vel Satis

The other night, my local MP, an up-and-coming Tory, told me over dinner that Tony Blair had banned smoking, smacking and hunting in just one week. 'So imagine what he'd be able to do in the next five years.'

I was thinking about this the next day as I drove through a 20 mph 'home zone' on my way to a no-smoking restaurant in Oxford when on to the radio came a man with news of a proposed law that would ban four-wheel-drive cars from 'green laning' in the countryside.

It seems that for some time now the infernal Ramblers' Association has been twittering on about maniacs in souped-up Land Rovers spoiling the peace and serenity of the countryside by chewing up the nation's footpaths and deafening the birds.

This seems fair enough, until you pause to consider. According to my calculations, there are in Britain 82,000 miles of countryside footpaths on which cars are not allowed. Then we have 18,000 miles of bridleway on which you may ride a horse (so long as you're not chasing a fox, obviously) but on which cars are still banned. In fact, there are only 2,500 miles of byways on which you can take a car.

So walkers have more than 95 per cent of the country's paths to themselves, plus all the land on which Tony says they're now allowed to roam. Yet they want more. They want it all. And, of course, because the ramblers are urban communists for whom the Labour Party has a natural affinity, they tend to get what they want.

So the government is looking at how this ban can be implemented, what it should cover and where. But I bet there's one thing they've overlooked . . .

Most of the people who go green laning, at heart, are murderers for whom *Deliverance* was not a film but an aspirational lifestyle choice. They wear combat trousers, collect knives and the only thing they like to do more than cataloguing all the heads they've severed is deliberately getting their car stuck in the mud so that they and their friends can spend the rest of the day digging it out again.

Over the years I have met several green laners and I could just tell they all were wondering what my head would look like on a spike. So if they're banned from driving in the countryside, I have very real concerns that the green and pleasant land will become a bloodbath. Ramblers may well cease to be troubled by the roar of big V8s, but they may well be deafened by the sounds of other ramblers being made to squeal like a piggy. Blair's Witch-Hunt will turn into The Blair Witch Project.

Of course I don't know why I'm bringing this up, because whenever Mr Blair's government gets the scent of a potential ban in its nostrils it can't be stopped. So 4×4s will be outlawed from the countryside; and then, after a period of extended congestion charging, they will be banned from city centres, too. Which means the country's murderers, footballers, school-run mums and black DJs are going to need a substitute.

Actually, they're going to need a substitute even without government legislation because off-roaders are a fad, just like hot hatchbacks were a fad in the 1980s. And obviously fads, by their very nature, eventually go away. It's hard to predict what might be next, but I keep looking at the Renault Vel Satis and thinking, 'Hmmm.'

You see, we buy a 4×4 for the same reason that we used to buy a hot hatch. It's because we have a latent fear of the four-door saloon. A four-door saloon is seen as being boring.

A four-door saloon is what Terry and June used. A four-door saloon is a repmobile, a car you choose when the boss has given you no choice at all.

So what are the alternatives? An MPV, which is a sign you've completely given up with life? A two-seater convertible, which would be no use for the family? A Volvo estate? What, like Jerry had in *The Good Life*? Puh-lease. So eventually we end up at the large and stylish door of the Vel Satis.

In essence this is a normal two-wheel-drive, five-seater, five-door executive car designed to compete with the BMW 5-series and the B-class Mercedes. But because Renault knows it has neither the technical flair nor the badge to compete with the Germans on level terms, it has gone its own way.

The result is a strange but rather fabulous-looking creation that doesn't look or feel quite like anything else on the market today. And that's because no car I know is so wilfully stylish. It's all form, and forget the function.

I love it, but there's a big question to be answered. Does the style of the thing mask some technical deficiency and, if so, does it matter? I mean, half the bottle openers you can buy these days look great but could no more open a bottle of wine than plough 400 acres of East Anglia. Doesn't stop you buying them, though, does it?

Well, when we step inside the Vel Satis, we find seats that, unlike the Germanic norm, are huge and squidgy. Strange for a country where mothers think it is their social responsibility to make sure their children have small bottoms, but very good news indeed in a country where mothers force-feed their children with lard to keep them quiet.

Then there's the space. All cars feel a little claustro-phobic when they are full of people, but having five in the Vel Satis is like having five in the ballroom of the Grosvenor. Partly, this is down to an enormous amount of head- and legroom, and partly it's down to the choice of colours.

You see, in a BMW or a Mercedes you have a choice of black, black, black or dark black, whereas every Vel Satis I've driven has been kitted out with lots of cream and beige. This means it feels what an estate agent would call light and airy.

Some of the detailing is exquisite, too, like the mar-quetry on the woodwork, and, as usual with French cars these days, the list of equipment that comes as standard is dazzling. The satellite navigation system is particularly noteworthy because it actually works.

I know this, because when I asked it to find a route into the middle of Oxford last week, which is a bit like asking it to find a route into the bowels of Fort Knox, it didn't simply explode. What's more, it didn't make a single mistake earlier in the day, even though I had to be in Chippenham for breakfast, Le Caprice for lunch and home for tea.

Unfortunately, on this eight-hour round trip, the rest of the car was not quite so competent. The 3.5-litre V6 in my top-of-the-range, £31,000 test car is the same 3.5-litre V6 you get in a Nissan 350Z. It's a good engine, with plenty of oomph, but it's too much for a front-wheel-drive car. So any request for more speed was met with a Gallic shrug and a puff of wheelspin.

Then there's the ride. Most of the time it's as soft as the seats, and that makes for an uncannily un-German feel, but when the road surface goes all blotchy, the suspension just can't cope at all and flicks into wobble-drive. This becomes wearisome after a while.

But the driving position becomes wearisome way sooner than that. Get the seat right for your legs, and the wheel is too far away for your arms.

And then some of the trim fell off. It was only a small piece and it didn't really matter, but it provides a clue to the Renault's shortcomings.

It's a large, luxurious car from a company that simply doesn't understand luxury at all.

Sadly, then, the Vel Satis is an appealing but ultimately hopeless replacement for your 4×4. But don't despair, because one day a company with more experience of quality engineering will follow suit and sell us a car that's not only properly stylish but good underneath as well.

BMW mechanicals. With a Conran look. It's the next big thing.

Sunday 13 February 2005

Maserati MC12

Cricket, obviously, is a monumentally dull spectator sport. And so is golf, and so is snooker. But the dullest, most excruciating sport of them all – and I'll brook no argument on this – is the day-long motor race at Le Mans.

At four o'clock on the Saturday afternoon, a grid full of cars from companies you've never heard of, and drivers whose names you can't even pronounce, set off on what in essence is a 24-hour economy run. And then it goes dark.

Now I'm sorry but how, in the name of Zeus's butthole, can anyone with even a tiny sliver of intelligence imagine that spectators will be interested in watching a sport they can't see? A pair of headlights is coming towards you and then, after a short, deafening roar, they are replaced by a set of red tail-lights whizzing off into the night. Was that a Courage that just went by, driven by Alfonso Percolinno? And if so, was it whining or coming last? There is no way on God's earth of knowing.

All you do know is that the race, when it finishes at 4 p.m. on the Sunday, will be won by the team with the most money. And that, for the past few years, has been Audi. Although, for marketing purposes, the car is not always called an Audi. Sometimes they replace the four rings with a flying B and call it a Bentley.

Frankly, it would be easier, and quieter, if each team were asked to roll up with a copy of its most recent bank statement. Then the champagne could be given to the one with the biggest number of noughts. That way we'd all be spared the public-relations-inspired test of a car's fuel consumption, held under cover of darkness, half a country away from where 80 per cent of the spectators live.

There's talk among the sport's fans that things will improve when the field is made up of proper road cars that everyone recognises. This, they say, is already happening, with Aston Martin entering a DB9, Chevrolet a Corvette, Lamborghini a Murciélago, and Ferrari a 575.

Apparently, if this new class becomes numerous and competitive enough, the one-off Audi-style prototypes will be banned and it will be the basis on which all endurance racing is founded. That sounds great, but there are still two problems. First, it will still go dark, so for a third of the race we won't see what's going on. And second, the Italians will bend the rules so hard that they are as near as dammit broken.

In fact, it's already happening. You see, the new class is supposed to be for GT cars. That would be 'grand tourers' like the Corvette, the DB9 and the 575. But what Maserati has done is go cap in hand to its sister company, Ferrari, and take away all the components from an Enzo, which is no more a GT car than my dog. From these it has made a racing car.

Of course, the rules say that 25 road versions must be sold, but finding 25 people from a customer pool of 6 billion isn't that hard. Even when the car in question costs £520,000 and doesn't even have a back window.

If I'd been running the governing body, I'd have smiled while they explained how this car obeyed the letter of the law, and then told them to get lost. But I'm not running the governing body, so, even though it's racing on wooden tyres, it's already out there winning races without breaking out of a canter.

More importantly, the 25 road cars have been sold, and last week I gave one of them a damn good thrashing.

Yes, it has the same carbon–fibre skeleton as an Enzo and the same 6-litre V12 engine. It has the same flappy paddle gearbox, too, and the same set of controls for raising the nose to get over speed bumps, firming up the dampers and altering the savagery of the gearbox change action. But because it was conceived as a racing car, it needed better aerodynamics than the Ferrari on which it's based. So it's a full 2 feet longer than the already bulky Enzo and a foot wider. The MC12, then, is absolutely bloody massive. And because you can't see anything out of the back, parking is jolly tricky.

But, amazingly, driving it isn't. You expect, when you see that air intake on the roof and those ludicrous over-hangs, that it's going to be a full-on racing machine, a fire-spitting bone-breaker. And when you step inside, to be confronted with proper race harnesses instead of seat belts, there is a sense of 'here we go'.

But the engine fires quietly, the gearbox slides into first, and the steering is no heavier than a Nissan Micra's. You can even remove the roof. The most astonishing thing, though, is the ride. This car glides over bumps, the suspension absorbing the road-worker Johnnies' laziness without transferring a single ripple to the cool blue interior with its Milanese fashion house upholstery.

It's weird. You climb into what looks like a racing car, and yet it behaves like a family saloon. I think I know why they've done this. It's so they can argue that it is a GT car, a comfortable long-distance cruiser with a boot. And we'll gloss over the fact that the boot lid needs an Allen key and three burly blokes to remove it.

I was still thinking along these lines when I first put my foot down. Oh. My. God. There's none of the aural histrionics you might expect from a car that churns out 623 bhp. You just get a savage punch in your kidneys as the huge rev counter explodes round the dial. Bang, you pull the right-hand paddle, and in a couple of milliseconds you have a new gear and a new kind of agony in your spleen. In less than 4 seconds you are past 60 mph and on your way to 205 mph.

It goes like a train, this car; but the most impressive thing is that it also feels like a train; one of those 180 mph TGVs that whistle through France while you sit in silence eating cheese.

Sadly, things aren't quite so satisfactory in the corners. Where an Enzo is flat and grippy, the MC12 wallows and understeers. And every time you go near the throttle, you're told via a dash warning panel that the traction control system is keeping you out of the hedge. But hey, driving a car like this with the traction control on is like eating boil-in-the-bag food at the Wolseley. So you turn it off. And once again. Oh. My. God.

When the understeer comes, you give the throttle a tiny nudge to unstick the back end and . . . whoa, it's as though the rear wing has been hit with a wrecking ball. Now you've got an armful of opposite lock and you know things are about to get messy.

It takes practice, getting this car to power slide. In the same way that it would take practice to get an aircraft carrier to power slide. But it is possible. And it's worth it, because then you feel the Enzo foundations. The sense of total balance. That said, it's not as good as an Enzo. It's not as savage or as exciting. And it's not as fast. But they only made 399 Enzos, so, if you weren't one of the lucky ones, the MC12 might appear to be the next best thing.

Yes, it is very, very quick and it will, if you concentrate, blow your mind clean in half in the corners. But you're always aware somehow that it's a big, ugly, cobbled-together con trick with no back window. And that for couple of hundred grand less you could have a vastly superior Porsche Carrera GT.

Sure, this car was built to win races. But I'm afraid it fails to win something more important. My heart.

Sunday 27 February 2005

Porsche 911

As you read this, a ship called the *Terrier* is forging a path across the bitter north Atlantic on its way from the eastern seaboard of America to the north coast of Germany. I hope she has a smooth and unruffled passage, because in her bowels is something very precious. My brand new Ford GT.

I first drove this 212 mph monster about two years ago in Detroit, and I pretty much knew as I flew home that I simply had to have one. I mean, it was a modern-day incarnation of my childhood dream machine, the GT40, the car that had been built to take a working-class sledge-hammer to Ferrari's aristocratic dominance of European motor sport. And a car that had done just that by winning Le Mans four times on the trot.

Unfortunately, by the time I got round to ringing Ford, it had already had 2,000 serious enquiries about the 28 GTs that would be coming to Britain. It seemed bleak, but I was at journalism college with Ford's head of PR, so guess what? I was squeezed on to the list of accepted customers between Damon Hill, Martin Brundle, Eddie Jordan and Ron Dennis.

This was certainly the first time I'd ordered anything without having a clue about how much it would cost. But in hushed whispers Ford was saying I should think along the lines of the Ferrari 360. So that meant a whisker under £100,000. And that seemed all right, for the realisation of a dream.

What's more, as the months rolled by, the dollar weakened until we were teetering on a two-to-one exchange rate. I even started to think it might be under £4.50. I was happy.

And then everything started to go wrong.

First of all, the cars went on sale in America, but there was no sign of any coming to Europe. 'Ah,' said my friend at Ford, 'that's because we have to change the lights and the exhaust system before it can be sold here.'

Now look: the BBC was recently asked to make 18 episodes of *Top Gear* for the American market in which all references to petrol, bonnets, pounds sterling, boots, motorways, footpaths and bumpers were altered.

On top of this, all mentions of Bolton Wanderers and wellington boots had to be expunged. And we did that in a week. So how come it had taken the world's third-biggest car firm six months to fit its flagship with a new exhaust pipe? Then I was sent a recall notice, saying the front suspension was likely to crumble and that the car must not be driven under any circumstances. Well, that was unlikely, since the parts for mine were still being dug out of the ground.

Then the delivery date slipped from Christmas to Easter, I suspect because Ford in America had lost its atlas and couldn't remember where Britain was.

And then they announced the price. Despite the whispers and the exchange rate, the car was going to cost

£120,677 plus £2,790 for stripes, £1,600 for the fancy wheels, £160 for the road fund licence, £38 for the first registration fee, £25 for number plates and £75 for the first tank of petrol. Which at 4 mpg wouldn't even get me home from the dealership. Gulp.

People kept telling me not to worry because GTs imported privately from the US were being sold in Britain for £180,000, and I was still in profit.

But I hadn't ordered this car to turn a buck.

I'd ordered this car because I have the mental age of a seven-year-old, and I wanted a 5.1-litre supercharged monster to play with.

I know of course that it won't fit in any parking space and that every penny I earn will be used to feed its fuel injectors. I also know that people will point as I rumble by and say, 'Ooh look. There goes someone who can't afford a Ferrari Enzo.'

I know too that it has no satellite navigation, no hands-free phone, no traction control and that the exhaust system, the very thing that has delayed the car for so long, will have to be replaced with the louder, squirrel-killing American set-up.

But I don't care. I don't care about the wait, the price or what anyone will think. Because I'm going to be travelling at 3½ miles a minute in the best-looking, most evocative, most exciting, muscle-bound meat machine the world has seen.

And now it's time to talk about Porsche. Yes, I know I talked about the Boxster last week, and there was a review of the new convertible the week before that, but

I haven't finished yet. Because I've just been driving the bog standard two-wheel-drive 3.6-litre 911.

As you may know, I've never really liked the 911 because over the years it's adhered to a flawed basic premise. That the engine should be in the back.

Yes, as the car squats under fierce acceleration, this layout gives you better traction. But in the bends it becomes a giant pendulum, using the laws of physics to swing you clean off the road. So, as you scream along your favourite bit of blacktop, there's always been a worry that you're messing with the forces of nature.

It's like being an anti-terrorist policeman. You get it right for year after year and nothing happens. But if you get it wrong just once, everyone in London ends up with 14 ears and lungs like walnuts. This makes the job a bit unrewarding somehow.

Now, though, after 40 years of constant development, the rear is held in place as firmly as Lake Mead. Which means the latest models are sculptured proof that, in a battle for supremacy between God and German engineering, beardy is always going to finish second. A modern 911 shouldn't work, but it does. Brilliantly.

There's a lightness to the steering that you just don't get in any other car. It whispers information to your fingertips about what the front wheels are doing and how they're feeling. Driving a 911 is like making love to someone you care for in the bridal suite of the Georges V Hôtel in Paris. It makes my GT feel like a knee-trembler among the empties outside a Rotherham nightclub.

And, on top of this, a 911 is beautifully made and small,

so you can use it every day. Also, it has two small seats in the back, a usable boot, and prices start under £60,000.

This, then, is a 177 mph car that you can choose with your head and your heart. It'll make love to your fingertips and stir your soul. There is no part of your body that it will not stimulate and caress. But don't, whatever you do, buy the convertible, because this won't stroke your penis. It'll make you look like one.

You can't, when you've got a hair hole, and a gut the size of one of Saturn's moons, drive through the middle of a populated area with the roof off any car. Trundling along with the sun on your face and a breeze in your hair may feel nice, but it's as stupid as walking into the Ivy with a 12-year-old Russian hooker. People are going to snigger.

And it's especially sniggersome in a 911. Because this makes you look like a prize vegetable even when the roof is up.

You see, all convertibles are engineering and dynamic compromises. They are heavier and less stiff than their hardtop brothers. That makes them slower and less wieldy, which doesn't matter if you're talking about a cut-down version of a car that wasn't much good anyway. But it does matter with a 911.

This is a purist's driving machine, an adrenalin pump. Every last detail was designed to maximise the score on the driver-o-meter. So removing the roof is like removing the laces from your training shoes. It's only a small change but it ruins everything.

And don't try to tell me that a convertible Porsche is

more finely honed and more delicate than my big Ford because, while this may be true, I have an answer already prepared. In my GT I shall look like Steve McQueen. In your drop-top 911 you'll look like Robert Kilroy-Silk.

Sunday 13 March 2005

Mercedes-Benz CLS 55 AMG

When Mercedes-Benz announced five years ago that it was going to make a car for everyone, I thought that was a figure of speech. But it seems Mercedes really is endeavouring to provide a different model for every single one of the world's 6.4 billion people.

If you are an African dictator with a fuel expenses account paid by Bono and the World Bank, you can have a large S-class with a sumptuous and turbocharged V12 engine. If you are a taxi driver in Geneva, you can have the same car, but with diesel power and wipe-down seats. Then there's the Maybach, which so far as I can tell was made specifically for Simon Cowell.

At the other end of the scale we find the A-class. It was developed after Merc bosses received a letter from a Mr Grant Neville of Huddersfield, who said he wanted a car with two floors and five seats. Fine. Mr Neville was very happy.

But then they got another letter from a Signor Olivio Pagnietta of Pisa, who said he wanted a car exactly the same size as an A-class and with exactly the same number of seats. But only one floor. So they came up with the Vaneo.

We see a similar everyman policy with the E-class saloon. They made a version for some chap in Ottawa who wanted a top speed of 145 mph. And then a businesswoman from Madrid said she liked the car very much but she wanted a top speed of 143 mph. So they did another model to oblige.

This opened the floodgates, so now there is an E-class with every top speed you can think of. There's even an E-class with a big Chrysler body on it, called the 300C. And if you want the same car but 250 millimetres shorter, they'll sell you a C-class, which comes with a range of engines more infinite than space. Does sir want 122 bhp, or 143 or maybe 150? We can also do 162, 177, 192, 218, 229, 255 or 367. Basically, you can pick any number you like.

Now this policy of meeting all requirements, no matter how ludicrous, is extremely good news for you and me. But it is jolly expensive from Merc's point of view. You see, when someone wrote to say they lived in Paris and wanted a small, easy-to-repair plastic car that could be parked nose-on to the pavement, Mercedes set up the Smart division, which last year lost a reported £250 million.

I'm delighted to say, however, that this hasn't stopped them, a point that becomes blindingly obvious when you look at the range of coupés. There's the C-class, the SLK, the SL, the CLK, the CLK convertible, and the CL. All of which are available with a choice of 2 million engines and 14,000 option packages.

But this wasn't good enough for Hans Beckenbaur, a flour merchant from Dortmund, who wanted a car that looked like a coupé but was in fact a four-door saloon.

Mercedes was horrified that he'd exposed a gap in its line-up and immediately set about filling it with the car you see here, the CLS.

It is a Marmite car, I know. You either love it or you've put down your book and run from the room, retching. I'm in the love camp.

So far as I'm concerned, this is certainly the most spectacular-looking car Mercedes has made, and possibly one of the all-time greats from anywhere.

Those slim windows and pillarless doors put me in mind of the Batmobile, while the rear lights are similar to the *Starship Enterprise*'s exhaust vents. But the best thing is that the CLS looks more expensive than it is. Prices start at a little more than £40,000, which is roughly half what I was expecting them to be.

I almost didn't want to drive it. I feared that it would be a bit like actually meeting Uma Thurman. It might be a let-down. It might not be able to cash the cheques that its glorious styling was writing.

So I started in the back, where you'd expect the sloping roofline to make the accommodation suitable only for Anne Boleyn. But no. There are only two seats, rather than three, but there is enough room for non-amputees to stretch out and relax. Even I fitted, and I have the body and legs of an ostrich.

The front, though: that's where you want to be. Because, although the CLS is based on the ordinary E-class, it's actually 40 per cent stiffer. Which means it's 40 per cent more sporty. And to make the recipe even better, the car I tested had a 5.5-litre supercharged AMG

V8, the engine that sounds like a Second World War fighter and goes like a modern-day rocket.

Sadly, because it has such a rich seam of weapons-grade torque, Herr Beckenbaur's car has to make do with the old five-speed automatic gearbox. It would rip Merc's new seven-speeder to shreds. They say, as always, that the power of this engine is so brutish that the top speed of the car has to be electronically checked at 155 mph. But I saw 175 on the speedo, and it was still climbing like a bat out of hell when I ran out of road and had to hit the brakes.

Aaaaargh. They were astonishing. Mash your foot on to the brake pedal, and I'm not joking, it really does feel like your face is being torn off. The G forces are so immense it actually hurts.

This is because the CLS uses the same technology we first saw on the McLaren SLR. When it's wet, the pads pulse slightly to keep the discs dry, and if you lift your foot off the throttle in a big hurry, the computer system notices and orders the braking system to tense so it's ready for some action.

And what's more, it's the brakes that are also used to keep the car in check, should you find yourself on a motorway exit road going a little bit faster than is prudent.

Even if you have the traction control system turned off, Big Brother is still awake, and if he detects the onset of a slide, the offending wheel is individually reined in without you having to do a thing. It all sounds too brilliant for words.

But after just 10 minutes of hard use, the Mercedes

Achilles heel reared its ugly head. The whole dashboard went bright red as the on-board Blair delivered the bad news. 'Brakes overheated. Drive carefully.'

Mercedes says it's cut its profits from £3 billion to £1 billion a year in a drive to improve quality. But I fear it may have to cut them still further.

Certainly, some of the trim pieces on the CLS are a bit low-rent. The plastic on which the seat massage button is mounted looks like it's come off a Hyundai.

But then, if I'm being honest, this is nit-picking and I really was brutal with the brakes. So let's give Herr Beckenbaur's car the benefit of the doubt. I certainly want to, because it was a gem: fast, handsome, well priced, comfortable and blessed with a handling balance that's pretty close to perfect.

And here's the thing. To hammer the point home about Merc's car-for-everyone policy, I was going to sign off by listing a number of stupid small changes that I'd like to see on a CLS if I were to buy one. It was going to be stuff like a green steering wheel and a 5.6-litre engine instead of a 5.5.

But you know what? In truth, I can't think of a damn thing I'd like changed. I'd take it as it is.

Sunday 20 March 2005

Fiat Multipla 1.9JTD

In two million years man managed to discover only three important things: fire, the fact that wood floats, and the horse.

Then within 100 years, starting in about 1820, he came up with everything else. Railways, cars, aeroplanes, horror stories, antibiotics, electricity, the telephone, the computer, the lawnmower, photography, the record player, the typewriter, barbed wire and, of course, linoleum.

One day you were painting bison on the side of your cave. The next, you were chatting on the 'phone' with Aunt Maud in Wakefield while listening to the news on your 'radio'. It must have been a nightmare for the new-fangled science-fiction writers. Because by the time they got round to finishing their books all their ideas had become science fact.

But then we arrived in, ooh, about 1920 and everything just stopped.

Mobile phones. Word processors. The Eurofighter. They're all just developments of ideas that came along in the nineteenth century. And it's easy to see what went wrong: the British Empire collapsed.

I'm going to use Isambard Kingdom Brunel here as a case study. When he fancied the idea of building a new train or a new bridge or a new tunnel, he had to find benefactors. And they were everywhere, gorged with cash from the empire's 11.5 million square miles and its 400 million inhabitants.

Initial estimates for his Great Western Railway, which was to link London with Bristol, suggested it would cost £2.8 million. But this, as things turned out, would only have got it as far as Slough. The actual cost was a truly astronomical £6.5 million.

And when it was finished he went back to the financiers and said: 'Let's keep going. Let's take the passengers off the trains in Bristol and put them on steamships to America.' And they agreed, paying for the SS *Great Western* and then the SS *Great Britain* and, when that ran aground, the enormous SS *Great Eastern*. The biggest ship the world had seen, or would see, until the *Lusitania* came along, 50 years later.

Now imagine if IKB were around today. And try to imagine how far he'd get if he suggested to Network SouthEast that it should finance an idea he'd had for scramjet flight to the space station, and then plasma drive rockets to the most distant of Saturn's moons.

Today nobody looks at the long term. Nobody builds great houses for the grandchildren and huge gardens for the generations to come. The quick-growing leylandii has replaced the oak as our tree of choice. And shareholders will fire any CEO who doesn't turn a profit within the next quarter of an hour.

'So thank you for your very kind offer, Mr Brunel. But would you mind awfully getting lost.'

Nowadays we celebrate James Dyson as a great engineer

because he invented a vacuum cleaner with no bag. And we swoon over the latest mobile phone because it can send a grubby 10-second video clip of your genitals to your girlfriend.

The single best invention I can think of in the past 20 years – 20 years! – is Sky Plus. But it's not really up there, is it, with the invention of flight or electricity or the car.

Speaking of which . . .

You may marvel at the new Aston Martin V8, but may I prevail upon you to stop and think for a moment. Yes, it is handsome and, yes, it is fast. But it is still propelled by a series of small explosions, just like Karl Benz's tricycle, more than 110 years ago.

I'm absolutely certain that, given a free rein and a bottomless vat of money, someone in Scotland, which is the font of all inventiveness, could by now have made a new type of engine that runs on brussels sprout peelings, perhaps, and develops limitless power.

But, instead, the great engineering minds are employed to think of new ways in which the cup holders can slide out of the dashboard. Honestly, they're talking about the fitment of MP3 players in cars these days as though they've created a cure for the common cold.

The last truly great piece of automotive ingenuity came from Toyota who, in the late 1960s, showed the world that cars didn't have to break down all the time. But since then the world's car makers have been playing around with the seven degrees of separation.

We've had engines with three cylinders and five and

ten. We've had engines at the front, in the middle and at the back. We've had air bags for your face, your wife and your children. We've even had air bags for your testicles.

And we've had the Fiat Multipla. In the middle of the 1990s Fiat noticed that you could buy cars with one seat, two seats, three seats, four seats, five seats and seven seats.

Which meant there was a gap. In the big scheme of things it wasn't a particularly big gap. But in the stagnant climate of late-twentieth-century industrial thrustiveness it was a yawning chasm. There was no car with . . . wait for it . . . six seats.

The solution they came up with was a family-sized hatchback that had three seats in the back and three in the front.

So radical and amazing was this that plainly the car needed a whole new look. And so the Multipla was born, the first car to resemble an Amazonian tree frog.

Unfortunately, this turned out to be a mistake. Customers liked their cars to resemble sharks or leopards or, er, cars. But not frogs. And so the Multipla was a monumental flop. And then it was dropped.

And now it's back again. But this time around the quirky styling has been replaced with a blandness that beggars belief. I have to say that this is the most boring-looking machine in the whole of human history. I've seen more exciting cardboard boxes.

And to make matters worse, while Fiat was fiddling about, Honda cottoned on to the six-seat idea and came up with the FR-V, which I suspect may be the second most boring-looking car in the whole of human history.

There's obviously a problem with this three-and-three layout. It means the car has to be square and, because it has to be tall too, to give an impression of space and practicality, it also has to be cubed. As a result, you end up with the Borg spaceship from *Star Trek*.

And there's another problem, too, which becomes evident when you take one into town. While it will fit comfortably into spaces denied to the longer and more traditional people-carrier, its girth makes it a nightmare in narrow streets. I spent most of my week with the Honda and the Fiat, backing up.

It's funny. I never really noticed this with the old Multipla. Maybe it's because that front end was so scary, other people backed up to get away from it.

Or maybe it's because the overpowering styling obliterated the faults. Asking how wide the old Multipla was would be like asking if Adolf Hitler had big feet. It sort of wasn't important.

Anyway, if you live in a Georgian town with broad streets and you have precisely four children, which is best? On the face of it the Fiat looks good. While the top models cost around the same, £16,500, there's a cheap entry-level Multipla for £13,300, whereas the least expensive Honda is £14,700. It should also be mentioned at this point that Fiat can sell you a diesel, whereas Honda cannot. Neither can do an automatic gearbox.

But I'm afraid that a test drive shows the Honda to be the better choice. It's noisy, sure, but it rides more smoothly, it's faster, and it feels as though it's made from materials that will last beyond next Tuesday.

Let's not forget that in the *Top Gear* customer satisfaction survey, Honda won and Fiat didn't. By a long way.

To be honest, though, I really didn't like either of them. They were dreary and bland, and the width really is a nuisance. So if you have three children, may I suggest you buy a packet of condoms. If it's too late, buy a Toyota Corolla Verso.

Sunday 27 March 2005

Peugeot 1007

So what, exactly, is God's most stupid creation? The pink flamingo, the avocado pear, Stephen Joseph from the pressure group Transport 2000? There are many choices even before you get to the koala bear.

It sleeps for 18 hours a day, only waking up to gorge on eucalyptus leaves, which make it stoned. So stoned in fact that whenever it sees anything that isn't a eucalyptus tree or another koala, it becomes so frightened it gives itself chlamydia.

This can't be much fun. Sitting around in a tree all day, in a big fur coat, in Australia, with a bent mind and a sexually transmitted disease that you caught without actually having sex.

Mind you, I've just come back from a couple of weeks in Barbados, where I had plenty of time to study something even more mad. The cicada.

Finished in brown and green, this small insect is so completely camouflaged when sitting in a tree that not even the most eagle-eyed predator would stand half a chance of spotting it. So why, you may be wondering, does it make such a monumental din? I mean, if you're hiding from certain death, it's best not to bellow. This is the main reason why snipers, for instance, don't crawl through long grass with ghetto blasters strapped to their backs.

And yet the virtually invisible cicada has been equipped with such a powerful voice that it must fold its own ears away before letting rip.

Scientists will tell you that this is because the poor thing is so well camouflaged it would never be able to find a mate without shouting. But come on. Moles manage. So does Steve Davis.

No, the real problem is that, contrary to the popular view in travel agency brochures, hot tropical nights are noisier than the opening of a new Las Vegas hotel. You've got the constant pounding of the surf, the frogs, which sound like a million wonky paddle fans, and the monkeys, who could give the Grateful Dead a run for their money. To be heard above this lot, you need to have a 400-watt mouth.

And now, to make matters even worse, the people of Barbados have started buying cars. Except that over there they are not really seen as cars as such. They are horns, which can also be used for moving people and stuff.

I have not seen a copy of the Barbados *Highway Code*, but plainly no one is told to mirror, signal then manoeuvre. There seems to be a commonly held view that you can do whatever you like, at whatever speed takes your fancy, so long as you are leaning on the horn at the time.

This means, of course, the cicada is safe from predators. No airborne hunter can hear it any more. But then neither can its potential mates, which means that from now to the end of its truncated time on the evolutionary cycle, the poor thing will be reduced to a life of onanism.

Interestingly, this brings me on to the new Peugeot 1007, which, for legal reasons involving James Bond, cannot be called the one-007 and must be referred to as the one thousand and seven.

The first and most striking thing about this car is its doors, which do not open in a conventional fashion. Instead, when you press a button, they slide backwards on runners.

At first it's hard to see why this should be a good thing. Being French, they'll be badly made and will therefore shoot backwards every time you accelerate. Though to counter this my test car had such a weedy 1.4-litre petrol engine and a power-sapping sequential gearbox that 0–60 mph took 18 seconds. This means there is no G force at all, and, as a result of that, the doors won't fly off the handle.

Fine. But then there is the problem of knowing which button on the key fob opens which door. There is absolutely no way of telling which one does the left and which one does the right, and in the same way that toast always lands butter-side down, I can pretty much guarantee you'll hit the wrong one.

So you'll be standing there, trying to look cool in front of all those pretty school-run mums, while electronically opening the wrong door.

We're told that electric sliding doors mean children can scamper into the back without having to fold the front seats forward, and this may be so, if your child was created by Lowry. But in these days of PlayStations and lard-burgers, most kids wouldn't have a hope in hell.

Of course, where the one thousand and seven's funny doors really do pay dividends is in narrow parking spaces.

If I lived in Paris I'd have one like a shot because there, where you're allowed to park anywhere so long as it's stylishly done, Starship Enterprise docking ports would open up a whole new range of possibilities. You could park on pavements and still be able to get out. Hell, you could even park between the tables of your local patisserie. I'd like that.

But I don't live in Paris. I live in Britain, where we have out-of-town superstores with clearly defined car parking spaces and city centres that are rigorously patrolled by Nigerians to make sure that no one parks at all.

We therefore simply don't need those doors in the same way that we don't need a 4-million decibel horn, because we're too polite to use it, and we don't need diesel engines because, unlike the Romans, we don't need massive torque for physically shoving other cars out of a parking space that's rightfully ours.

This is what I love about the world of cars: that we can see national characteristics oozing out of every rivet and every weld. Indian cars have huge back seats because all the nephews and nieces will want to come too. Italian cars have a buzz. American cars wobble. German cars are resolute. Swedish cars have bigger wheels for the deep snow. And so it goes on. It's why there has never been a truly global car. And it's why, when we look at the Peugeot one thousand and seven, we have to completely ignore those doors, I'm afraid, and concentrate on the rest of it.

Well, that was my plan, but the doors, I'm afraid, kept cropping up, partly because they make the little Peugeot very expensive – at £12,000 it's £1,000 more than its closest rival from Renault – and very heavy. Not only does this result in the woeful acceleration (I think it's the slowest car from 0 to 60 on the market today) but less economical than it should be, too.

Then you have problems with practicality. Unlike, say, a Honda Jazz, which can accommodate five, the Peugeot is strictly a four-seater. And while the rear bench can be moved hither and thither in a number of amusing ways, the boot is never what you'd call generous. There's also a high sill over which all your shopping must be humped.

On top of this, it's about as much fun to drive as a smallish bus, leaning badly in the corners and never ceasing to amaze you with its complete lack of grunt.

Good points? Well, it scored very highly in the big independent safety tests and you can change various bits of interior trim if someone is sick on them or if you're bored with the colour. They've even produced one version with interior trim designed by Sadie Frost and Jemima French, which I'm sure would be great, if you had the first clue who these people were.

The 1007, then, is the motoring world's cicada. Blessed with only one notable feature which, at best, is useless and at worst isn't notable at all.

Sunday 1 May 2005

Lexus GS430

Do you remember when you were growing up and all your friends were allowed to go on school exchange trips to exotic places like France and Germany? Well, how's this for progress? We now have an 11-year-old girl from Tokyo in the spare room.

Now, I've been to Japan and it was strange. The bath in my hotel room was vertical and made from wood, the food was mostly still alive, there weren't any chairs, the walls were made from rice, I was fed by a woman with a completely white face and a shoe size of minus three, all the bars were full of men in slippers, singing, the traffic hadn't moved since 1952 and all you could buy from vending machines on the streets were cans of drink called Sweat. And soiled pants.

Once I tried driving from Tokyo to Yokohama but it was impossible because none of the road signs made any sense. Elsewhere in the world 'centre' is *zentrum*, or *centro* or some such derivation, but in Japan it's just a meaningless squiggle. Honestly, I would have found more cultural reference points if I'd gone to Venus.

So after a week I went back to my hotel and spent the rest of the trip under my bed, hiding. And I was 40. So how on earth would an 11-year-old girl cope over here? To get round the fact that the poor little thing didn't speak a single word of English, she was sent with one of those gadgets that only exists in *Star Trek*, the mind of Stephen Hawking and most Japanese high street electrical stores.

You type a message in Japanese and it speaks the words in a sort of Daleky Engrish. And the first words it spoke, just five miles from the airport, were 'car sick'. Plainly, after 11 years in a Tokyo traffic jam, our visitor was unused to travelling at speeds in excess of 3 mph.

She was also confused by her supper on that first night, picking up a spoon and staring at it in much the same way that a traveller from the future might pick up and stare at a gramophone record. Plainly it made no sense. But then neither did any of the foodstuff that had been placed on her plate.

I couldn't even use her gadget, partly because all the keys were in Japanese and partly because it had stopped saying 'car sick' and was now saying 'broken', over and over again.

We'd been told that the whole point of her trip was to provide an experience of England, but after the spoon episode we did give her some chopsticks. And then, after watching her use them to wrestle with a six-inch York-shire pudding, I'm afraid I relented and drove all the way to London for some sushi. To be honest, I felt so sorry for her I'd have gone out and harpooned a whale if that's what she'd wanted.

To make matters worse she had arrived with a suitcase full of presents, all of which were exquisite but completely unfathomable. I mean, what kind of face are you supposed to pull when you've just been given what looks like a squidgy test tube full of pink and green sticky tape? It turned out to be a pen that writes a musical score as you drag the nib across the paper. Honestly, I'd never seen anything so amazing in my whole life. But then everything's relative. She'd never been to a house that had dogs on the inside and trees on the outside.

It's said that genetically the human race is defined at one end by the tribesmen of New Guinea and at the other by the Basques. These, apparently, are the bookends. But I'm sorry. I reckon the genetic North Pole is a 6 ft 5 in. Brit and the genetic South Pole an 11-year-old Japanese schoolgirl.

And that brings me to the new Lexus GS430 I've been driving these past few days.

Like all cars, it has doors, seats, pedals, a steering wheel and lights at the front and the back. But how can this be, when it comes from a people who are baffled by a spoon? How do they make something so instantly recognisable as 'a car' when they can't eat mashed potato without vomiting? We have knives and forks. They have chopsticks. We lie down in the bath. They stand up. We cook food. They don't. Their culture is completely different from ours, and yet the Lexus, on the face of it, is just the same as a Jaguar, a Mercedes or a BMW.

Except it isn't. It is much, much quieter. At 70 mph it's so silent you can hear your hair growing. Sitting in your garden after a lovely lunch is more frantic. In the cabin you are so isolated from the real world that you get some idea of what it might be like to be dead.

The six-speed automatic box swaps cogs like an albatross changes direction, and even if you do put your foot down, the big V8 responds by humming, quietly, like it's in a church arranging flowers. Driving this car is like being wrapped up in a duvet and carried from place to place by a small white cloud. Only faster. It is far from being a sports car – driving this car with gusto would be like going into a sword fight armed with a cushion – but in a straight line, at least, the 4.3-litre engine delivers the goods. It'd easily hang on to the coat-tails of a similarly priced BMW 5-series.

But the best thing about this car is the layout of the interior. If we ignore the spectacularly horrible wooden trim we find a sense of order and logic that would make Mr Spock look like a swivel-eyed madman. All the major controls are where you want them to be, and do what you want them to do, and all the minor controls are hidden away in a flap by your right knee.

Problems? Well, apart from the wood trim you have to dig deep to find anything tangible. The boot's an awkward shape, I suppose, and there isn't quite as much space in the back as you might expect. But neither of these things is a good enough reason for buying something else. As a long-distance cruiser this car is quite simply outstanding. Better than a Gulfstream V, and maybe even a rival for teleporting.

Unfortunately, I didn't like it at all, partly because it's about as attractive as a sponsored town centre roundabout and partly because Lexuses these days are driven by people who play golf, or people who like to slap their hos and drive around at night shooting at business rivals with sub-machine guns. Gangstas? Golfers? I don't want to look like either.

Mostly, though, I don't like this car because it feels like a facsimile of the real thing. And that's hardly surprising because that's exactly what it is. A copy. A Mercedes clone.

Cars sit in the Japanese psyche along with spoons and mashed potato. They don't come naturally. Oh sure, they can copy a Mercedes and use it to earn vast lumps of foreign currency, but how do you copy flair and panache and feel? The simple answer is: you can't, so you end up with a completely soulless driving experience.

It's a bit like those vegetarians who insist on eating hamburgers that are designed to look, feel and taste like the real thing. But they're just not.

Technically, this new Lexus is probably better than a Mercedes, in the same way that a golden egg made by laser is going to be technically better than one of Karl Fabergé's originals. But which one would you rather have?

Sunday 8 May 2005

Nissan 350Z Roadster

A recent piece in the motoring section of Her Majesty's *Daily Telegraph* contained a bold claim. That south of a line through Stoke-on-Trent, Derby and Norwich, and excepting Bodmin Moor in winter, there is almost nowhere in England where it might be a pleasure to drive a car for more than 10 consecutive minutes between 7 a.m. and 7 p.m.

The writer suggests that with 31 million vehicles on the road the country is now too congested to allow for untrammelled liberty at the wheel, and that these days nobody buys into the suggestion by car makers that their products are indispensable instruments of self-expression.

I'm sure this strikes a chord, but actually I think the last time someone was so wrong he was standing by an aeroplane at Croydon airport in 1938 waving a piece of paper around.

First of all, contemporary car advertisements feature dancing robots and windscreen wipers crawling across the floor and Gene Kelly breakdancing in the rain. The days when they showed a car whizzing hither and thither on some deserted mountain road to the musical accompaniment of Steppenwolf are long gone.

That's because advertising agencies think like you do, and you think like our friend from the *Daily Telegraph*.

You think that because of the traffic and the speed cameras and the idiot in front it is no longer possible to enjoy more than three-tenths of a car's performance envelope. And that it's a waste of time buying a 155-mph BMW when you'll get to work just as quickly in a £2.50 Perodua.

You've probably worked out – as I have – that if you parked all of Britain's 31 million vehicles nose to tail the traffic jam would be a staggering 82,000 miles long. And what's more, on Friday evening, coming home from work, you probably thought you were at the end of it.

I'm sure, too, that you look at all those empty roads on *Top Gear* and think,' Yeah, right . . .' Even my nine-year-old boy, whose school run takes a torturous 90 minutes, said the other day that the big wide shots of deserted tarmac were 'unrealistic'.

But you know something: they're not. We have neither the time nor the inclination, frankly, to digitally erase other traffic. We don't film on Sundays at four in the morning. And nor do we have the power to close roads for our own gratification.

What's more, I have a test route on which I take all the cars I borrow. And not once in 10 years have I had the run spoiled by traffic. Of course, I encounter other cars trundling along from time to time, but that's what a 500-bhp engine is for, surging you past the dunderhead in a torrent of g-force and noise.

Last night at 6.30 p.m., just 70 miles from Trafalgar Square, I was able to fully explore the outrageous performance characteristics of a TVR Sagaris, changing down two gears for the corners, feeling the loaded tyre straining for grip, then feeding in the power after I'd kissed the apex just so.

Last week I was in a Mercedes SLK 55 in Norfolk, on that arrow-straight road going past Lakenheath air force base. And had I been so inclined I could have kept my foot buried in the shag pile for about half an hour.

In essence, for every clogged-up road you can show me, I'll show you ten that provide the driving enthusiast with every conceivable challenge and every conceivable view. I'll show you roads that still provide the Steppenwolf soundtrack, roads you used to see in the car advertisements, roads that can still tingle the very follicles of your soul. Bikers know what I'm on about here. You ask one.

And then name any county you like, even the ones that snuggle up to London itself, and I'll find you a damn sight more than 10 consecutive minutes of high-octane red-line thrills. I'll find you a round trip that'll pluck the strings of your heart like it's a harp. These roads are there, I promise you. All you need to bring along is a decent car.

So, not the new Nissan 350Z convertible then.

In many ways this new two-seat drop top, with a V6 engine, many speeds and lots of rear-wheel-drive action for those tricky left/right moorland switchbacks, seems ideally suited to the forgotten dream of a balls-out Sunday afternoon thrash.

You climb into what's undoubtedly a well-made car, press a button and marvel as the canvas roof is scooped up and electrically folded into a cubbyhole between the seats and the boot.

Then, with the sun making pretty patterns in the pollen, and 'Born to be Wild' on the stereo, you stamp on the throttle and marvel as you're whisked in a blur of light and colour and sound from 0 to 60 in 5.5 seconds, then onwards to 155. Mmmm. A tasty prospect, I'm sure you'll agree.

Unfortunately there's quite a lot of marzipan in the mix. I see that it has a carbon-fibre prop shaft and an aluminium bonnet, and I can tell from the scuttle shake that they've skimped on underfloor strengthening to replace some of the rigidity lost when the roof was removed. But the weight-saving programme hasn't worked. This car still feels like it's made from ebony and lead. It feels as though it's dragging an anchor.

I wasn't taken with the driving position either. The seat doesn't go back far enough. And while the cockpit layout is logical and concise, there's not much flair. Nor is the gearbox much cop, and the fuel tank's too small as well.

Then there's the noise. A car like this should sing or howl or impersonate thunder. Whereas it sounds like . . . a noise. A drone that just gets louder and louder as the revs begin to wage their war with the weight.

There's a small red light that comes on in the middle of the centrally mounted rev counter to tell you when it might be a good idea to change up. But I can pretty much guarantee you'll never see it illuminated, because your ears and your fingertips sense you're out of revs long before you really are.

The one light you will see, however, is small and yellow and comes on to say the traction control is active. This flickers constantly because the suspension cannot cope at all with mid-corner bumps. It just seems to rattle and then hand over all responsibility to the electronic nanny.

The 350Z, then, feels like a mishmash: like a Japanese car designed by an Indian from Leicester in America and then altered for Europe. Which shouldn't be a surprise because that's exactly what it is. And worse, when you're at a party and someone asks what you're driving, you have to say: 'A Datsun with a Renault engine.'

It's not even what you'd call good-looking. The boot seems to go on for a mile and a half, which might be acceptable if the space inside were large and commodious. But peering into the cavity beneath that huge back end is a bit like peering into the lower decks of an aircraft carrier and finding only a broom cupboard. It's disappointing.

It wasn't the road, then, or the traffic that spoiled my drive in this car. It was the car itself.

But then again I could be wrong. It wouldn't be the first time I've been out of step. I, for instance, didn't like the hard-top 350Z whereas it made my colleagues in the specialist motoring press all weak at the knees.

What's more, I think Britain is still able to provide a wonderful driving environment. And I can pretty much guarantee you're with the chap from the *Telegraph* on this one.

Sunday 29 May 2005

BMW M5

I worked today with a young naked girl whom we shall call Teri. She wasn't actually naked, but such was the smallness of her clothing you could tell she wanted to be.

Teri wasn't a model. She was absolutely adamant about that. 'I'm not a model,' she said. 'I'm a television presenter.' And proceeded to reel off a list of her shows, all of which are beamed only into homes with satellite dishes the size of New Mexico.

Teri was one of the most annoying people I've ever met because at no point in the day did she do or say anything even remotely surprising. From the moment you saw her hair, you could tell where she lived, what her friends looked like and that she almost certainly has the *News of the World*'s newsdesk on speed dial.

It's the same deal with those thin-lipped, angry-looking women you see in Caffe Nero reading the *Guardian*. You know everything about them before even saying hello. And then there was the berk in the Boxster that cruised past me in Docklands last week. I saw the parting in his hair and knew he'd have a plasma television, an appointment to play squash that night with someone called Dom, and no carpets.

Don't these people realise that it's much more fun

to pick and mix opinions rather than buying a sort of compilation album. It's why I'm so supportive of the European Union and have donkeys. Because these are the last things anyone would expect.

And it's also why I have such a downer on BMWs. Sure they're great cars, but they're like magnolia paint. It's warm and practical and goes with anything, but what it says most of all is I Have No Imagination.

The M5, however, has always been a little bit different. The best was the first. Launched in the late 1980s, it looked exactly like my dad's dreary 525e, but, thanks to its 286 bhp straight-six engine, it went with a ferocity and a panache that had no place in a four-door saloon.

It was, quite simply, the best Q car ever made (it looks ordinary but goes like a rat up your trousers).

That said, the M5s that followed were fairly stupendous as well. Quiet, unassuming cars for people who wanted to get home very quickly without making a song-and-dance about it. And here's the clincher. These cars lost money like gin palaces, halving in value overnight and then halving again before breakfast was over.

So whenever I see someone in an M5 I'm overcome with a wave of respect, because here is someone who has paid a fortune to hide his light under a bushel. I like that, and as a result I was desperately looking forward to my first go in the new model.

It has a 5-litre V10 engine that churns out 400 bhp. It'll do 0–60 in 4 seconds and could, if it didn't have an electronic Bill Oddie under the bonnet, hit 204 mph. And yet, apart from a few fancy air ducts on the front, it looks pretty much identical to your doctor's normal 5-series. Sounds like quite a recipe.

Unfortunately, however, the recipe has been spoiled somewhat by someone who thinks pure engineering can be improved with a blizzard of technobabble.

So before setting off for a 50-mile journey home on a lovely summer's evening, I had to choose from 11 different settings on the seven-speed flappy paddle gearbox. Then I had to decide how ferocious I wanted the gear-shifts to be: very fierce, quite fierce, moderately fierce, boring or very boring. And then I had to choose from three settings on the electronic differential.

And then, since I didn't know where I was, I had to set the sat nav, which meant hitting a knob, twiddling it, moving it to the side and then twiddling it again.

It's a good job this car has so much power because, by the time you've set it up for the journey that lies ahead, you're already very late.

Anyway, off I toddled, cursing the BMW gearbox's inability to cope with town traffic, no matter what setting you choose. Pretty soon, however, the road opened up, Bob Seger came on the radio, and with a determined shove I put my foot down.

And pushed a knob on the steering wheel that I assumed controlled the volume. It didn't. It changed the station, so now instead of *Hollywood Nights* I had some fat opera bint warbling on Radio 3. Damn. So I had to get the screen out of sat nav mode into entertainment mode and then tell it I wanted an FM station, whereupon it presented me with a million local alternatives that nobody who has £61,000 to spend on a car would ever listen to. I just want one button for Radio 2 and one for Radio 4. And that's it.

Eventually I relocated Bob Seger, but unfortunately I was approaching a roundabout and the sat nav woman had decided I was an idiot. So she told me to go straight over and then repeated herself and then repeated it again. And by the time she'd shut up Bob had been replaced with a miserable-sounding girl called Dildo.

Happily, by this stage I knew where I was, so I thought, 'OK, I'll turn the sat nav off.' Well, you can't. It doesn't matter what button you press, she continues to give her instructions over and over again until you want to bludgeon her and her family to death with an axe. Even if you pull over and turn off the engine, she lies in a state of suspended animation, waiting to spew electronic diarrhoea all over the cockpit when you set off again.

To make matters worse, in the desperate search for the right button I'd hit something called 'power', which had ruined the ride. And then I'd made the mistake of reaching for the indicator. You can't turn that off, either. It doesn't matter what you do with the stalk, it just goes on blinking until it's decided you've made the turn.

By this stage I was properly angry, and now the sat nav cow was not only giving me audible instructions but also flashing them on to a head-up display on the windscreen. And the indicator was still on and I couldn't find Radio 4. And then I hit another button on the steering wheel called 'M'.

This brought up a rev counter in the head-up display and caused the seat to start attacking my back. I'm not joking. Every time I went round a corner, some electronic chip decided I needed more support and firmed up the appropriate bolster.

They say a Dutch bargee can swear for two minutes without repetition or hesitation. But in the new M5 I beat that easily. Why, I wailed to myself, can there not just be one big red button in the middle of the steering wheel which turns all this crap off? Why do I have to live in some German geek's wet dream? And then, to improve my mood still further, I came up behind a Rover that was being driven by someone who was a hundred and seventy twelve. In a temper I put my foot down to get past and couldn't believe what happened.

It seems that the M button, in addition to electrifying the seat, had told a computer deep in the bowels of the engine that I was in the mood for some fun and games. So now the V10 was no longer developing 400 bhp. It was handing over a massive 507. That's right, 507. And as a result the M5 just flew.

In the last five miles of my journey I discovered that deep beneath the layers of utter and complete electronic nonsense, and the rather ugly body, there's one truly amazing car.

Just when I was thinking that BMW had made yet another car for yet another software consultant, it did something I really wasn't expecting.

It became a full-on M5. And praise doesn't come higher than that.

Sunday 12 June 2005

Vauxhall Monaro VXR

Last week the *Daily Mail* broke off momentarily from writing about immigrants, Princess Diana and the value of your house, and published a photograph of my wife and me walking down the road.

Why? Well, I was carrying nothing while my wife was lumbering along beside me weighed down with a heavy suitcase.

'Look at him!' it screamed. 'Making his long-suffering wife carry his bags.'

What this proves, most of all, is the absolute hopeless-ness of the *Daily Mail* as a newspaper. My wife was carrying my bags not because I'm a male pig, but because moments earlier an MRI scan had revealed that I've slipped two discs. And that carrying heavy suitcases is something I'm not allowed to do any more.

More importantly, and this is the story those blinkered people on the *Mail* managed to miss, I'm no longer allowed to drive. Yup, for the next few months I'm off the road.

Partly this is because I can't look left or right, partly it's because my left arm doesn't work at all, and partly it's because I'm on a cocktail of drugs so bright and vivid I spend half the day wondering if I'm a horse and the other half answering only to the name of Stephen.

The only good news is that I'm taking steroids, so by the time I'm fixed I shall have breasts and a handbag, and as a result the *Daily Mail* will write stories about my brave battle with a spinal injury and how I'm an example to women everywhere.

In the meantime, however, my pain in the neck means I'm not allowed to drive, which will be a pain in the backside. Mostly for my wife, actually, who will have to carry my bags to the car and then drive me to work. She may even have to write this column because, while I have a few cars stockpiled up, the list is not endless.

Maybe I'll do some features on what life is like in the back of a Rolls-Royce or a Maybach until the steroids have worked and I'm mended. Unless they don't, in which case I'll need an operation, and that could turn me into a drooling vegetable. In which case I'll do some stories about wheelchairs and mashed food.

Whatever. In this world where everything is always someone's 'fault', the most important thing right now is to work out how I, the world's least active man, managed to slip not one but two discs. I went through all the possibilities with my doctor and we decided that the blame for my condition lies fairly and squarely at the door of Vauxhall.

Apparently, if you spend too long driving round corners much too quickly it will pull all the gooey stuff out of your spine; and last week I spent a very great deal of time going round many, many corners much too quickly in the new Vauxhall Monaro.

It's been around for a while now, the Monaro, and

nobody seems to have paid it much attention. Small wonder, really, when you consider that it's an Australian car, with an American engine. Sure, we'll buy colonial wine and we'll concede that they're good at sport, but that's chiefly because they plainly do very little else.

In the past 200 years Australia has only invented the rotary washing line, and America's sole contribution to global betterment is condensed milk. The notion of these two great nations coming together to make a car doesn't fill anyone from the world's fountain of ingenuity with much hope.

Especially when it lumbers into battle sporting a Vauxhall badge.

The thing is, though, that the original Monaro was a little gem. Or, to be more specific, a rough diamond. With a 5.7-litre V8, and nineteenth-century technology feeding all that torque to the road, it was a crude but devastatingly effective mile-muncher.

Think of it as an Aussie from the Outback. Maybe he can't quote Shakespeare. Maybe he's never heard of Terence Conran. But he can smash all the teeth clean out of your mouth with a single punch. That was the Monaro.

And now there's a new version. At first glimpse the prospect is even more exciting because it has a restyled bonnet full of aggressive vents and holes, and because underneath it gets an even bigger engine. A 6-litre V8 from the last Corvette.

Sadly, all is not sweetness and light, because the Monaro is sold in America as a Pontiac GTO and the new version was designed specifically for Uncle Sam. That means it's all gone a bit soft. And for some extraordinary reason they've moved the 60-litre fuel tank to a point directly above the rear axle. This means the car's handling will change, depending on how much fuel you have on board, and also that the boot is nowhere near as big as it should be.

So, does the extra power from the bigger engine compensate for this? Or is this the automotive equivalent of the American version of *The Office*: a good idea ruined by the Septics? To find out, I took it to a track and drove round and round until, as we know, my spine disintegrated.

The first thing worth noting is that the power isn't delivered in a zingy, revvy, European way. It's more a suet pudding than a champagne sorbet, but there's certainly no shortage. And as a result you'll go from 0 to 60 in 5.3 seconds and onwards to 185. That's pretty quick.

The lazy engine certainly suits the whole feel of the car. It lumbers rather than darts, it feels heavy and lethargic. But then you might have said all this about Martin Johnson. And that really is the point of the big Vauxhall. It's second row, not a winger.

The gearbox, especially, is worthy of a mention. The lever looks like it's come from the bridge of a nineteenth-century ocean liner, and the effort needed to move it around is huge. But then this is a muscle car. It's not for sheilas.

My favourite part, however – and you'll only really trip over this on a track – is the way it goes round corners. The angles of oversteer it can achieve, thanks mainly to its long wheelbase, are absolutely ludicrous, and, if you keep your foot planted, so too is the volume of smoke from the back wheels. If you have the mental age of a six-year-old, and I have, you would never tire of sliding this massive car from bend to bend.

In fact, after I wore one set of tyres down to the canvas, I went straight round to a tyre shop, bought two more, and then proceeded to wear those down to the canvas as well. This car is that much fun.

Of course, it's not what you'd call luxuriously appointed. There are plenty of toys to play with, and lots of space for four, too, but the quality of the plastic and the feel of the carpets beggars belief. Until you look at the price. This car, this 6-litre V8 185 mph muscle car, is less than £37,000 – the same as a BMW 535 diesel.

Yes, the BMW is more of a quality product, but which would you rather have, a night out with a vicar or a few pints with your mates at the pub? When it comes to fun, the Monaro is truly wonderful, and it's not bad at cruising either.

The seats are sublime, it glides over bumps, and at 70 mph the engine is barely turning over, so it's quiet as well.

It all sounds great, but there's one problem. You can still buy the original, harder, 5.7-litre car. Yes, this only offers up 349 bhp compared with the 6-litre's 398 bhp. But you're pressed to spot that difference on the road.

And here's the clincher. The 5.7 is only £29,000. Put simply, there is no better bargain on the market today.

Thank you, by the way, for all your emails on the Ford

GT. There have been hundreds and hundreds. Now that I can't go anywhere I have time to read them. And I'll let you know what you've all decided.

Sunday 10 July 2005

Rolls-Royce Phantom v. Maybach

Travelling. The unfortunate end result of internal combustion and jet propulsion. The scourge of the modern
age. It's dangerous, it's time-consuming and it's irretriev-
ably boring.

In the olden days when men wore hats made from
wolves, no one wasted their lives by travelling from A to
B, because B was too far away. Now, though, people are
quite happy to spend 10 hours in an aluminium tube,
watching all their veins clog up with lard, simply so they
get a tan.

When you are on a plane you are achieving nothing
and you are not enjoying yourself, so you are wasting
the most precious commodity you have: time. If you're
middle-aged now, you only have 200,000 hours left, and
are you prepared to spend 20 of those being squashed,
plus another 20 waiting to be squashed while someone
confiscates your knitting needles? Especially as a recent
survey found that, on average, the modern Briton now
spends four years of their life in a car. That's four years
moving from place to place. Four years just travelling.

This is why I like cars that are fast. In the same way
that an F-15 fighter can enliven air travel, a powerful
engine can turn the most tedious slog into an adrenalin
rush. I like the feel of G when a quick car accelerates, I

like the cornering forces as it slices through the bends, and I love the sense of danger when you pull out to overtake and you're not sure you're going to make it.

Drive quickly and you turn the act of travelling into an adventure. You make those four years in a car exciting. You give them a point. And you will arrive at your destination sooner, too, which means you have more time to have fun. Put simply, 500 bhp enriches your life.

Unfortunately, our present government has somehow arrived at the conclusion that it's possible for there to be no accidents at all on the road, and that this can be achieved by removing the thrill of driving. So we're being watched, and controlled and punished if we break its rules.

What's more, ministers are saying that if we all drive around in Toyota Priuses at 17 mph we will save not only ourselves but the planet as well. They cannot see the car as a thrill machine. They view it simply as an alternative to public transport. And as a result it is becoming increasingly difficult these days to hurtle round a corner, because hidden in a bush on the other side is a civil servant in a van.

So, if we can't go quickly in a bid to make travelling more fruitful, then we must turn our attention to other alternatives. And that brings me neatly on to the question of club class.

Flying in the front of an aeroplane does not make the journey pass any more quickly, but at least you don't have to spend 10 hours with your face in a fat man's armpit. The jump in price from economy to club is vast, but there's no doubt in my mind that it's worth every penny.

So does this apply on the road, I wonder. Is it worth spending £300,000 on a Rolls-Royce Phantom or a Maybach? Are they really three times better than a Mercedes S 55 AMG? And is the last word in automotive luxury a realistic alternative to power and speed and excitement? We shall begin with the Maybach 62, which nosed through the gates to my house, as requested, at 7.30 a.m. The rear arrived about 40 minutes later. It is a vast car this, more than 20 feet long and almost 6½ feet wide.

So I think it's fair to call the back-seat area generous. It's so generous in fact that, stretched out on one of the airline-style seats, my legs did not even touch the partition that separates those in the rear from the driver.

With barely a sound, the twin-turbocharged V12 engine whispered into life and off we went, with me already starting to experiment. After a while I had one television set showing a sat nav display and the other showing breakfast news. Then I found the fridge, the button to move the headrest just so, and both the mobile phones.

And then I found the roof. It's made of photochromatic glass, which at the twiddle of a switch can be fully frosted, very frosted, not frosted at all or completely opaque. I liked playing with this feature. In fact, by the time I was bored with it we were in west London, at a set of lights where many Eastern European builders were hanging around waiting to be picked up by contractors.

I don't think they liked me very much, so I pushed another button and closed all the curtains.

Ah, the curtains. They were hideous, unless your name is Hyacinth Bucket and even your bog-roll cosy is ruched. In fact, come to think of it, the whole car was hideous. The exterior styling, the polished wood, the chromed uplighters. It was like one of those really expensive cabin cruisers that back up to the harbour wall in St Tropez.

What's more, in a brief idle moment I caught sight of the dashboard on which, picked out in the finest plastic, was the legend 'SRS Airbag'. Just like you find on a Mercedes S-class. And that's the Maybach's biggest problem. When all is said and done, and there's much to say and lots to do, it is only an elongated Mercedes. So I always think of it as bespoke tailoring from Marks & Spencer. Fine, I'm sure, but not quite the same as bespoke tailoring from Rolls-Royce.

There's a lot less to do in the back of the Phantom, even in the new long-wheelbase version I tried. This is 10 inches longer than the standard car and about £30,000 more expensive. That's £3,000 an inch, and that's expensive. Every day I receive emails offering me extra inches for a lot less.

But when you climb into the back of this car and wade through an acre of thick pile carpet to your seat, let me tell you, it feels very good. Stepping out of the Maybach into this is like stepping out of a Sunseeker Camargue 47 and into the library at Blenheim Palace. Only with the most fabulous art deco fixtures and fittings.

Despite the BMW ownership these days, there's nothing on the dash to suggest that this is anything but pure Rolls-Royce. You don't have a rev counter, for instance.

Instead you get a dial telling you how much power the engine has in reserve. Even at speed it usually reads 95 per cent.

I'm sure the Phantom has an airbag, but there's no sign advertising the fact. It's probably a brown paper bag and arrives in the cabin after a discreet 'Ahem'.

My test car was fitted with a Stuart. The Stuart's ability to accelerate and brake without causing my champagne to fall over was remarkable, and in direct contrast to the Gary that was installed in the Maybach. The Gary hustled. If you're in a hurry you need a Gary. The Stuart drove like a Buddhist butler.

And that sums up how the cars feel. In the Maybach you sense all the time that you're connected to the road, that you're in a car. Whereas in the Rolls you get the sense that you've been picked up by a huge velvet glove. In the Maybach I played. In the Rolls I dozed.

It had a computer and televisions, of course. But if I were to buy a Phantom I'd specify it with a nice coal fire and a chimney. It already comes with wingbacks.

I spent four wonderful days being driven around in these monsters and can report that they are a realistic alternative to speed. Yes, you can get home faster in a Ferrari, but in the back of a Maybach or a Phantom you are doing what you'd be doing at home anyway. Sitting back, watching the news, with a glass of something chilled.

Are they worth three times more than a top S-class Mercedes? Oh, absolutely. In the same way that a Gulfstream V is worth a damn sight more than a Piper Cherokee.

And now we arrive at the big one. Which is best? I've mocked the Maybach for being a jumped-up Mercedes, but that's unfair. The sheer volume of gadgetry in its rear quarters means you quickly forget you're on Mercedes suspension, behind a Mercedes engine. It is a wonderful way to travel if you are a northern businessman or a Kuwaiti or you have the mental age of a six-year-old. Which is not a criticism, by the way.

However, I would choose the Rolls. I like the engineering, I like the style, I absolutely adore the looks, but most of all I love the sensation that you're inside something that was designed to be 'the best car in the world'. I think, though, it's more than that. I think that in these difficult and dark days it's actually the best way to travel.

Sunday 24 July 2005

Aston Martin V8 Vantage

What with the bombs and everything, we haven't really learned much about Britain's big Olympic sports day. It's almost as though the whole thing has simply gone away. But don't worry. Behind the headlines, the organisers are hard at work and have already made one important decision. These will be a low-carbon, sustainable, public transport Games with no provision for any car parking whatsoever at any of the major sites.

Can you believe that? No, really. Can you honestly believe that with all the things that need to be achieved in the next seven years, the powers that be have decided that global warming is somehow the most important issue.

'Right. We need to compulsorily purchase half of east London, we need to bulldoze it, we need to get some stadiums designed, we need to find some steel that isn't on its way to Shanghai, we need to build a whole village for the athletes and we need to ensure nobody explodes. But first things first, comrades. Are we all agreed that these Games should be car-free?' Don't these idiots remember the Millennium Dome? Over the years, many enquiring minds have speculated on why this billion-pound umbrella failed. But there's only one reason, really. Even if you wanted to see the multi-faith exhibits and learn how a turd was made, you couldn't get there. Because there was no car park.

Of course, those in charge of the Olympics will say that the Games give us a chance to show the world that London is a shining beacon of environmental responsibility . . . in the same way that London was a shining beacon of multiculturalism, right up to the moment when a small group of deranged Muslims started blowing themselves up on Tube trains. The Olympics are a test designed to quantify and celebrate human physical achievement. They are not an opportunity for a bunch of stupid, left-wing, weird-beard failures to make political points.

I make this prediction now. The woolly-pully brigade will be so busy over the next seven years ensuring that the Games are eco-friendly that they'll forget to build a running track. And the health and safety department will outlaw the swimming pool on the basis that someone might drown.

This will make Britain a laughing stock in the eyes of the whole world, so consequently we must quickly find something else to crow about. And that brings me neatly on to the Aston Martin V8 Vantage.

In the past few weeks this new car has been subjected to a torrent of crowing as various motoring correspondents have vomited eulogies on to the page. But I'm afraid that I must be the voice of reason here.

First of all, Aston Martin is owned by the Americans and run by a German whose most recent decision saw engine production being moved from Newport Pagnell to Cologne. So it's about as British as Budweiser.

And then there's the price. At £80,000, the Vantage is £20,000 more than was originally suggested and, crucially, £20,000 more than the car with which it was designed to compete: the Porsche 911.

Of course, with a three-year waiting list, the Aston is unlikely to depreciate much, so that makes the premium more palatable. And that leaves us with the next problem. A lack of power.

Eventually there will be a faster version called the Vantage Vantage probably, or the Vantage Squared, but for now, when you change down and pull out to overtake, the baby Aston accelerates briskly but with none of the savagery you might have been expecting. It's fast. But it's not blistering.

The engine starts out in life as a 4.2-litre Jaguar V8 but is then extensively reworked to become a 4.3 that churns out 380 bhp and 302 torques. This isn't enough. It's less torque than you get from a Mercedes SLK, less bhp and torque than you get from a Vauxhall Monaro. And more worryingly it's less bhp and torque than you'll get from the next Jaguar XK, which will be cheaper as well. And just as beautiful.

Annoyingly, with a 4.3-litre V8 allied to a chassis made from air and a body fashioned from the froth on a cappuccino, the Vantage could have been really quick, cartoon quick, fast enough to fan a forest fire with its wake. But if they'd done that, why would anyone have spent about £20,000 more on a DB9? It's not like the Vantage is different in any other way. Apart from the lack of back seats, the new V8 has exactly the same Volvo sat nav system as the DB9, exactly the same hard-to-read dash as the DB9 and exactly the same Ford trim as the DB9.

In other words, like the DB9, the Vantage was built using whatever the Aston engineers could get their hands on cheaply. As opposed to the 911, which was built using whatever took the Porsche engineers' fancy.

I'm sorry if this all sounds negative but I'm being realistic here. And I'm also being realistic when I tell you that in a straight fight, on any road or track, the 911 will be faster. Not just because of its superior grunt but also because it brakes better, steers better and corners more confidently.

But, and this is what makes cars such fun to write about, given the choice of a Porsche 911 or a V8 Vantage, I wouldn't hesitate for a moment. I'd buy the Aston.

While it may not be as nippy or as thrilling as the 911, it has a he-man feel on the road that I like. Thanks to heavy steering, heavy brakes and a heavy six-speed manual gearbox, they've made the syllabub-light body feel like a meat pie. The 911 is for nancy boy racing drivers. The Aston's for gentleman thugs.

That said, it's by no means uncomfortable. Be in no doubt that it's a firm car, designed for the bends, but the suspension never gets panicked by ridges and potholes in the same way that it does in, say, a Mercedes SL. It's always controlled. Down. Up. Stop.

And then there's the noise. Oh my God. What a sound-track. From inside, all is quiet and serene. At normal speed, when the European Union testing people are listening, all is quiet and serene.

But put your foot down and a little valve in the exhaust system changes everything. Under full-bore acceleration, this car doesn't rumble or howl. It sounds like all the most exciting bits of the Bible. It sounds like Revelation.

And it's just so loud. When my wife went for a spin on a balmy summer's evening, I heard her change from fourth to fifth a full two miles away.

A Porsche may well have the power and agility to get past, but stuck in the sonic boom from those exhausts, I suspect the German car would probably disintegrate before it ever got the chance.

The way it sounds is a good enough reason to buy the Vantage but there's more: the way it looks.

This, of course, is the Aston party trick. A Vanquish is so pretty you overlook the fact its flappy paddle gearbox is useless. A DB9 is so pretty you overlook the fact it goes wrong quite a lot. And now we have the V8, which is so pretty you overlook the fact it's not quite as good as a 911.

In the same way you'd overlook the undoubted charms of Cherie Blair with her law degree and her international connections for a chance to spend the night with – I was going to say Jordan, but I think Keira Knightley is a bit nearer the mark somehow.

Oh, and one more thing. The amount of global-warming carbon dioxide produced by the Aston's big V8 is roughly equivalent to the amount produced by a dozen sprinters in a 100-metre race. Just thought I'd mention it.

Sunday 18 September 2005

Ford Mustang

The new Pontiac Solstice is America's first attempt at making a sports car in more than 50 years. And not since David Beckham's wayward penalty kick against Portugal have we seen anything go so wide of the mark. It is comically awful.

And that sets a question. How come America's massive car industry can't make what is basically beans on toast? A light, zesty, pine-fresh car with an engine at the front, a simple foldaway roof in the middle and rear-wheel drive at the back? Lotus can make a sports car using nothing but a melted-down bathtub and the engine from a Rover. Alfa Romeo can make a sports car using steel so thin you can read through it, and an engine that won't start. Then there was Triumph, which made a sports car even though its entire workforce was outside the factory warming its hands around a brazier and chanting. So what's America's problem? Well, here in Europe early cars were expensive coach-built luxury goods for the tweedy and well-off. It wasn't until the 1940s that cars for the common man came to France, Germany and Britain, and it wasn't until the 1950s that they came to Italy. They haven't arrived in Spain even today.

As a result we still have an innate sense that a car is something you save up for, something a bit decadent and

exciting. Whereas in America the everyman Model T
Ford came quickly after the introduction of internal
combustion, so there was never a chance for cars to earn
that upmarket cachet. As a result, they've always seen the
car as a tool: nothing more than an alternative to the
horse.

In Europe we talk about style and how fast a car accelerates. In America they talk about how many horse boxes
their trucks can pull and how much torque the engine
produces.

If you do encounter someone over there who's fond
of performance cars they're only really interested in how
much g can be generated in the bends, whereas here those
of a petrolhead disposition don't care at all about grip,
only what happens when it's lost and the car is sliding.
Then you are into the world of handling. A world where
nothing but skill keeps you out of the hedge.

There's more, too. From day one American motor
sport was all about sponsorship, which is why the oval
raceway was developed. It meant the whole crowd could
see all the sponsors' names all the time. The cars never
zoomed off into a wood.

Here, they did. Motor racing was a rich man's game,
held far from hoi polloi on airfield perimeter roads.
And on twisty tracks like this, grip was nowhere near as
important as decent handling.

Add all this together and you start to understand why
we have Lotus, Ferrari, Maserati and Aston Martin. And
they have the Ford F-150 Lightning pick-up truck:
0–60 mph in a millionth of a second. Enough space in

the back for a dead bear. And on a challenging road about as much fun as a wasabi enema.

They also have the Ford Mustang and last week that's what I was using to cruise up the 101 from Monterey to San Francisco. The sun was shining, 104.3 the Hippo was massaging my earbones with soothing West Coast sounds and, like everyone else, I was doing a steady 65 mph, my heart beating in slow monotonous harmony with the big V8.

This new version has been styled to resemble the original from 1965, and that's a good thing. Less satisfactory is the news that it's also been engineered to resemble the original with all sorts of technology that in Europe would have been considered old-fashioned by Edward Longshanks.

There's no complex double-stage turbocharging here; no elegantly machined swirl chamber to extract the best possible power and economy from the smallest possible engine. It's a 4.6-litre V8 with just one camshaft, three valves per cylinder and the sort of power output the average European would expect from a juicer.

The platform for the new Mustang comes from a Jaguar S-type. But then the Americans take it back in time by fitting a solid rear axle such as you'd find on a Silver Cross pram, and a Panhard rod, dismissed by Newcomen as being 'a bit too last year'.

So what's it like to drive? Well, the previous day I'd taken it on a hard lap of the extraordinarily beautiful Laguna Seca raceway, which, because it's the curliest track in North America, is regarded by racing drivers all over the world as one of the greats. Mansell. Villeneuve. Even *Top Gear*'s Stig goes all misty-eyed at the mention of it.

And frankly it was more than a match for Ford's big daft horse. Its brakes were cooked by turn six; the final slow corner completely overwhelmed the live rear axle; and through the fearsome Corkscrew, which twists down a gradient so steep you can't even walk up it, I'm afraid Mr Ed was about as pin-sharp as a punt gun. I damn nearly soiled myself.

Is it fast? Well, you get 300 bhp, which is about 200 bhp less than BMW gets from a similarly sized engine. But nevertheless it will get from 0 to 60 mph in 5 seconds and reach a top speed of 150. That's not bad for an ox cart.

But by European standards this car is rubbish. Its engine has wasteful, unused capacity that turns fuel into nothing, it couldn't get from one end of a country lane to the other without running out of brakes, and it handles like a newborn donkey.

There's more, too. It's got a gruff engine note, its interior has the panache of an Afghan's cave and . . . and . . . and I can't go on. You see, I'm running through all this car's bad points, but I'm afraid my mind is consumed by the bit where I was doing 65 mph on the 101, listening to some Eagles on 104.3.

And then by the subsequent memory of grumbling along the waterfront in San Francisco itself, the city setting for *Bullitt*, the film that etched the Mustang for all time on the petrolhead's radar.

You see, I kept thinking, I'm in a Mustang in San Francisco on a glorious September afternoon. And I liked that a lot. I liked it so much that I became consumed with the notion of maybe taking a small part of the experience home with me.

The numbers look good. Because the Mustang is made from pig iron and lava it is extraordinarily cheap: $25,000. And £13,800 for 300 bhp is tempting. Even if you factor in the cost of shipping, changing the lights and paying Mr Blair some tax, it'll still only be £22,000.

For that you could have a Golf GTI, which alongside Ford's canoe looks like the Starship *Enterprise*. It's more practical, easier to run, and around Laguna Seca undoubtedly it'd be a whole lot more competent. Whenever I drive a GTI I'm always full of admiration for its abilities, but when I was driving that Mustang I liked it. And that's sort of more important.

Of course, the American way means they'll never be able to build a sports car. It explains why the Pontiac Solstice is so dire. But the simplistic, covered-wagon approach doesn't really matter on a car like the Mustang, not when you're doing 65 mph in the sunshine and the Doobies are serenading you with *Long Train Running*. Not when it means you get a car this handsome for 13 grand.

The only worry is that if I did buy a Mustang, I'd get the car over here and on a wet November night realise that, actually, what I wanted to bring home was San Francisco.

The Mustang, then, is a great car in America. But here you're better off with a Golf.

Sunday 25 September 2005

Volkswagen Golf R 32

It was Sheikh Yamani, the former boss of Opec, who pointed out that the Stone Age didn't end because the world ran out of stone. Nor did the Iron Age end because we ran out of iron. And you can be fairly sure the Oil Age won't end because we run out of oil. Nobody knows when this will be because nobody knows how much there is down there, and equally nobody knows how much demand there will be for it in the future. In the past 40 years the population of the world has doubled.

So will it double again in the next 40? Or will we all be killed by parrots? Only the world's environmentalists, with their crystal balls and their tarot cards, seem belligerently certain about what's going to happen next.

Oh, and the car firms. Toyota says that in the next 10 years one million of the 7 million cars it'll be making every year will be part-petrol, part-electric hybrids. And now BMW, Daimler-Chrysler and General Motors have joined forces to provide some competition.

Sounds great, but this technology is not designed to replace oil, merely to eke it out. And it's only catching on because the world is awash with hippies who really do think that by driving around in a Prius they're saving the world's water beetles. Think of hybrids as council-run bottle banks: almost completely useless marketing tools designed to make you feel all warm and fuzzy about being green.

More realistically, the future will bring extraordinary advances in efficiency. I remember, in the mid-1980s, Daihatsu shocked the world by producing an engine that could produce 100 bhp per litre. But soon you can reckon on being given 150 bhp per litre and more. Already Volkswagen has a 1.4-litre motor that uses turbocharging, supercharging and direct injection to produce 167 bhp. That's way, way more eYcient than any complex triple-engined hybrid.

Ultimately it's possible we'll all be driving cars powered by hydrogen. Maybe it will be burned internally, as a substitute for petrol, or maybe it will be used in a fuel cell to generate electricity that's then used to provide power. Either way the only emissions are heat and water. That keeps the hippies happy and it should keep normal people happy, too, because there's a limitless supply of hydrogen. Britain, we're told, would only need four nuclear power plants to keep every car, van and truck in the land going.

Don't hold your breath, though. We're a fair way off this clean dream becoming reality. It'll be a technology familiar only to our children. And that's the beauty, because who knows what might happen between now and then. Maybe some extraordinary new science will be discovered, or perhaps limitless power will be found on Mars. We can predict only that something will replace oil, in the same way that something replaced stone.

And we could leave it at that. But no. The world's motor industry, in a desperate bid to sound caring and kind, says that soon your car will be directed to a parking space by satellite spies in the sky, it will park itself and it will be safe if you have a crash. With nothing but water coming out of the exhaust you'll be able to run down as many pedestrians as take your fancy on the way to work, safe in the knowledge that neither they, nor you, nor the planet will be hurt in any way.

And then, when the car has reached the end of its life – currently that's after an average of 14 years – it will be melted down and turned into a water sprinkler for what, in the past, had been the developing world. Think about that. Lots of smiling Ethiopians sitting in their gardens, watching your old Range Rover water their lawns.

The world's motor mandarins paint a picture of a world with no war, no poverty and no pollution. It'll be a world where George Monbiot sits every week staring at his computer wondering what on earth to worry about. Transport 2000, the eco-pressure group, will be gone. And every Sunday night *Top Gear* will smile its way through yet another review of yet another completely safe, completely slow, completely dull p.o.s. Oh yeah? Well, if that's the case, why are we in the middle of a power battle not seen since the Second World War. Mercedes and BMW are making bigger, heavier and increasingly powerful cars that can't park themselves, can't crash without injuring everyone within six miles, and produce enough carbon dioxide to fry a whole flock of great crested grebes.

Then there's Volkswagen, crowing about its 1.4-litre engine that produces 167 bhp. But not half as loudly as it crows about its Bentley Flying Spur, the fastest four-door saloon in the world, and the new Bugatti Veyron, which churns out 1,000 bhp.

These motor industry guys are like errant husbands, whispering sweet nothings to their wives about love and affection while pouring half a gallon of baby oil over their lover's breasts. What you see is not what you get. But then again, what you get isn't half brilliant.

And that brings me neatly on to the new Volkswagen Golf. Think about what that name means. A car for everyone, a sensible, safe, practical tool in which people and luggage can be transported reliably, efficiently and as cheaply as technically possible. The Golf, remember, was the successor to the Beetle.

Yes, so why's the new model got a 250-bhp narrow-angle V6 engine? Why does it go from 0 to 62 mph in 6.5 seconds? Why, if VW is so bothered about the world, does it keep on going all the way to 155 mph? Why? Because it's great, that's why.

No, really, this is a fabulous car. Apart from a bit of jewellery at the front and some blue brake callipers it looks like a normal Golf. You really have to stare at it for quite some time to notice it's riding a little lower than usual and that the tyres are suspiciously wide.

It's much the same story on the inside. The chunky, flat-bottomed steering wheel hints at something that really doesn't seem to be there. It just feels Golf-ish. And it keeps on feeling Golf-ish when you turn the key and set off. The ride is comfortable, there's no unnecessary noise and everyone has lots of space. A lot more than they'd get in, say, a BMW 1-series.

Then you put your foot down and suddenly the world starts to go backwards. Not harshly or sportily. It's not like the GTI, this. It's a big, refined power, more like gravity than internal combustion, so you feel like you're in a Mercedes. Only I'd like to bet the VW is better made.

And cheaper. Prices for a three-door start at less than £24,000, which is exceptional value for money, and even if you go for a five-door with a double-clutch DSG flappy paddle gearbox (which is what I'd do) you're still asked to pay less than £26,000. And that's a lot of car for the money. It's more than that in fact. It's every car you could ever reasonably need. Fast, well made, practical, surprisingly economical and above all discreet. Nobody's ever going to mistake you for a footballer, that's for sure.

We don't know what the future holds, so we can't plan for it. We only know what's in the here and now, and this Golf R32 is as good as it gets. Which is why I'm giving it the rare accolade of a *Sunday Times* five-star rating.

Sunday 20 November 2005

Bugatti Veyron

When you push a car past 180 mph, the world starts to get awfully fizzy and a little bit frightening. When you go past 200 mph it actually becomes blurred. Almost like you're trapped in an early Queen pop video. At this sort of speed the tyres and the suspension are reacting to events that happened some time ago, and they have not finished reacting before they're being asked to do something else. The result is a terrifying vibration that rattles your optical nerves, causing double vision. This is not good when you're covering 300 feet a second.

Happily, stopping distances become irrelevant because you won't see the obstacle in the first place. By the time you know it was there, you'll have gone through the windscreen, through the Pearly Gates and be halfway across God's breakfast table.

It has always been thus. When Louis Rigolly broke the 100 mph barrier in his Gobron in 1904, the vibration would have been terrifying. And I dare say that driving an E-type at 150 mph in 1966 must have been a bit sporty as well.

But once you go past 200 mph it isn't just the suspension and the tyres you have to worry about. The biggest problem is the air. At 100 mph it's relaxed. At 150 mph it's a breeze. But at 200 mph it has sufficient power to lift an

800,000-lb jumbo jet off the ground. A 200 mph gust of wind is strong enough to knock down an entire city. So getting a car to behave itself in conditions like these is tough.

At 200 mph you can feel the front of the car getting light as it starts to lift. As a result you start to lose your steering, so you aren't even able to steer round whatever it is you can't see because of the vibrations. Make no mistake, 200 mph is at the limit of what man can do right now. Which is why the new Bugatti Veyron is worthy of some industrial-strength genuflection. Because it can do 252 mph. And that's just mad – 252 mph means that in straight and level flight this car is as near as makes no difference as fast as a Hawker Hurricane.

You might point out at this juncture that the McLaren F1 could top 240 mph, but at that speed it was pretty much out of control. And anyway it really isn't in the same league as the Bugatti. In a drag race you could let the McLaren get to 120 mph before setting off in the Veyron. And you'd still get to 200 mph first. The Bugatti is way, way faster than anything else the roads have seen.

Of course, at £810,000, it is also jolly expensive, but when you look at the history of its development you'll discover it's rather more than just a car . . .

It all started when Ferdinand Piëch, the swivel-eyed former boss of Volkswagen, bought Bugatti and had someone design a concept car. 'This,' he said, 'is what the next Bugatti will look like.' And then, without consulting anyone, he went on, 'And it vill have an engine that develops 1,000 horsepower and it vill be capable of 400 kph.'

His engineers were horrified. But they set to work anyway, mating two Audi V8s to create an 8-litre W16. Which was then garnished with four turbochargers. Needless to say, the end result produced about as much power as the earth's core, which is fine. But somehow the giant had to be cooled, which is why the Veyron has no engine cover and why it has 10 – count them – 10 radiators. Then things got tricky because the power had to be harnessed.

For this, VW went to Ricardo, a British company that makes gearboxes for various Formula 1 teams.

'God, it was hard,' said one of the engineers I know vaguely. 'The gearbox in an F1 car only has to last a few hours. Volkswagen wanted the Veyron's to last 10 or 20 years. And remember, the Bugatti is a damn sight more powerful than any F1 car.'

The result, a seven-speed double-clutch flappy paddle affair, took a team of 50 engineers five years to perfect.

With this done, the Veyron was shipped to Sauber's F1 wind tunnel, where it quickly became apparent that while the magic 1,000 bhp figure had been achieved, they were miles off the target top speed of 400 kph (248 mph). The body of the car just wasn't aerodynamic enough, and Volkswagen wouldn't let them change the basic shape to get round the problem.

The bods at Sauber threw up their hands, saying they only had experience of aerodynamics up to maybe 360 kph, which is the effective top speed in Formula 1. Beyond this point Bugatti was on its own.

Somehow they had to find an extra 30 kph, and there

was no point in looking to the engine for answers because each extra 1-kph increase in speed requires an extra 8 bhp from the power plant. An extra 30 kph then would need an extra 240 bhp. That was not possible.

The extra speed had to come from changing small things on the body. They started by fitting smaller door mirrors, which upped the top speed a bit but at too high a price. It turned out that the bigger ones had been keeping the nose of the car on the ground. Without them the stability was gone.

In other words, the door mirrors were generating down-force. That gives you an idea of how much of a bastard the air can be at this speed.

After some public failures, fires and accidents, and one chief being fired, they hit on the idea of a car that auto-matically changes shape, depending on what speed you're going.

At 137 mph, the nose of the car is lowered by 2 inches and the big rear spoiler slides into the slipstream. The effect is profound. You can feel the back of the car being pressed into the road.

However, with the spoiler in place, the drag is so great you're limited to just 231 mph. To go faster than that you have to stop and insert your ignition key in a slot on the floor. This lowers the whole car still further and locks the big back wing down. Now you have reduced downforce, which means you won't be going round any corners, but you have a clean shape. And that means you can top 400 kph.

That's 370 feet a second.

You might want to ponder that for a moment. Covering the length of a football pitch, in a second, in a car. And then you might want to think about the braking system. A VW Polo will generate 0.6 G if you stamp on the middle pedal hard. You get that from the air brake alone on a Veyron. Factor in the carbon ceramic discs, and you will pull up from 250 mph in just 10 seconds. Sounds good, but in those 10 seconds you'll have covered a third of a mile. That's five football pitches to stop.

I didn't care. On a recent drive across Europe I desperately wanted to reach the top speed, but I ran out of road when the needle hit 240 mph. Where, astonishingly, it felt planted. Totally and utterly rock steady. It felt sublime.

Not quiet, though. The engine sounds like Victorian plumbing – it looks like Victorian plumbing as well, to be honest – and the roar from the tyres was biblical. But it still felt brilliant. Utterly, stunningly, mind-blowingly, jaw-droppingly brilliant.

And then I reached the Alps, where, unbelievably, it got better. I expected this road rocket to be absolutely useless in the bends, but it felt like a big Lotus Elise.

Occasionally, if I accelerated hard in a tight corner, it behaved strangely as the four-wheel-drive system decided which axle would be best equipped to deal with the wave of power. I won't say it's a nasty feel or dangerous. Just weird, in the same way that the duck-billed platypus is weird.

You learn to raise an eyebrow at what's only a foible, and then, as the road straightens out, steady yourself for Prince Albert's boiler to gird its loins and play havoc with the space–time continuum. No, really, you come round a bend, see what appears to be miles and miles of dead straight road, bury your foot in the carpet and, with a big asthmatic wheeze, bang, you're instantly at the next bend, with your eyebrow raised again.

From behind the wheel of a Veyron, France is the size of a small coconut. I cannot tell you how fast I crossed it the other day. Because you simply wouldn't believe me. I also cannot tell you how good this car is. I just don't have the vocabulary. I just end up stammering and dribbling and talking wide-eyed nonsense. And everyone thinks I'm on drugs.

This car cannot be judged in the same way that we judge other cars. It meets drive-by noise and emission regulations and it can be driven by someone whose only qualification is an ability to reverse round corners and do an emergency stop. So technically it is a car. And yet it just isn't.

Other cars are small guesthouses on the front at Brighton and the Bugatti is the Burj Al Arab. It makes even the Enzo and the Porsche GT feel slow and pointless. It is a triumph for lunacy over common sense, a triumph for man over nature and a triumph for Volkswagen over absolutely every other car maker in the world.

Sunday 27 November 2005

Mini Cooper S Convertible

Sir Ian Blair, the preposterous London police chief, said recently that the newspapers whipped up far too much of a hullabaloo about the murder of Soham schoolgirls Jessica Chapman and Holly Wells. And that nowhere near as much coverage is given when some poor black kid is killed. Obviously the case of 10-year-old Damilola Taylor must have slipped his mind. And Stephen Lawrence, for that matter.

Anyway, the ginger idiot announced the very next day that the best thing he can do to bring peace and tranquillity to the streets of the nation is barge into middle-class executive homes and bust everyone for taking cocaine. For their own good? I should cocoa. According to Blair, it's for the good of people in the 'developing world', who somehow have their legs blown off every time someone in Chelsea buys a gram.

The message here is simple. Sir Ian is prepared to ignore the Turkish heroin smugglers and Albanian people traffickers in his quest to rid the capital of hideous middle-class white people. He hates their children, their institutionalised racism, their la-di-da accents, their private schools and their weekend cottages, and if they're going to liven up a Saturday night with some marching powder he'll be on hand to make sure their Volvos are confiscated.

Unfortunately, if you're middle class you may as well take cocaine and spend Saturday night talking to yourself because there's bugger all else to do. You can't go into town because it's been overrun with drunks and all the police are too busy filling in hazard assessment forms to do anything about it. And you can't stay at home because there's nothing you want to watch on the box.

This is because the Islingtonites who run television these days don't really like the middle classes either. I was told the other day by a senior bod in the industry not to use the phrase 'dinner party' on *Top Gear* because it's 'elitist'. For the same reason I was told by a director last month it'd be best if I didn't mention my children's nanny. I gave him one of my special hard stares.

Interestingly, however, whenever a middle-class programme is shown on television, and I'm thinking here of *Have I Got News for You*, or *Who Do You Think You Are?*, the viewing figures shoot through the roof. And everyone in the TV business calls hurried meetings so they can work out why.

'We put out a programme last week about a disabled Somali woman whose benefit cheques have been stopped and no one watched that. So why did 5 million tune in to see Stephen Fry wandering around some sugar beet fields in Suffolk?' I wonder. Could it have something to do with the 40 million middle-class people in Britain who are so starved of entertainment they'll tune in to anything with proper vowel sounds? No, really. How well do you think *What Not to Wear* would have gone down if it had been presented by two fat slappers for whom the letter 'h' was as difficult to master as that clicking sound made by African bushmen? No one likes a thicko to sit in the corner of their front room, which is why the people who do well in that celebrity jungle thing are usually well-spoken and bright. Tara P-T. Tony Blackburn. And, of course, Carol Thatcher. Then there was Jack Dee, who won the first *Celebrity Big Brother*, a result that plainly alarmed the producers so much they subsequently ensured that all future contestants aren't even middlebrow, leave alone middle class. The last lot, so far as I can tell, were essentially zoo animals.

And who can forget the moment when Judith Keppel, the woman from Fulham, was first to scoop a million out of Chris Tarrant's pocket. You could almost hear the Blair brothers screaming: 'Aaaargh. Why couldn't it have been someone with one leg from the Taliban?' There's a quiet war being waged against the middle classes. All this talk, for instance, about what might be done to stop people buying second homes in the country: you think that's because of the locals being priced out of the market? Really? So how come no one's bothered about kids in the inner city who can't afford to get on the property ladder either? No, I'm afraid second homes are under attack for the same reason they decided to save the fox. It's payback for Judith Keppel. And Arthur Scargill.

You may think the reason people spit at 4 × 4s these days has something to do with Greenland's blanket of ice. It isn't. It's because you're well-off. And that's not allowed.

So, what's to be done if you want a nice car but don't want to drive through a blizzard of phlegm every time you go to the shops? Well, obviously you could buy a van, or a Hyundai, but what we're really after here is a cheap car that doesn't feel it. And that leaves us with a choice of one. The Mini.

The lovely thing about the new Mini is the very same lovely thing about the old Mini. When one goes by you have no idea what sort of person is at the wheel. It is hard to think of any product that is quite so classless. Branston Pickle, maybe, but that's about it.

So what about the convertible version? Well, even though it's been around for 18 months I've never driven one. However, having written about the new Mazda MX-5 last week I thought I'd give it a go.

You see, the Mazda was wonderful: a proper, charming and fun little sports car, but that in itself creates problems. Because it also sounds and feels like a sports car when you're on the motorway, and it's a Tuesday, and it's a bit cold, and you just want to get home. That's not a criticism so much as an observation. But it is the reason I thought I'd try the drop-head Mini – to see whether it's a sports car without the sports car drawbacks.

Don't laugh. Beneath the veneer of cool-this and brushed-aluminium-that the hardtop Mini has a properly good little chassis. The steering, the turn-in and what happens when you exceed the available grip are all excellent. And it's the same story with the ragtop. Yes, there's a whiff of dreaded scuttle shake, that awful sense the front and the back are connected with nothing more than spit and Kleenex, but for the most part this is a little car that laps up the bends and snorts rortily on to the straights.

Sure, unlike the Mazda it doesn't have rear-wheel drive, and it's a bit of a fatty, so the straightforward 1.6-litre engine struggles a bit, but here's the good part. When it's cold and wet and you just want to listen to the radio it's fairly quiet and comfortable. Providing you don't spec it up with the big wheels.

What we have here, then, is a fun, comfortable and, providing you don't spec it up with anything at all, extremely well-priced car that's so classless it could drive through Ian Blair's legs and he wouldn't even notice.

There are, however, two things that you really ought to consider. First of all, while it bills itself as a four-seater, there is no legroom in the back at all. And the boot is barely big enough for the gram of coke you can't buy any more. But the worst thing is the rear visibility.

Of course, this is always an issue in a softtop car – even the Mazda isn't all that easy to see out of – but driving the Mini is like driving with a box on your head. For parking you need to use the force. And when pulling out of oblique junctions, might I suggest you get rubbing those rosaries.

I certainly don't recommend having a bump of any kind, either, because if the police come and find you to be in possession of the 'h' sound, and a Harvey Nicks credit card, you'll be playing hunt the soap in Strangeways from now till the end of time.

Sunday 12 February 2006

Volkswagen Jetta

At my old school, detention usually involved being asked to write a 1,000-word essay about the inside of a ping pong ball. So I'm well qualified to write about the new Volkswagen Jetta. Because I spent every Saturday afternoon for five years writing about the precise chemical breakdown of air, it's a breeze to fill these pages with prose about what is unquestionably the most boring car in the whole of human history.

Even James May, my colleague from *Top Gear*, agrees. I spoke to him yesterday. 'I'm driving the most boring car in the world,' I said, and though he's known as Captain Slow and practises the art of what he calls Christian motoring, he said: 'Oh, you must have a Jetta then.' I wouldn't mind if it were awful or ugly or spontaneously combusted every time there was a day in the week. That at least would make it characterful and interesting. But it does none of these things. It does nothing.

I can't abide bores. There's a man I meet every week – I shan't say where in case he's reading this – and never, not once, in four years has he been able to make a single story interesting. Even if he'd just been mugged by a gang of Terminators or gang raped by a rampaging swarm of goblins he'd still fail to bring the tale alive. And pretty soon you'd be wishing you were a horse; so you could fall asleep standing up.

Unfortunately, he never has been raped by goblins or beaten up by Terminators. All that happened in his life last week was a new delivery of paperclips. And staggeringly, he believed that this was interesting enough to bring up in conversation. Honestly, after a few minutes I gave serious thought to stabbing him in the heart.

I believe that the greatest gift bestowed on a human being is not beauty, intelligence or wealth. It's the ability to make a story live. To take a tale and know instinctively what to leave in, what to leave out and when to lie a bit. If you do not have this, then you should learn to shut up.

Of course, it helps if you do actually lead an interesting life. I mean, if Ranulph Fiennes had been an office boy or an IT consultant he probably wouldn't be much fun down the pub. But when he tells you about sawing off his own fingers using a garden-shed fretsaw – well, it's kind of hard to mess that up.

I have such a pathological loathing of bores that, and I mean this, I'd rather have dinner with Myra Hindley than dinner with a dullard. I'd rather spend time with Richard Brunstrom, the mad mullah of the traffic Taliban who runs the North Wales police, than spend time with someone from the Aston Martin owners' club.

Once, when I was working on a local newspaper, I came home at night and told my girlfriend that we'd had some new office furniture delivered to the office. Moments later, when I realised what I'd said, and how deeply uninteresting this was, I left her and the job and moved to London.

Now I have children and I'm forever to be found in the kitchen telling them that if the story they've embarked on has no point then they shouldn't have begun. Simply reeling off the lessons they've had at school that day is just not good enough, not unless it's an anecdotal device, some kind of calm before the climax in double Latin when the teacher exploded.

I can't be bored. I have no ability to deal with it. That's why I can't do church sermons, or *Big Brother*. It's why I was so irritated by the game of squash in Ian McEwan's *Saturday* and why I won't go to America any more. Those two-hour queues for immigration are just killers.

It's also why I'm fidgety and distracted today. Because I came to London yesterday in the Volkswagen Jetta, and tomorrow I must go home in it. Which will be like spending an hour in a coma.

I'd love to meet the man who styled the exterior, to find out if he'd done it as some sort of a joke. But mostly I'd like to meet the man who simply didn't bother at all with the interior. Because looking at that dashboard gives you some idea of what it might be like to be dead.

It's black. And so are the buttons, and so are the dials, and so are the carpets and so are the seats. To give you some idea of how dull and featureless life is in there, put a cardboard box over your head. And leave it there for 10 years.

Then there's the engine. This is the 2-litre direct-injection jobbie you find in various other VWs and Audis and it's normally not bad. But like a bloke who could make a UFO encounter seem boring, the Jetta seems to suck all the life out of it.

It's the same story with the ride and handling. It's really not bad at all. But it's hard to spot this when you are stuck in that vegetative no-man's-land with a face that's so numb you don't even know you're dribbling.

And now we arrive at the boot lid, which is supposed to boing up when you press a button on the key. But it can't be bothered. It springs from the traps, rises about a foot and then just gives up.

There's a similar lack of enthusiasm from the satellite navigation system. Every request is met with a shoulder-sagging teenage harrumph. Perhaps this is because the car's made in Mexico: so it just wants to sit under a tree all day dozing.

Volkswagen itself was plainly bored to tears when trying to think of things to say about the car. So what you get in the press blurb is chapter and verse on the windscreen wipers, which apparently perform a number of tasks. Further investigation reveals these tasks to be (1) sitting still and (2) moving hither and thither clearing raindrops.

What I'm most interested in is why on earth this car was made in the first place, because it's actually a Golf with a boot. Or to put it another way, a Golf that's a bit uglier, a bit heavier, a bit slower, a bit less practical, a bit less economical and a lot more boring to drive. To mis-quote Mark Twain, then, it's a good Golf ruined.

And yet the model I drove cost £18,500. And to that you must add another £1,200 for an automatic gearbox and £1,675 if you want leather upholstery instead of the Pleblon that comes as standard. I'd also go for the £13.99 'life hammer', which is designed to be used to break the windows after an accident. But it could also be used by a passenger to hit you on the head when you start dribbling. Or as a tunnelling tool, like the rock hammer in *The Shawshank Redemption*.

Because, believe me, being trapped inside a Jetta is just like being trapped in a 1930s jail. You really would want to escape, whatever the cost.

Anyway, my point is that the Jetta is a £21,000 car. So why not buy a bigger, better and (marginally) more interesting Passat instead?

Or why not save a few bob and buy a vastly superior Golf GTI? Or why not buy 2.1 million penny chews? What really pisses me off about the Jetta is that Volkswagen is a company that makes the Bentley Continental and the Lamborghini Gallardo. It has the flair and the panache to make the Bugatti Veyron, and we know it can make a Golf saloon interesting because they've proved it with various Seats and Skodas.

But what they've come up with here is an automotive Belgium, Tim Henman with wheels. The inside of a ping pong ball. I therefore cannot recommend it to you in any way.

Sunday 19 February 2006

Jaguar XK Convertible

I was bored. I'd eaten everything in the fridge, learned to play the piano and beaten myself at chess. And then someone from Jaguar rang to see if I wanted to go to South Africa for the weekend. Damn right I did. Getting there is very easy – you go on a plane – but working out what to expect when you arrive is rather more tricky. On the one hand you think you'll spot Peter Gabriel with a bone in his nose, chanting. Or maybe Charlie Dimmock bouncing up and down in Nelson Mandela's rose beds. But on the other hand you suspect you may be hacked to pieces by a machete-wielding mob.

You certainly don't go to South Africa for the viniculture. We stayed at a vineyard and on one evening they took us to the cellar, which was full of huge steel vats and pressure gauges. It was like being in a nuclear power station.

And what did the finished product taste like? Well, pretty much like the stuff that comes from the outlet pipe at Sellafield. I doubt the French would put it in their windscreen washer bottles.

So what about ebony and ivory getting along in perfect harmony? Yes, apartheid is over but all the black people seem to have got now is the vote, and a carrier bag each. I'm not kidding. Even if you go far out into the blazing heat of the hinterland, you will find the roadside littered with people who are just sitting there, with a plastic bag, doing nothing.

Occasionally one will stick out his thumb so you can give him a lift to a new bit of roadside where he can sit with his bag, doing nothing. But the back seats in the Jag were too small so I'm afraid I just cruised on by.

I don't think I've been anywhere where the rich, behind their razor wire and automated sprinkler-fed lawns, live quite so close, and yet quite so far away, from the poor and their plastic bags. I don't think a *Guardian* reader could cope.

Frankly, though, I had more important things on my mind. For 30 years I've toured the globe looking for the same light that we saw in *Butch Cassidy and the Sundance Kid*, when Paul Newman takes Katharine Ross for a spin on his new bicycle. You know what I'm talking about: that dandelion-flecked morning promise of warm summer breezes to come. Well, it's there, in South Africa.

And Christ almighty, it gives good mountain. It's a bit like Greece, and Yorkshire and northern California. But of course it's not, because the clouds are pure Wilbur Smith; they could only be African. And then you have the Lowry trees, with their Lionel Richie hairdos. You don't find those anywhere else either.

Then you spot where the post-sanctions money was spent. On the roads. They're amazing.

Now they've worked out that tyres go on cars, rather than round one another's necks, they've created one of the best driving countries anywhere on earth.

Eventually I got to Cape Town and oooh, what a place. It's often said that London, New York and Rome are the world's three great cities but none has much of a back-drop. That's why I prefer Hong Kong, Wellington and Reykjavik. You have the restaurants and the shops and the bars. And all the time you can admire God's axe work in the background.

In many ways Cape Town is like Sydney or Vancouver. It has a Britishness to the architecture and there's a sort of touristed-up dock area where you can pay too much for stuff you don't need. But in Cape Town you have Table Mountain just there, right at the end of your nose.

This – and I'll take no argument, thanks – is one of the world's great cities. And South Africa, despite the hilarious attempts to make wine, is one of the world's great countries. I loved it.

Jaguar had made the most of the three-day trip, too, providing helicopters to take us into the mountains and ribs to take us round the coast. They provided choirs every time there was an embarrassing silence and at night they provided telescopes so we could look at Saturn.

They'd also provided 16 chauffeur-driven long-wheelbase XJs to ferry us around when we were drunk. And 45 XKs for when we weren't. Although by the time I got there 700 journalists from around the world had been through the programme, so there were only 39 left.

So, what's the XK like? Well, if you go faster than 130 mph I can report that the front end starts to get a bit light. You lose some of the 'feel' from the wheel. And this, in one of the strangest games of consequences ever, is because of the need to provide a decent-sized boot.

Here's why. EU rules say that the compulsory high-level centre brake light has to be mounted within a certain distance of the rear window. And because the rear window on the XK convertible is small, so it'll fit in the boot without taking up too much space, the only place to fit the brake light is on top of a big rear spoiler. And because it's so big, the front of the car starts to 'lift' at speed.

Of course, you wouldn't expect there to be a similar problem in the coupé, which has a big rear window, but this is Jaguar, a small company that's been losing money hand over fist in recent years. So thanks to a need to economise, both models get the same spoiler. So both have the same high-speed handling issue.

You see a similar thing going on with the aerial. Most cars these days have one inside the front windscreen, hidden away. But because the Jag has a heated front windscreen, and the heater elements mess with the reception, it comes with exactly the same sort of electric antenna you used to fit as an after-market accessory to your 1976 Ford Cortina.

And to think this car is made in the same factory that used to churn out Second World War Spitfires. Though, of course, back then British ingenuity wasn't at the mercy of American next-quarter accounting.

Because of these two little things the Jaguar is not a car from which you walk away saying, 'I have got to have one even if it means cutting out my own tongue.' It's not a car that stirs the soul and breaks your heart. Instead it's a car you'll decide to buy after a logical process of elimination.

Yes, a 6-series BMW is faster, but come on. This is not a car that stirs your soul either; just your stomach. It's hideous. And with that silly iDrive malarkey it's also far too complicated.

So what about the Mercedes SL? Well, unless you can have the AMG growler, the answer's no. It's just a bit too boring.

The Jag, on the other hand, isn't. It is pant-wettingly pretty and it makes just the most visceral, animal snarl when you boot it. On the move this turns into a muted version of the noise you got from 1970s American muscle cars. You'll adore it.

You will also adore the simplicity of the undersides. It rides on proper suspension, not some oleohydryopneumatic nonsense, the controls work brilliantly, and while the back seats aren't big enough for hitchhikers, or even their carrier bags, the front is spacious and wonderful.

There's only one small thing. The Aston Martin V8 Vantage. This comes from the same company, Ford, was designed in essence by the same man and has basically the same engine. But it sounds even better and is even prettier to behold. So, would you always think, if you had the Jag, that you'd bought second best? Honest answer? Yes. But there is another way of looking at it. Aston Martin has a properly crap reliability record, whereas the latest figures put Jag ahead of every other car maker in the world except Lexus. So what you have with the XK is a reliable way of enjoying at least some of the Aston magic.

It's like Cape Town, then. You have a taste of Africa without the malaria, the flies in your eyes or having your genitals cut off by angry locals. Yes, the wine's rubbish, but like the aerial and that high-speed lift it's a small price to pay.

Sunday 5 March 2006

Alfa Romeo 159

How many actors are there in the world? I'm counting everyone, from the 'boy' in an amateur dramatic society's performance of *The Winslow Boy*, to the Latvian teenager who appears only on webcams, covered in baby oil.

I'm counting people in Bollywood, people in French art house films, people at provincial Brazilian drama colleges. And if you do that, the number must be into the millions. Some of them must be very good. It stands to reason. But they'll never make it. The hand of fate will continue to deal them low diamonds and mid-range clubs until eventually they wind up teaching Stanislavski to self-harming inmates at Pentonville. Even those who make it to the top struggle to become Tom Cruise. The big-name star. The guarantee of bums on seats.

Take Christopher Walken as a prime example. He's big, all right. He could get a table at the Ivy any time he wanted. And he's also fabulously watchable. That gold watch scene in *Pulp Fiction* was, I think, the finest performance from any big screen actor since . . . well, ever.

But he still couldn't fill a theatre. I mean, since *Pulp Fiction* he's appeared in *Kangaroo Jack*, *Engine Trouble*, *The Country Bears*, *Poolhall Junkies*, *The Affair of the Necklace*, *Joe Dirt*, *Jungle Juice*, *The Opportunists*, *Kiss Toledo Goodbye*, *Mousehunt* and countless other movies that I can pretty much guarantee you haven't seen. Since *Top Gun*, how-ever, there isn't a single Tom Cruise film I've missed. In fact there isn't a single Tom Cruise film I don't own on DVD. Of course, Tom's a fine actor. His performance alongside Dustin Hoffman's twitchery in *Rain Man* was especially memorable. But is he better than Walken?

So it goes with all things, especially cars. Last week, after a hard day's filming, I drove home in a new 3-series BMW. The Tom Cruise of motoring. The machine you would automatically choose if you wanted a well-made, reasonably sporty four-door saloon. And it was fine. But the next day an Alfa Romeo 159 arrived at my house. Now, this is a car you would automatically not choose if you wanted a well-made, reasonably sporty four-door saloon. This is Christopher Walken.

Actually, that's one of my less risible metaphors. Because in its long history of making cars, Alfa only rarely produces a *Deer Hunter* or a gold watch scene in *Pulp Fiction*. The vast majority of its offerings are complicated, silly and badly made. And as a result most go straight to the discount DVD bin at Blockbuster.

The thing is, though, with the exception of the simply appalling Arna, I've loved all Alfas. In fact I've argued time and again that nobody can be a petrolhead until they've owned one. It's a rite of passage. Think of it as the great sex that leaves you with an embarrassing itch.

Take the old GTV6 as a prime example. I owned one once and it was a nightmare. The worst car I've owned. Deeply uncomfortable, spectacularly impractical and blessed with steering so heavy that navigating into a

London parking space was like navigating a donkey into
a budgie cage.

Then there was the complete lack of quality. Nothing
worked. And when you got one thing fixed something
else would break on the way home. Once it tried to
murder me. The linkage from the gear lever to the rear-
mounted gearbox fell off and jammed the prop shaft,
causing a sound not heard on earth since Krakatoa blew
up, and the rear wheels to lock.

But behind the oyster-like impregnability of its ergo-
nomics and hidden in the sea of snot were two perfect
pearls. The styling. And the howl from its V6 engine. In
a tunnel, at 4,000 rpm, it was more sonorous than any
music. It was like having your soul licked by angels.

In essence, then, Alfa has always understood what
makes driving a thrill. But it has never been able to make
a car. Well, not a car that a rational, normal human being
might want to buy.

Think of them as underground German art films. Great
for serious-minded critics but not quite in the same
everyman league as BMWillis on an asteroid.

At first I thought the 159 would be more of the same.
The boot release button is in the roof, just where you
wouldn't expect it to be, the electric windows have a
mind of their own, and like the Fiat Grande Punto I
reviewed last week, it couldn't find or hold Radio 2. It
could pick up pigs squeaking on Io, and Radio Leicester.
But not Johnnie Walker.

These, however, are trivial faults. No more annoying
in the big scheme of things than the iDrive in a BMW

or the harsh ride you get on an Audi. Unlike Alfas of old you have to look long and hard in a 159 to find something deeply disturbing. But I found it all right.

The greatest sensation of speed afforded to ordinary man is not on a go-kart or a rollercoaster. It comes when you've got the cruise control set at 70 mph, the traffic in front is stopping and momentarily you can't find the button to turn it off. In that hiccup of time it doesn't feel like you're doing 70 mph. It feels like you're doing three times the speed of light.

That's why, in most cars, the cruise control 'off' button is clearly visible and easy to use in a hurry. Not in the Alfa it isn't. It looks like one of the pieces from a game of Risk and it's mounted on a stalk just below and slightly behind the indicator.

So when the traffic ground to a halt on the M40 I bet the chap behind me was keen to know why I didn't slow at all and then, for no obvious reason, suddenly indicated left. This, then, is proper swivel-eyed Alfa lunacy but it is the only thing in the car that's truly wrong and there's a simple way round the problem. Ignore it. Pretend it isn't there.

But do not pretend the 159 isn't there next time you want a mid-range four-door saloon because that would be a mistake. A bad one. First of all, it is exactly one million times better-looking than a BMW 3-series. And with those triple headlamps, and perfect proportions, at least half a million times better-looking than any rivals from Audi, Mercedes or Jaguar.

Inside, it's even better. The driving position is spot on,

the dials look like they've come from a Swiss watch and the quality of the leather, especially if you have it in red, gives the impression that it costs Rolls-Royce money.

But it doesn't. A 159 Lusso, which is the luxury version, is £22,395. That's about what BMW charges for a 320i SE, but Alfa gives you far more equipment as standard and lots more power as well. The 2.2-litre engine is a peach that just begs to be taken outside and given a damn good thrashing. Porsche engineered an exhaust rasp into the Boxster at 5,000 rpm to reward the sporty driver. Alfa hasn't bothered. It just gives you a simple four-cylinder engine that, all on its own, sounds better and better until you're up at 6,500, when it sounds like a metallic werewolf.

You can pootle around slowly but somehow you tend to drive the 159 very hard and very fast. But the engine, torquey, powerful and smooth though it may be, is not the best part of this car. That accolade goes to the steering. It's fast, sharp, more informative than the internet and more tactile than a freshly carved stone otter.

The handling is also sweet and yet the ride isn't even slightly uncomfortable. Which means that the 159 drives and feels like no other car in its class. If you have even the faintest trace of petrol in your veins, if you are even on nodding terms with the concept of simple, good engineering, you should drive this car. Because it doesn't matter what you have now, you'll be smitten. I was.

This is one of those cars that's demonstrably and appreciably better than any other mid-range four-door family saloon. And unlike any Alfa of the past, you don't have to machete your way through a million inconveniences to find the point. This car does not hide its gold watch up its behind. It is an absolute gem.

Sunday 26 March 2006

JEREMY CLARKSON

THE WORLD ACCORDING TO CLARKSON

Jeremy Clarkson has seen rather more of the world than most. He has, as they say, been around a bit. And as a result, he's got one or two things to tell us about how it all works – and being Jeremy Clarkson he's not about to voice them quietly, humbly and without great dollops of humour.

With a strong dose of common sense that is rarely, if ever, found inside the M25, Clarkson hilariously attacks the pompous, the ridiculous, the absurd and the downright idiotic ideas, people and institutions that we all have to put up with at home and abroad, whilst also celebrating the eccentric, the clever and the sheer bloody brilliant.

'Hilarious ... it'll make you appreciate the ludicrousness of modern life and have you in stitches' *Sun*

JEREMY CLARKSON

I KNOW YOU GOT SOUL

Some machines have it and others don't: Soul. They take your breath away, and your heart beats a little faster just knowing that they exist. They may not be the fastest, most efficient, even the best in their class – but they were designed and built by people who loved them, and we can't help but love them back.

For instance,

Zeppelin airships, whilst disastrously explosive in almost every case, were elegant and beautiful bubbles in the air.

The battleships were some of the least effective weapons of war ever built, but made the people who paid for them feel good.

Despite two tragic crashes, the *Space Shuttle* still leaves you with a rocket in your pocket.

Some might dismiss this list as simply being for boys and their toys, but, as Jeremy Clarkson shows, that is to miss the point of what makes the sweep of the Hoover Dam sexier than a supermodel's curves; why the *Princess* flying boat could give white elephants a good name; and why the *Flying Scotsman* beats the Bullet Train every time.

In *I Know You Got Soul*, Jeremy Clarkson celebrates, in his own inimitable style, the machines that matter to us, and tells the stories of the geniuses, boffins and crackpots who put the ghost in the machine.

JEREMY CLARKSON

MOTORWORLD

There are ways and means of getting about that don't involve four wheels, but in this book Jeremy Clarkson isn't interested in them.

Taking himself to twelve countries (okay, eleven – he goes to America twice), Clarkson delves deeply into the hows, whys and wherefores of different nationalities and their relationship to cars.

For instance, why is that Italians are more interested in looking good than looking where they are going? Why do Indians crash a lot? How can an Arab describe himself as 'not a rich man' with four of the world's most expensive cars in his drive? And why have the otherwise neutral Swiss declared war on the car?

From Cuba to Iceland, Australia to Vietnam, Japan to Texas, Jeremy Clarkson tells us of his adventures on and off four wheels as he seeks to discover just what it is that makes our motorworld tick over.

Jeremy Clarkson

CLARKSON ON CARS

Jeremy Clarkson is the second best motoring writer in Britain. For twenty years he's been driving cars, writing about them and occasionally voicing his opinions on *Top Gear*.

No one on in the business is taller.

Here, he has collected his best car columns and stories in which he waxes lyrical on topics as useful and diverse as:

The perils of bicycle ownership

Why Australians – not Brits – need bull bars

Why soon only geriatrics will be driving BMWs

The difficulty of deciding on the best car for your wedding

Why Jesus's dad would have owned a Nissan Bluebird

… And why it is that bus lanes cause traffic jams

Irreverent, damn funny and offensive to almost everyone, this is writing with its foot to the floor, the brake lines cut and the speed limit smashed to smithereens. Sit back and enjoy the ride.